THE EUROPEAN COMMISSION

The European Commission is the result of a special collaboration between Kogan Page and Redline Wirtschaft, Germany's leading business publisher. Selected best-selling titles previously published by Redline Wirtschaft and their sister companies, such as Economica, are translated into English and published by Kogan Page to ensure a worldwide distribution.

This English version is a translation from the German title *Das Räderwerk der Europaïschen Kommission*.

THE EUROPEAN COMMISSION

An Essential Guide to the Institution, the Procedures and the Policies

Gerhard Sabathil, Klemens Joos & Bernd Keßler

KOGAN PAGE

London and Philadelphia

Publisher's note

Every possible effort has been made to ensure that the information contained in this book is accurate at the time of going to press, and the publishers and authors cannot accept responsibility for any errors or omissions, however caused. No responsibility for loss or damage occasioned to any person acting, or refraining from action, as a result of the material in this publication can be accepted by the editor, the publisher or any of the authors.

4th updated edition published in Germany in 2005 by economica, Verlagsgruppe Hüthig Jehle Rehm GmbH, Heidelberg/München/Landsberg/Berlin
First published in Great Britain and the United States in 2008 by Kogan Page Limited

120 Pentonville Road
London N1 9JN
United Kingdom
www.koganpage.com

525 South 4th Street, #241
Philadelphia PA 19147
USA

ISBN 978 0 7494 5266 7

British Library Cataloguing-in-Publication Data

A CIP record for this book is available from the British Library.

Library of Congress Cataloging-in-Publication Data

Sabathil, Gerhard, 1954–
The European Commission : an essential guide to the institution, the procedures, and the policies / Gerhard Sabathil, Klemens Joos and Bernd Keßler. 1st ed.
p. cm.
ISBN 978-0-7494-5266-7
1. European Commission. I. Joos, Klemens. II. Keßler, Bernd. III. Title.
JN33.5.S23 2008
341.242'2—dc22

2007047404

Typeset by JS Typesetting Ltd, Porthcawl, Mid Glamorgan
Printed and bound in Great Britain by MPG Books Ltd, Bodmin, Cornwall

Contents

List of tables

Editors' Foreword

The European Commission under President Barroso, the fifteenth Commission since the founding of the European Coal and Steel Community and the beginning of the High Authority on 10 August 1952 under the legendary first President, Jean Monnet, enters its last year. As unique as the character of this Authority is as the motor of integration, guardian of the European Treaties and enforcer of European policies, it is judged in an equally controversial manner by both European and world opinion. Some view the Commission as one of the most efficient and most innovative administrative bodies in the world, while others see it as a bureaucratic giant and the gravedigger of the ideal of a united Europe.

This book does away with these superficial, simplified and stereotyped views and ideas. It shows how the Commission acts with other players as part of a balanced system of decision-making. It explains its internal structure and provides a compact overview of the interconnected European policies with clear added value above and beyond that offered by current and short-lived sources of information.

Readers active in the areas of politics, science, the media and business, and above all the interested citizens of Europe, will better understand how the machinery of the Commission functions, and thereby gain access to the complicated, daily work processes in Brussels thus often perceived as oblique.

Dr Gerhard Sabathil
Dr Klemens Joos
Bernd Keßler

1

The Commission and the other institutions and bodies of the European Union

INTRODUCTION: THE TASKS OF THE EUROPEAN UNION

The European Union is a unique organization, unlike any other within the world community. For decades academics and other experts have been discussing what exactly the European Union is. Traditional theories of political science and internal relations have been used to try to define this unique model, and to force it to fit into existing political forms and theories. However, all attempts to do so have failed as it has proved impossible to come up with one single concept to describe the innovative core of Europe. This is why political scientists today define the model of Europe as a 'supranational' structure, to a certain extent as an additional, fourth political level of its Member States in Germany and Austria.

The European Union is neither a super state taking the place of its individual Member States, nor an international organization like the United Nations. It is a union of states in which the Member States have combined a large amount of their powers. It now encompasses 27 European countries with a total population of around 494 million people and has set itself the goals of maintaining peace on a continent that has historically been conflict-ridden, and improving the prosperity of its citizens.

The structure known today as the European Union has to date legally been made up of several 'communities'. The European Union has its origins in founding treaties related to common mergers in three policy areas, two of which still exist: the European Coal and Steel Community (ECSC, 1952), whose treaty expired in 2002; the European Economic Community (EEC, 1958); and the European Atomic Energy Community (Euratom, 1958). These three communities were amalgamated in April 1965 by the Merger Treaty. Once this treaty came into force, the High Authority – the present-day European Commission – of the European Communities (EC) thus created began its work. The Single European Act (SEA) of 1987 developed the single European market, while the Maastricht Treaty (or, more correctly, the Treaty on European Union, or TEU), signed on 7 February 1992, created the European Union as we know it today. Due to difficulties during the ratification process, the Treaty of Maastricht came into force later than planned, on 1 November 1993.

The 'three pillars principle', which to date has constituted the valid and generally applied description of the European Union's areas of activity and its basis in the Treaties, is based on the Treaty of Maastricht. The first pillar encompasses European integration on an economic level, in other words, at the core of the EC. The second pillar creates a common foreign and security policy (CFSP) and the third pillar contains a common policy on justice and home affairs. The division of the individual policy areas of the EU into three pillars can be illustrated as shown in Table 1.1.

The 'first pillar' of the Union contains the EU's policy areas; in this respect, most progress has been made with regard to integration within the EU. The European institutions can enact legal acts in these areas that immediately become valid in the Member States and can have precedence over national laws. The European economic and monetary policy is in the centre.

The 'second pillar' of the EU is embodied in European co-operation in the areas of foreign and security policy. Although decisions in these areas are to a large extent taken as part of co-operation between states, the EU now has at its disposal a range of instruments of its own that it can use to take action. These relate to decisions in principle, common

Table 1.1 The EU's 'three pillar diagram'

The European Union		
First pillar	Second pillar	Third pillar
European Communities	**Common Foreign and Security Policy**	**Police and Judicial Co-operation**
ECT	*Title V EUT*	*Title VI EUT*
• Customs union and Internal market • Economic and monetary union • Competition policy • Trade policy • Agricultural policy • Structural policy • EU citizenship • Education and culture • Transport policy and trans-European networks • Consumer protection and health • Research policy • Environmental policy • Social policy • Asylum policy • External borders and immigration policy	**Foreign policy** • Co-operation, common positions and actions • Peacekeeping • Human rights • Democracy • Help for third-party states **Security policy** • Common security policy • Disarmament • Economic aspects of armaments • European Security Order (long term)	• Judicial co-operation in civil and criminal matters • Police co-operation • Fight against racism and xenophobia • Fight against drugs and arms trafficking • Combating organized crime • Combating terrorism • Crimes against children and human trafficking

Source: Office for Official Publications, 2004

strategies, common positions, actions, measures and framework decisions. Although these instruments do not enjoy direct legal validity in the Member States, the Member States are obliged to co-operate loyally and to implement decisions taken in this area, so that a form of supranationality has actually been created on a political level.

The 'third pillar' of the European Union is formed by police and judicial co-operation within Europe. The common fight against criminality, terrorism, racism and xenophobia is increasingly being effected by means of international co-operation. The creation of the European Police Office, known as Europol, and judicial co-operation in legal proceedings and extraditions (e.g. the European Arrest Warrant and the limited cross-border co-operation between police forces) have steadily increased European integration in this area.

The Treaty on European Union has twice been revised since the Treaty of Maastricht came into force on 1 November 1993. The Treaties of Amsterdam (signed on 2 October 1997; came into force on 1 May 1999) and Nice (signed on 11 December 2000; came into force on 1 February 2003) have as a result of their changes consolidated (in other words, brought up to date) the original treaties. While the Treaty of Amsterdam above all expanded the European Parliament's decision-making powers, the focus of the changes in the Treaty of Nice was the Eastern enlargement of the EU.

The enlargement to take in the countries of Eastern Europe meant that the European Union and its then Member States were confronted with new expectations and demands. All the decision-makers within the European Union agreed that the new Eastern European states had to be integrated into a large and unified Europe. The countries that culturally and historically belonged together were to be brought together.

The enlargement of the European Union which took place on 1 May 2004 was a unique occurrence in world history. Ten states declared themselves ready to submit themselves to the European Union and to bring their laws and regulations into line in many policy areas. The aim was to create a Europe in which human rights, democracy and the rule of law are guaranteed everywhere and at all times. However, during the negotiations on accession it became clear that the existing structures of the EU would not be able to cope with an enlarged EU.

In order to guarantee the ability to act of an EU made up of 27 or more countries, the consolidated Treaty of Nice introduced a number of institutional reforms, including the change to the number of seats allocated in the European Parliament, the reorganization of the voting system in the Council, and the restriction of the number of members of the European Commission. Although the reforms dealt with the challenges faced by a larger EU only to a limited extent, the Treaty of Nice still determines the current rules within the European Union. All of the regulations mentioned below relate to the Treaty of Nice.

To remedy the defects of the Treaty of Nice and to have a fundamental rethink of the future goals and shape of Europe, the European Council in December 2001 called a 'Convention on the Future of

Europe', which consisted of representatives of the governments, the European Parliament, the Commission and the national parliaments. Between February 2002 and July 2003, the Convention worked out most of the draft for the European Constitution.

The working goals of the Convention were ambitious: to simplify EU law and the structures of the EU, to clarify responsibilities, democratization, to reduce bureaucracy and to move closer to the citizens of the EU. In fact, as a result of very broad co-operation between the relevant governments, non-governmental organizations, churches, associations, trade unions and other groups, the Convention submitted a draft treaty that succeeded in clarifying a large number of constitutional responsibilities and in strengthening and stabilizing as well as increasing the democratic legitimacy of the European institutions and European policy. By standardizing the framework structure – doing away with the pillar model – the aim was also to make the whole legal structure easier for the citizen to understand.

The majority of Member States with the majority of the population of the EU ratified the Constitution (including Spain and Luxembourg in plebiscites). However, the citizens of France and the Netherlands rejected the Constitutional Treaty, which was signed in Rome on 29 October 2004, in referendums. In France, 54.8 per cent of voters voted against the Constitution, on 29 May 2005, while in the Netherlands around 63 per cent voted 'No', on 1 June 2005. This temporary failure in the ratification process was regrettable, particularly as the important simplification of the decision-making process provided for in the Constitution would not now come into effect. As a way out, the European heads of state and government after a 'period of reflection' agreed on a new treaty called the Reform Treaty, which was signed in Lisbon in December 2007. If this new Reform Treaty will be ratified and come into force is unclear at the present time. Due to this uncertainty, concrete provisions of the Reform Treaty were not taken into consideration in the following pages.

THE INSTITUTIONAL TRIANGLE

The European Commission

http://ec.europa.eu/index_en.htm

The European Commission is the body of the European Union that takes initiatives aimed at promoting integration, guarantees that

Community legal acts are complied with and puts political decisions into effect. It represents the joint interests and is thus the heart of the EU. The nature of its tasks can be described using three key terms: motor of integration, guardian of the treaties and executive body of the EU.

Motor of integration

Due to its right to initiate legislation, the Commission has the privilege of submitting new draft legal acts in areas of Community policy (first pillar). Its area of responsibility is regulated in the treaties, and ranges from trade, industrial, competition and regional policy to issues of agriculture, the environment, energy and research. The Commission acts in accordance with the principle of subsidiarity and proportionality where its initiatives and draft legal acts are concerned. This means, first of all, that it is active only in the areas of responsibility in which it can take more effective measures than the individual Member States alone; furthermore, the measures taken must be in suitable proportion to the objectives to be achieved.

The Council of Ministers and the European Parliament have the opportunity to put proposals forward to the Commission and to arrange investigations. For example, the European Parliament can propose new budget headings, which the Commission must then elaborate. The Council of Ministers and the European Parliament also take part in the decision-making process later on. In the vast majority of cases, the Parliament and the Council jointly decide on the introduction of new legal acts. The Reform Treaty provides for a fundamental extension of the powers of the European Parliament in relation to the EU's decision-making procedures. The co-decision procedure created in 1991 by the Treaty of Maastricht is to be extended to additional policy areas (in this respect, see Section 2.4 on the interplay between the Commission, the Council and the Parliament). When proposed legal acts are being elaborated, the Commission has close consultations with representatives from the Member States, the business community, trade unions and other interested bodies.

Although the Council and the Parliament can propose legislation, it is incumbent on the Commission to check that these proposals are compatible with the objectives of the EU and, if necessary, to initiate steps that lead to Community initiatives or Community law. In this respect, if necessary, the Commission discusses these proposals with the Council or the European Parliament or jointly with both institutions.

The Commission interprets this monopoly on initiatives, which is in accordance with the way in which it perceives itself as a political/policy-making institution, as a duty to initiate. Through innovative and creative draft legal acts it has become the driving force behind European integration and acts not on behalf of national or group interests, but for the EU and its citizens in general. It is thus not surprising that the Commission often meets with resistance from the Member States due to its activities.

The Commission also works out announcements and proposals for draft legal acts in the form of Green and White Papers. While Green Papers, as published announcements from the Commission, only contribute to the consultation process at European level, White Papers contain formal proposals for the Community to become active in a specific policy area. The Commission's activities are presented in the 'Annual General Report on the Activities of the European Union', which appears in the first quarter of each year.

Guardian of the treaties

Second, the European Commission, as guardian of the treaties, ensures that Community legal acts are applied on a continuous basis and in a proper manner. It watches over the treaty provisions and, as the body in charge of Community interests, guarantees that no Member State or company is failing to comply with the provisions of Community law. Whether it is a question of meeting steel quotas, incorporating EU directives into national law or limiting state aid, the Commission must assert its authority and intervene if a treaty is being violated. In this respect, it can take action against both state bodies and private companies, irrespective of the means by which the Commission received notice of the infringement. If requests for statements and actions in accordance with the treaty in question are ineffective, the Commission can take disciplinary measures, such as imposing monetary fines and instituting proceedings in the European Court of Justice.

As an example, due to the deficit limit in the EU's Stability and Growth Pact being exceeded several times, deficit proceedings have been instigated against nine Member States, including Germany and Portugal, since July 2002. The Commission submitted recommendations for combating the high deficits to the countries in question and set a deadline for the taking of effective measures.

Executive body of the EU

The third task of the Commission, as one of the executive bodies of the EU, is to ensure that Community decisions are put into practice. The European Council has not transferred executive powers to the European Commission in all policy areas. For example, the incumbent High Representative for the Common Foreign and Security Policy, Javier Solana, was appointed to the European Council by agreement between the European Member States and acts for the European Union as a whole and not on behalf of or in the name of the Commission.

Through specific treaty provisions and authorizations from the Council of Ministers, the Commission now has a broad and interesting range of areas of activity at its disposal. It deals with implementation of the EU budget and has important decision-making powers in the areas of agricultural, trade and competition policy. The Commission is authorized to act independently in relation to support programmes in the area of regional and structural policy, research and education.

Together with the Council, the Commission is responsible for representing the EU outside of its borders. The Commission can conclude trade and co-operation agreements with third-party and candidate countries, for example within the framework of the World Trade Organization (WTO). One of the most important innovations created by the Reform Treaty is the creation of the post of a 'double-hatted' High Representative for Foreign Affairs, who is intended to provide greater coherence where the EU's stance on foreign policy is concerned. If the Reform Treaty comes into force, this person will fulfil the tasks of both the High Representative for the Common Foreign and Security Policy and the Commissioner with responsibility for foreign affairs as a Vice-President of the Commission. He is also due to take on the tasks assumed by the Council presidency in the area of foreign affairs and chairmanship of the 'Foreign Affairs' Council formation within the Council of Ministers.

The European Parliament

http://www.europarl.europa.eu/news/public/default_en.htm

The European Parliament of the EU is the body that directly represents the citizens of Europe on a democratic basis. The Parliament functions and acts to a great extent like a typical national parliament and, since

1979, has been directly elected every five years by the citizens of Europe. Citizens from all the Member States elect their MPs directly in their own countries, and the number of seats for each country is calculated in accordance with a key. Due to its size of its population, Germany has the most Members, with 99.

After the 2004 and 2007 enlargement of the EU, which involved taking in ten countries located in central and eastern Europe, as well as Cyprus and Malta, the European Parliament now has 785 MPs. The allocation per country is shown in Table 1.2.

The European Coal and Steel Community (ECSC) had a consultative assembly and the subsequent European Economic Community (EEC) and European Communities (EC) were given a parliamentary assembly that was named the European Parliament after the first direct elections took place in 1979. The European Parliament carries on its work in three places: Luxembourg, Strasbourg and Brussels. The tasks fulfilled by the European Parliament were originally divided up among the three cities in accordance with the historical development of the EU. When the EU was established as the EEC, there was only a parliament assembly instead of a real parliament; its members were delegated by the national parliaments. The logic involved in dividing up the power and prestige of the EEC decreed that all of the institutions be located in several places, but have only one headquarters. The High Authority (the future European Commission) was thus established in Brussels and Luxembourg, though its headquarters is in Brussels. The Council of Ministers meets in Luxembourg, but its Secretariat General moved to Brussels. The Parliamentary Assembly was established in Luxembourg and Strasbourg, though plenary meetings are held in Strasbourg, where the headquarters are located.

When the influence of the Commission increased due to advancing integration within the EU, the importance of Brussels also gradually increased. The Council moved more and more of its work to Brussels and the European Parliament also decided to hold its committee meetings there because these were increasingly dependent on the Commission's technical expertise, and to continue to hold only its plenary meetings in Strasbourg. The monthly, mainly weekly, journeys made by all of the Members and a large number of officials and employees of the European Parliament to Strasbourg have their origin in these developments. The European Parliament's translation service and personnel management division are the main bodies located in Luxembourg.

Table 1.2 Members of Parliament per Member State

Country	**Number of Members with 27 Member States**
Belgium (BE)	24
Bulgaria (BG)	18
Czech Republic (CZ)	24
Denmark (DK)	14
Germany (DE)	99
Estonia (EE)	6
Greece (EL)	24
Spain (ES)	54
France (FR)	78
Ireland (IE)	13
Italy (IT)	78
Cyprus (CY)	6
Latvia (LV)	9
Lithuania (LT)	13
Luxembourg (LU)	6
Hungary (HU)	24
Malta (MT)	5
Netherlands (NL)	27
Austria (AT)	18
Poland (PL)	54
Portugal (PT)	24
Slovenia (SI)	7
Slovak Republic (SK)	14
Finland (FI)	14
Sweden (SE)	19
Great Britain (UK)	78
Romania (RO)	35
Total	785

Election results

General elections to the European Parliament took place from 10 to 13 June 2004. Turnout at the elections varied greatly in the different countries, but the average was very low, at 45.7 per cent (similar to the turnout at US presidential elections). As this book went to press, the sizes of the different political groups were as follows:

European United Left (EUL)/Nordic Green Left (NGL), 44
Party of European Socialists (PES), 218
Greens/European Free Alliance (EFA), 42
Independence/Democracy Group (IND/DEM), 24
Alliance of Liberals and Democrats for Europe (ALDE), 104
European People's Party (EPP)/European Democrats (ED), 278
Union for Europe of the Nations (UEN), 41
Non-aligned (independent Members), 34

Division of seats in the European Parliament

As is common for European elections, the elections resulted in no clear majority. Although the conservative grouping, the European People's Party (EPP)/European Democrats (ED), with 268 Members, was the strongest group, due to the complicated way in which numbers are calculated within the European Parliament, it is only the largest minority, followed by the Party of European Socialists (PES) with 200 Members. The Liberals (Alliance of Liberals and Democrats for Europe, or ALDE) had 88 Members, the Greens (Greens/European Free Alliance or EFA) had 42 Members and the Communists and United Left (European United Left/Nordic Green Left) had 41 Members. Due to the significant amount of success achieved by populists hostile to Europe during recent elections, the influence of the different groups, which want to lead the EU back to being a confederation, has greatly increased (Independence/Democracy Group, or IND/DEM, with 37 Members, and Union for Europe of the Nations, or UEN, with 27 Members). The large number of independent Members is also a new phenomenon.

Organization of work

The first President of the European Parliament in the new legislative period was the Spanish socialist Josep Borrel Fontelles. According to parliamentary custom, the President's term of office is two and a half years. The chairperson of the German European People's Party (EPP) grouping, Hans-Gert Pöttering, was elected President in 2007.

Most of the important decisions are not taken by the President alone, but by the Presidium of the Parliament, which consists of the President, 14 Vice-Presidents and five Quaestors. The Quaestors regulate the Parliament's internal administrative processes and those of its Members. Most of the important political preliminary decisions are made during the Conference held by the chairpersons of the political groupings, where the two largest groupings, the EPP/ED and the PES, have the greatest influence.

As is usual in parliaments, the European Parliament's political work takes place in committees. During its 2004–2009 period of legislature, the Parliament decided to divide its work up among 20 permanent committees and also to set up two non-permanent committees to deal with special issues.

The Council of the European Union

http://ue.eu.int/cms3_fo/showPage.ASP?lang=en

Together with the European Parliament, the Council of the European Union is the EU's legislative decision-making body. The governments of the 27 Member States are represented in the Council.

The Council is principally made up of three plus one levels: ministerial level, the level of the Permanent Representatives (i.e. the Ambassadors) and the level of the Working Groups. The additional level consists of the European Council, which is made up of the heads of state and government of the Member States.

In accordance with a regular cycle, the Council is chaired by one Member State for six months. In 2007 it was chaired by Germany and Portugal[i]. Together with the European Commission and the High Representative for Common Foreign and Security Policy, the chairperson is responsible for representing the EU in the area of foreign affairs. He also co-ordinates the work of the Council at all levels and establishes each agenda.

---

[i] The Council's current valid decision applies to the period from 2007 until the first half of 2020. The following process has been laid down: 2008 Slovenia and France, 2009 Czech Republic and Sweden, 2010 Spain and Belgium, 2011 Hungary and Poland, 2012 Denmark and Cyprus, 2013 Ireland and Lithuania, 2014 Greece and Italy, 2015 Latvia and Luxembourg, 2016 Netherlands and Slovakia, 2017 Malta and Great Britain, 2018 Estonia and Bulgaria, 2019 Austria and Romania, 2020 (first half) Finland.

Table 1.3 The Council of the European Union

The Council meets in the form of special Councils of Ministers	
Committee of Permanent Representatives (CPR)	
CPR II	**CPR I**
Ambassadors responsible for, among other things, • Foreign affairs • Important political questions • Economic and budgetary policy • Preparing the European Council	**Deputy Ambassadors** responsible for, among other things, • Single European Market • Transport • Environment • Budget • Social affairs • Research • Energy
Political and Security Committee (for preparing the Council of Foreign Ministers)	
Special Agriculture Committee (for preparing the Agriculture Council)	
Economic and Budgetary Committee (for preparing the ECOFIN Council)	
Groups Technical level for special officials	

Where practical/political work is concerned, the fact that the Council of Ministers usually takes decisions based on the principle of consensus is particularly important. Although the treaties stipulate that decisions can be made in specific policy fields based on the right to qualified majority voting, the Council is oriented towards taking into consideration the doubts and wishes of as many Member States as possible. In accordance with the principle of consensus, small countries such as Luxembourg and Slovenia, and large countries such as Germany, France and Poland, have the same voice in the decision-making process. According to a criticism that was frequently made in the past, this can lead to far-reaching proposals made by the European Commission being watered down and, ultimately, a vote being made in favour of the lowest common denominator. On the other hand, this intensive process of discussions, in which all the Member States voice their problems and put forward their conditions, results in the creation of what is known as 'stakeholding'. This means that all the Member States feel themselves to be represented as part of all political decisions and can then justify those decisions (whether directive, regulation or framework) to their citizens. However, this is the typically ideal way of looking at things.

Since the consensus-oriented procedure is desirable, but can lead to blockades in an EU with more and more Member States, the qualified majority voting provided for in the treaties has increased in recent years.

The decision-making procedure within the Council

All the Commission's political and legal initiatives are discussed both in the Parliament and the Council. Normally, discussions on a proposal from the Commission begin at section level in the Council within the competent Working Group. This is where the experts from the 27 Member States sit in different configurations. They are either diplomats from the Permanent Representations or envoys from the capitals and ministries. During this round, the initiatives are discussed and joint decisions are taken on changes to the texts. When a Council Working Group has come to an agreement between all Member States, the text in question is sent to the next highest body, the Council of Permanent Representatives (Committee of Permanent Representatives, Comité des Représentants Permanents, or COREPER).

This also happens when, after several rounds of discussions, agreement has still not been reached on particular points. An attempt must then be made by the ambassadors themselves to achieve agreement at a higher level. If they succeed in doing so, a draft is sent to the Council of Ministers for voting. Here, the competent ministers or the General Affairs Council (in which the countries' foreign and Europe ministers are represented) vote on the drafts. In very rare and politically awkward cases, when the Member States cannot reach agreement on certain details at Working Group level or in the Committee of Permanent Representatives, a proposal is repeatedly discussed at ministerial level and voted on. Only at this level and in rare cases can it happen that a proposal from the Commission is actually voted on with a qualified majority.

During this procedure, each country is allocated a specific voting weight, depending on its size. The voting weights were laid down in the Treaty of Nice:

The total number of votes is thus 345 and the qualified majority is reached with 236 votes.

A decision is thus approved when the 236 votes come from at least the majority of Member States. Furthermore, a Member State may have a check carried out to see if the majority reached by the Member States represents at least 62 per cent of the population of the EU. This clause, which was negotiated in the Treaty of Nice, was a concession made by

Table 1.4 Voting weight in accordance with the Treaty of Nice

Country	**Number of votes**	**Country**	**Number of votes**
Belgium (BE)	12	Luxembourg (LU)	4
Bulgaria (BG)	10	Hungary (HU)	12
Czech Republic (CZ)	12	Malta (MT)	3
Denmark (DK)	7	Netherlands (NL)	13
Germany (DE)	29	Austria (AT)	10
Estonia (EE)	4	Poland (PL)	27
Greece (EL)	12	Portugal (PT)	12
Spain (ES)	27	Slovenia (SI)	4
France (FR)	29	Slovak Republic (SK)	7
Ireland (IE)	7	Finland (FI)	7
Italy (IT)	29	Romania (RO)	14
Cyprus (CY)	4	Sweden (SE)	10
Latvia (LV)	4	Great Britain (UK)	29
Lithuania (LT)	7		
Total:			**345**

France to Germany, which at that time accepted that it would have the same number of votes as France (both had 29), although, at around 82 million, the population of Germany is more than one-third larger than that of France (59 million). In any case, it is easy to ascertain that, when votes are being allocated, the smaller countries of the EU receive more weight than they would if the votes were allocated proportionally and based purely on the population of each country. In this way, a certain amount of political weight is guaranteed for smaller Member States, for example, the Netherlands.

As soon as it enters into force, the Reform Treaty will settle the issue of qualified majority voting once and for all, and without any artificial allocation of votes using what is known as the 'double majority'. If a majority of 55 per cent of the Member States, which represents 65 per cent of the population of the EU, votes in favour of a proposal, then a qualified majority has been reached. Certain Member States have achieved some procedural modifications to this general rule, which relate to certain delays in voting when they do not agree with a position (called the Ioannina compromise). However, this will not substantially affect the application of the double-majority.

During the Council's everyday working life, almost all points (80–90 per cent) are cleared at diplomatic or ambassadorial level. The decisions are thus brought to the agenda of the competent Council of Ministers in the form of what are known as A-points and are only voted on as a package. Very few serious points of contention, which could not be resolved at lower levels, reach ministerial level. They can be voted on by qualified majority.

Only when this does not happen – because an issue is considered too politically important by one or several countries for a decision at ministerial level – the issue is the European Council referred to[i]. According to the Treaty, it is the core function of the Council to decide on the broad guidelines of EU development and its foreign and security policy. Decisions that affect the core of the EU's identity and conception and policy areas of great importance are taken by the European Council. Typical examples are important decisions related to economic and monetary union (e.g. accession to the euro zone or the deficit procedure), issues related to EU enlargement and important steps in the accession process, as well as rules that affect protection of the common external borders (e.g. access to the Schengen zone). Furthermore, decisions that commit the institutions of the EU for many

[i] This arbitration role, which is fulfilled by the European Council (i.e. the heads of state and government), was developed in the 1980s and 1990s.

years, such as establishing the financial perspective, can also be taken only by the European Council.

The interplay between the Commission, the Parliament and the Council

The previous chapters explained the decision-making process within the three most important institutions of the EU. However, the EU's legislative procedures and political processes also, or above all, consist of political mechanisms of negotiation existing between the institutions. As described in Chapter 2.1, with the exception of a few policy areas, the Commission possesses the exclusive right of initiative. It submits proposals for directives and regulations and accompanies them through the Council and the Parliament, which function as decision-making bodies.

Through a number of changes to the treaties, the balance of power between the Council and the Parliament has slowly shifted in favour of the Parliament. In the current version of the treaties, amended by the Treaty of Nice, the Parliament has the same decision-making powers as the Council in almost all important policy areas. The equality of decision-making power was achieved in particular by the introduction of the co-decision procedure (Article 251). In the Reform Treaty, the co-decision procedure, which is important for the democratic legitimacy of the EU, was expanded once again to include a large number of policy areas.

There are a total of six important legislative procedures within the EU:

- the procedure whereby the Commission alone enacts a legal act;
- the non-consultative procedure;
- the consultation procedure;
- the co-operation procedure;
- the co-decision procedure; and
- the assent procedure.

The Commission procedure

Here, the Commission enacts a generally valid legal act unilaterally. This only happens in very rare cases, for example, in the area of public services (Article 86[3]) or in relation to employees' rights of residence (Article 39[3]).

The non-consultative procedure

During this procedure, following a proposal by the Commission, the Council passes a legal act without the involvement of the Parliament or one of the consultative bodies (the Economic and Social Committee or the Committee of the Regions). In this respect, the Council can request that the European Parliament take a position, but the Council is not obliged to do this. According to the Treaty of Nice, this procedure applies in many cases. Examples includes legal acts in the area of the Common External Tariff (Article 26), the freedom of citizens of third-party states to provide services (Article 49) and the establishment of the principles for the Member States' economic policy (Article 99).

The consultation procedure

During this procedure, which has existed since the first treaties came into force, a proposal for a legal act by the Commission is transmitted to the Council and Parliament. The Parliament has the right to take a position, which is then passed on to the Council with the Commission's comments. The Council can examine and comment on the changes proposed by the Parliament, and it has the power either to accept or reject these changes. The Council takes the final decision on the proposed legal act. Following recent reforms made to the Treaties in Nice, it has been possible to pass many legal acts after the consultation procedure has taken place in the Parliament, for example, in the area of voting rights in local assemblies (Article 19) or when state aid is being granted (Article 89).

The co-operation procedure

The co-operation procedure (Article 252) was introduced in 1987 by the Single European Act and strengthened the powers of the European Parliament for the first time.

The Act introduced a type of system involving two readings. In this respect, the Council can ignore the Parliament's proposed changes during a first reading and adopt its common position. However, if the Parliament rejects this position by an absolute majority of its members during the second reading, the Council can only adopt its position unanimously. If the Commission supports the changes proposed by the Parliament, the Council can also reject these only unanimously. The Single European Act introduced this procedure into many of the policy areas affecting the Single Market.

The co-decision procedure

Table 1.5 The co-decision procedure

Commission's proposal sent to EP and Council

Parliament's position

Council approves all EP's amendments	No changes made by EP	Council's Common Position	Commission's position on Common Position

Council can enact the amended legal act	Council can enact the legal act

EP approves the Commission's position or takes no decision	EP rejects the Common Position by an absolute majority of its members	EP accepts amendments to the Common Position by an absolute majority of its members

Law considered as enacted	Law not considered as accepted

Within three months the Council approves the EP's amendments (I) Through BQM if the Commission's position is positive (II) Unanimously if the Commission's position is negative	Within three months the Council has not approved all of the EP's amendments

Amended law adopted	Conciliation Committee convened within three weeks by agreement between Council and EP

Agreement within conciliation committee	Conciliation fails

Within six weeks approval by the EP (by simple majority) and by the Council (by BQM)	Within six weeks no approval by the EP and Council	Legal act not adopted

Legal act adopted	Legal act not adopted

Source: European Commission, 2005

Good experience with a Parliament which, with its fledgling legislative responsibilities, was acting prudently and circumspectly as a result of the co-decision procedure, and the wish to improve the democratic deficit criticized by many within the European Community (as it was still called then), led in 1993 to the introduction of a new procedure when the Treaty of Maastricht came into force. In the areas in which it is applied, this procedure (Article 251) finally created parity between the Parliament and the Council. It was simplified by the Treaty of Amsterdam and the Treaty of Nice, and is shaped as set out below.

After the Commission has adopted a proposal, this is sent to the Parliament. The Parliament adopts a draft during a first reading, which is sent to the Council with the Commission's comments. The Council has two possibilities. It can accept the proposal amended in this way and thus adopt the changes agreed by the Parliament. At this point the text of the legal act is considered as adopted during a first reading. If the Council does not agree with all of the Parliament's changes, it can adopt an amended text, which does not correspond to the Parliament's text. For example, this text may contain some of the Parliament's proposals, but in certain sections realizes formulations and ideas put forward by the Council. At this point the text goes back to the Parliament and the second reading of the legal act begins. The Parliament may once again comment on the proposed legal act. It can adopt or reject the Council's changes to the text. If the Parliament accepts the text adopted by the Council, this is considered as adopted during the second reading. If this is not the case, the text, which was adopted by an absolute majority by the plenary during the second reading, goes to the Council for a second time.

At this stage, the Council once again has the opportunity to accept the Parliament's draft in its entirety – the legal act is then considered as adopted during its second reading – or not to accept it. If the latter is the case, the Presidency of the Council contacts the Parliament and both institutions convene a Conciliation Committee. This Conciliation Committee consists of representatives from the 27 Member States and an equal number of Members of the Parliament. The Commission participates in the meetings of the Conciliation Committee in a consultative manner. This committee now has to reach a joint solution during negotiations. To be adopted within this body a text requires a qualified majority of Member States (in accordance with the method for calculating the qualified majority, described above) and a majority of the votes of the Members of Parliament. If this 'dual majority' is achieved, then the draft of the text of the legal act is considered adopted within the Conciliation Committee. It then goes to the Parliament and the Council for a third and final reading. Both the Parliament and the Council can now only adopt or reject the whole text. If both institutions adopt the compromise text, it is signed by the President of the Council and the President of the Parliament and thus enters into force. If the text is rejected by only one or even by both institutions, the legislation has failed.

An important modification in this procedure, which is applied in individual policy areas (e.g. in the areas of the environment, as well as the free movement of people, services and capital), stipulates that the Council must act unanimously for all decisions.

The assent procedure

Compared with the complex nature of the co-decision procedure, the assent procedure is really aesthetically simple in nature. It is mainly applied when important international treaties are being concluded, when new countries are joining the EU or in relation to specific requirements for economic and social cohesion. During this procedure, the Parliament must agree to a legal act or a treaty simply in the form of the majority of its Members. If this majority is not reached, the legal act is considered rejected.

The power of the Parliament

In public debate and even among people knowledgeable about politics, there are recurrent claims that the European Parliament has no influence on European legislation. An objective consideration of the facts actually reveals the opposite.

Since the process of harmonization of the Single European Market began in 1987 with the Single European Act, the European Parliament has been allocated more and more participation rights. Since the introduction of the co-decision procedure in 1993, in the Treaty of Maastricht, application of this procedure has been extended to additional policy areas whenever the Treaty has been revised (Amsterdam 1997, Nice 2000), as well as within the Reform Treaty that still has to be ratified. This means that the Parliament has been acquiring a growing influence. The older co-operation procedure is still applied in very few policy areas. It is mainly restricted to economic and monetary union (Articles 99, 102, 103). As a result of the co-decision procedure, the Parliament and the European citizens it represents decide in equal terms upon important policy areas such as discrimination on the grounds of nationality (Article 12), the Law on the Right of Establishment (Article 46), harmonization of the Single Internal Market (Article 95) and social policy (Article 141). The European Parliament is an equal partner of the Council in a total of more than 30 policy areas.

THE EUROPEAN COURT OF JUSTICE

http://curia.eu.int/en

The European Court of Justice (ECJ) – not to be confused with the European Court of Human Rights in Strasbourg, which is an institution of the Council of Europe, or with the International War Crimes Tribunal of the United Nations in The Hague – is made up of the Court of Justice and the Court of First Instance. It guarantees the uniform interpretation and application of Community law in all Member States and decides on legal disputes between Member States, EU institutions, companies and private individuals. At the request of the Council or the Commission, the European Court of Justice can, for example, relieve Members of the Commission from their office if they are no longer fulfilling their tasks satisfactorily or they show serious misconduct.

The Court of First Instance was created in 1989, to relieve the strain on the ECJ. It deals with specific legal procedures (e.g. with actions related to competition law). Both the ECJ and the Court of First Instance are made up of one judge from each Member State; the Court of Justice also has eight 'Advocates-General'. The judges and Advocates-General are appointed for a term of six years – two reappointments each lasting three years are possible – by the governments and Member States and sent to the Court. They must act completely independently of their country of origin. Every three years the judges of the ECJ and the Court of First Instance elect a president from among their ranks.

The European Court of Justice deals with different types of actions. In an infringement procedure, it checks at the request of the Commission or another Member State whether an EU state is contravening Community law. If a Member State is found guilty by the ECJ, it has to cease the activity immediately. Furthermore, Member States, European institutions and private individuals can request that an EU legal act be declared in contravention of the treaty and thus annulled during annulment proceedings. When an action for failure to act is

Table 1.6 Procedures within the Court of Justice of the European Communities

Court of Justice of the European Communities		
Procedure for taking actions and making appeals		**Preliminary ruling procedure**
Bill of complaint Delivery of the bill of complaint to the respondent by the Registry Publication of the complaint in the *Official Journal of the EU* (Provisional order) (Application to be joined to proceedings) Response to action (Plea of inadmissibility) (Rejoinder and counter-rejoinder) (Other pleas)	(Application for legal aid) Appointing of associate judge and Advocate-General	Advance judgement or decision by the national court Translation into the other official languages of the EU Delivery to the Parties involved in the main proceedings, the Member States, the Organs of the Community, the European Economic Area (EEA) and the European Free Trade Association's (EFTA) supervisory authority Publication of the request for a preliminary ruling procedure in the *Official Journal of the EU* Written Statement by the Parties, the States and the Organs
Conclusion of the written procedure		
Drawing up of the preliminary report by the associate judge General hearing, consisting of judges and Advocates-General (Allocation of the case to a chamber) (Taking of evidence) (Renouncement of an oral hearing) (Renouncement of closing submissions) (Oral hearing; report of hearing) (Advocate-General's closing submissions) Judges' deliberations JUDGMENT		

Source: European Court of Justice, 2005

ongoing, the ECJ and the Court of First Instance examine the legality of one of the bodies of the Community failing to act after being explicitly requested to do so. If its failure to act contravenes the treaties, the body in question is requested to take appropriate measures.

Within the EU, references for a preliminary ruling are particularly important. During this procedure, the European Court of Justice attempts to guarantee that the European legal acts are being uniformly applied by the national courts. In this respect, the national courts contact the European Court of Justice either to request an interpretation of a Community legal act or to apply for an examination of the compatibility of Community law with national regulations. They may also challenge the validity of a legal act.

Proceedings in front of the European Court of Justice and the Court of First Instance are divided into two phases. The first – the written – part of the proceedings involves the exchanging of pleas, the drawing up of a report by the competent judge, the writing of the closing submissions by the Advocate-General, who presents the legal issues in the case and puts forward a proposal for the court's decision, as well as formulation of a draft judgment by the judge. The Advocate-General plays a role only during the initial proceedings and not when the judgment is being deliberated; the court is not bound by its legal judgment.

These proceedings are followed by the public sitting, which takes place in front of the whole European Court of Justice or, depending on the scope of the proceedings, in front of smaller chambers made up of three or five judges. After the advocates have been heard in front of the judges and Advocates-General, the closing submissions are made. Finally, these are followed by a majority judgment.

All proceedings held before the ECJ are free of court fees. The internal working language is French although petitioners can speak in any of the 20 official languages and declare any of them to be the language of the proceedings.

THE EUROPEAN COURT OF AUDITORS

http://eca.europa.eu/portal/page/portal/eca_main_pages/home

The European Court of Auditors, the 'financial conscience of the EU', has been carrying out its work in Luxembourg since October 1977. It checks that EU income and expenditure are legal and above board, and thus ensures that EU citizens get maximum value for their money and that the EU budget is implemented in an economic manner. The Court of Auditors makes a significant contribution to guaranteeing the effectiveness and transparency of the Community system. It is made up of one independent member per EU state, who is appointed for a period of six years. The current President of the European Court of Auditors is the Austrian Hubert Weber.

To carry out its tasks the European Court of Auditors checks the books of all institutions handling EU income or expenditure and carries out on-site checks while doing so. The results of its work are recorded in reports, which are intended to draw the attention of the Commission and Member States to existing problems. Irregularities must always be reported to the competent bodies because the European Court of Auditors itself cannot take any legal steps. The annual audit report on the previous budget year sent in November to the Parliament and the Council is the most important basis for the Parliament's approving or rejecting management of the budget by the Commission. If the European Court of Auditors is satisfied with the budget plan and its management, it sends the Parliament and the Council a guarantee in the form of a statement of assurance confirming that the European taxpayers' money has been properly used.

The European Court of Auditors is free to determine the way in which its work is organized and how much time is spent on particular tasks. It can determine the focal points of its audits by itself, select individual policy areas and draw up related special reports. When the Work Programme of the European Court of Auditors was being presented in front of the Budget Committee of the European Parliament, on 17 February 2004, the President announced various projects including an audit of the structural funds for the new Member States, an assessment of the support measures for the private sector and an investigation into expenditure on translation and interpreting services.

FINANCIAL INSTITUTIONS

The European Central Bank

http://www.ecb.int/home/html/index.en.html

The European Central Bank (ECB), which was established in Frankfurt am Main, Germany, in 1998, manages the European single currency and defines and implements the EU's monetary policy. It co-operates with the European System of Central Banks (ESCB), which includes the ECB itself and the Central Banks of all 27 Member States. The countries that have introduced the euro form the 'euro zone'; their Central Banks and the EZB were merged to create the 'euro system'. Like the European Court of Justice and the European Court of Auditors, the ECB is wholly independent. The ECB may not seek or accept directives from any other bodies. The EU bodies and the Member States must also abstain from influencing the ECB.

The main task of the ESCB is to secure price stability in order to safeguard the purchasing power of the euro. The ESCB also supports the achieving of a high level of employment and sustainable growth, as long as this does not endanger price stability. In order to keep annual inflation under 2 per cent, and thus to safeguard price stability within the euro zone, the ECB uses two strategies. First of all, it controls the relationship between the money supply and the supply of goods and services. Second, it monitors price developments and estimates the related risk for price stability. Establishing the interest rates is one of the most important instruments of the ECB where control of the money supply is concerned. The European Central Bank devises and manages the monetary policy for the euro zone, it carries out foreign exchange transactions, supervises the Member States' currency reserves and ensures that the payment systems function in a problem-free manner. It also deals with the issuing of banknotes within the euro zone and the supervision of the stability of the financial systems and credit institutions.

The ECB's work is organized by different decision-making bodies. The Council of the Central Bank presidents, consisting of the members of the management committee and the presidents of the 12 central banks within the euro zone, establishes the monetary policy for the euro zone and, in particular, the interest rates. The management committee is made up of the President, Vice-Presidents and four additional members, and deals with the monetary policy decided on by the Council of the Central Bank Presidents by issuing corresponding directives to the national central banks. It also prepares the meetings of the ECB and is responsible for the daily business of the Central Bank. The General Council of the ECB is made up of the President, Vice-President, and the presidents of the central banks of all Member States of the EU. It consults with the ECB and plays a significant role in preparations for the future enlargement of the euro zone. The second President of the ECB, appointed in November 2003, was the Frenchman Jean-Claude Trichet, who succeeded Wim Duisenberg.

The European Investment Bank

http://www.eib/org

The European Investment Bank (EIB) is the financing institution of the European Union. It invests in projects that to a large extent contribute to integration, balanced development and economic and social union, in other words, to the EU's most important objectives. As a public financial institution it has to take into consideration a bank's operative constraints and to conduct a dialogue with the political bodies of the EU, in particular with the Economic and Financial Affairs Council (EFAC), the Commission and the Economic and Social Affairs Committee. The EU Member States' shares in the bank's capital are determined in accordance with their economic weight. Since the accession of the 10 new Member States in 2004 and 2007, the capital of the EIB is more than 163.6 billion euros.

When selecting projects to be financed, the EIB expressly takes care to obtain maximum expediency and pays particular attention to the transparency of its operations. The EIB deals with, among other things, investments in the area of trans-European networks in the transport, telecommunications and energy sectors; with contributions to the EU's policy on climate protection; and with supporting the development and integration of the new Member States as well as with consolidating a financial partnership with the countries of the Mediterranean zone. Due to its majority shares in the European Investment Fund (EIF), the EIB supports small- and medium-sized enterprises (SMEs) through investments. The overall total of signed loans reached 42.3 billion euros in 2003.

The board of governors, made up of 27 ministers from the Member States, issues guidelines for the bank's loan policy, approves its annual balance sheet and authorizes its financing of projects outside the EU. The administrative board grants loans, manages the bank and checks that its transactions are in accordance with the provisions of the EU Treaty. The management committee, which is made up of nine members, is the executive body of the EIB. It prepares, checks and implements decisions for the administrative board. The current chairman of the administrative board is the Belgian Philippe Maystadt, who is also a member of the management committee and President of the European Investment Bank.

ADVISORY BODIES

The European Economic and Social Committee

http://www.eesc.europa.eu/index_en.asp

The European Economic and Social Committee (EESC) was established in 1957 by the Treaty of Rome. It represents the interests of employers (Group I), employees (Group II), farmers, craftspeople, consumers and other interest groups (Group III) that make up what is known as the 'organized civil society' of the EU. The aim of the contacts existing between the EESC and the Commission, the Parliament and the Council is to build a bridge between the institutions and the citizens and to encourage European citizens to take pleasure in integration and develop a democratic frame of mind. Although the EESC does not play a role in determining policy, it is impossible to imagine the EU's decision-making process without it. Its position must be obtained on every decision taken with regard to economic and social policy and, at its own discretion, it is free to issue statements on important policy areas. Lastly, the EECS is active in consolidating the role of civil society in third-party states and contributes to the establishment of advisory bodies in these countries.

In preparation for the accession of the new Member States, the number of members of the EESC was fixed at 350 at most. Its seats are simultaneously divided up among the different Member States (more or less depending on the size of the population) and among the aforementioned groups. For example, countries such as Germany, France and Italy have 24 seats, while Spain and Poland have 21, the Czech Republic and Hungary 12, and Cyprus 6.

The members are proposed by the governments of the Member States, but are politically independent for the period during which they work for the EESC. Their term of office is four years; members may be reappointed.

The EESC contains a plenary session whose opinions are prepared by study groups. The issues dealt with by these sub-committees are clearly defined. For example, they deal with agriculture, rural development and the environment, with questions related to economic and monetary union, economic and social cohesion and external relations. Every two years the EESC elects a President and a Vice-President from its ranks chosen from each of the three groups in rotation. Dimitris Dimitriadis has been President since October 2006.

The Committee of the Regions

http://www.cor/europa.eu/En/index.htm

The local and regional authorities have been represented in the Committee of the Regions (CoR) since 1994. The CoR guarantees that their points of view are heard and that their interests are represented. In this way the aim is to safeguard regional identities and claims. When the Treaty of Maastricht, which established the CoR, was being drawn up, two considerations were of particular importance. First of all, a body made up of representatives of the communes, towns, cities and regions seemed a reasonable idea because three-quarters of EU regulations are implemented at local and regional level. Second, direct participation of the elected members closest to the largest number of citizens was seen as an opportunity to bridge the gap between the EU and its citizens, thereby helping to acquire more democratic legitimacy for the EU. The Commission and the Council are obliged to consult with the Committee of the Regions in the policy areas that can have an effect at regional and communal level. These areas are the following: economic and social cohesion, trans-European infrastructure networks, public health, education and youth, the labour market and social policies, environmental protection, vocational training and transport. The Commission and the Council can also listen to the CoR in relation to other issues when these appear relevant to them. The Committee of the Regions can also take a position on issues which, in its opinion, are of importance to the communes and the regions. By doing so, it exercises its right to draw up an opinion on its own initiative.

Like the Economic and Social Committee, the CoR can be made up of no more than 350 members. The seats are allocated in accordance with the pattern applied in the EESC and thus roughly correspond to the population of each Member State. The members are elected communal or regional politicians. They are mainly deputies from regional parliaments, presidents of regions or mayors from larger towns and cities, most of whom, of course, have specific party political leanings. This results in an interwoven matrix made up of communal, regional, national and party political interests. The representatives are nominated by the Member States, but act independently while they are working for the CoR. They are appointed by the Council of the European Union for four years, and may be reappointed.

The Committee of the Region's plenary sessions take place five times a year. They are used to establish the general policy direction and objectives of the CoR and constitute the forum where positions are taken. The consultative work is subdivided into six thematic commissions which prepare the CoR's positions. Peter Straub, President of the state parliament of Baden-Württemberg, has been President of the Committee of the Regions since February 2004.

MISCELLANEOUS

The European Ombudsman

http://ombudsman.europa.eu/home/en/default.htm

The task of the European Ombudsman is to mediate between the citizens and the authorities of the European Union. He is authorized to receive complaints from every EU citizen. These are levelled against insufficiencies and defects in the administrative structures of the European institutions, for example, unfair treatment, discrimination, abuse of power, lack of or refusal to provide information, unnecessary delays and incorrect procedures. If he considers it sensible, the European Ombudsman can send recommendations to the European Parliament, which may also accept the obvious political consequences of the revelation of irregularities or shortcomings. He carries out investigations on his own initiative or based on complaints sent to him. The results are initially sent to the body in question, which is requested to make a detailed statement. The Parliament and the complainant are also informed consequently. The Ombudsman is elected by the European Parliament every five years and must act in a completely independent and impartial manner. Nikiforos Diamandouros from Greece has been the European Ombudsman since April 2003.

The European Data Protection Supervisor

http://www.edps.europa.eu/EDPSWEB/epds/lang/en/pid/1

The Data Protection Supervisor is a body responsible for guaranteeing protection of the private sphere when personal data is being processed by the European bodies and institutions. This means that they supervise compliance by the Community's institutions with the strict data protection laws, for example, with regard to handling data containing information on a person's origins, religious convictions and political views. He carries out his investigations with the help of a secretariat, issues appropriate advice to the institutions and deals with complaints sent to him by EU citizens. He publishes an annual report on his activities every year. The Data Protection Supervisor is appointed by the Parliament and the Council every five years. If he neglects his duty to be absolutely neutral and independent, he can be removed from office by the European Court of Justice. The Dutchman Peter Hustinx was appointed Data Protection Supervisor in January 2004.

AUTONOMOUS INSTITUTIONS AND AGENCIES

The institutions of the European Union also include a range of decentralized bodies with their own legal personality, which were established to take over specific technical, scientific and administrative tasks within the Community's policy areas that are precisely defined in its basic regulations. By establishing the agencies, it was hoped above all that the Community's activities would be decentralized and spread over a wide geographical area, that transparency would be promoted by specific descriptions of tasks, that specific knowledge in technical and scientific areas would be developed, and that third-party state would be able to participate in this process. The agencies' head offices are divided up among the EU Member States.

There are currently 17 autonomous institutions and agencies, which are all financed by the EU budget. The word 'agency' forms part of their name in some cases (European Environmental Agency, European Medicines Agency, European Aviation Safety Agency), but they may also be called 'offices' (Office of the European Union for Trade Marks and Designs, Community Plant Variety Office), 'authorities' (European Food Safety Authority), 'foundations' (European Vocational Training Foundation, European Foundation for the Improvement of Living and Working Conditions) or 'centres' (European Centre for the Development of Vocational Training, Translation Centre for the Bodies of the European Union). (The tasks and activities of the autonomous institution and agencies are presented at the end of the chapter on their particular policy area.)

In general, the agencies have a similar basic structure. They usually contain an administrative board on which the members are always representatives of the Member States and the Commission.

Furthermore, persons appointed by the Parliament and representatives of the social partners can also be involved. The Director of the agency is its legal representative. The division of competencies between the administrative board and the Director is specifically laid down in the Regulation on Establishing an Agency. An academic committee made up of experts often supports the administrative board in the formulation of positions on questions submitted to it.

The following 25 agencies and autonomous institutions are described and assigned to the relevant policy areas in this book:

DG Employment, Social Affairs and Equal Opportunities
European Foundation for the Improvement of Living and Working Conditions (EUROFOUND)
European Agency for Health and Safety at Work (OSHA)

DG Education and Culture
European Centre for the Development of Vocational Training (ECDVT)
European Training Foundation (ETF)

DG Internal Market and Services
Community Plant Variety Office (CPVO)
Office of the European Union for Trade Marks and Designs (OAMI)

DG Fisheries and Maritime Affairs
European Fisheries Control Agency (EUFA)

DG Health and Consumer Protection
European Food Safety Authority (EFSA)
European Centre for Disease Prevention and Control (ECDC)

DG Information Society and Media
European Network and Internet Security Agency (ENISA)

DG Justice, Freedom and Security
European Monitoring Centre for Drugs and Drug Addiction (EMCDDA)
European Monitoring Centre for Racism and Xenophobia (EUMC)
European Police Office (EUROPOL)
European Police College (CEPOL)

DG Environment
European Environmental Agency (EEA)

DG Enterprise and Industry
European Medicines Agency (EMEA)

DG Energy and Transport
Euratom Supply Agency
European Maritime Security Agency (EMSA)
European Aviation Safety Agency (EASA)
European Railway Agency (ERA)
Intelligent Energy Executive Agency (IEEA)

DG External Relations
European Union Satellite Centre (EUSC)
European Union Institute for Security Studies (EUISS)
European Defence Agency (EDA)

EuropeAid – Office for Co-operation
European Agency for Reconstruction (EAR)

COMITOLOGY

Comitology within the EU is one of the clearest signs of its unique character. The 1,000 or so committees established around the Council of Ministers and the Commission supplement and support the executive function of the Commission. The comitology system is to a certain extent the institutional frame of the executive function of the Commission through the Member States. Although the Commission is principally assigned the EU's executive tasks in the treaties, the establishment of committees is provided for in individual legal acts in relation to many executive tasks. It is therefore difficult to estimate the exact number of committees. What they have in common is the fact that they are chaired by the Commission and each of the 27 Member States is represented on each committee. The committees are divided up in three ways:

1. In the consultative committees the representative of the Commission submits the measures to be implemented to the committee.

The committee indicates its position, which must be taken into consideration by the Commission. However, in this case the Commission can to a large extent carry through its policy-related plans.

2. In the administrative committees the Commission has the right to propose implementation measures, which have to be viewed positively by the Member States. This position must be adopted by a qualified majority of the Member States. If the Commission's measures are not in accordance with this position, the Commission must inform the Council of the situation immediately. It can then implement the measure or delay it for three months. During this period, the Council can adopt another resolution by qualified majority.
3. Regulatory committees basically carry out the same sort of work as administrative committees although, when a different position is taken, the Commission cannot implement the measure, but must first send it to the Council and inform the European Parliament. The European Parliament can then investigate whether a measure proposed by the Commission goes beyond the powers of the Commission in the legal act used as the basis for the proposed measure. A decision to this effect can be sent to the Council. The Council now decides on the Commission's proposal. If its decision (again taken by qualified majority) results in the proposal being rejected, the Commission must examine its proposal and submit a new one, either in amended or in the same form. If the Commission has not complied with the three-month deadline, the Commission's implementing act is enacted.

Further special procedures are agreed for some special areas such as procedures for protective measures.

2

The 27 Commissioners: the political college

THE COLLEGIAL ORGAN OF THE 27 COMMISSION MEMBERS

Composition and appointments

If the European Commission resembles the executive of the European Union, then the Commission's college resembles its government. The Treaty of Nice stipulates that the number of Commissioners, including the President, corresponds to the number of Member States. The exact number can be changed by a unanimous vote of the Council. This means that the Commission currently has 27 members.

The first step in the nomination of a new Commission is the appointment of the President by the European Council.

Since the treaty in Nice, a qualified majority is sufficient for this appointment; however, in political practice, no Commission President has yet been appointed without the consensus of all Member States. Even when President Barroso was being appointed it became clear during the decision-making process that a qualified majority decision was not on the agenda. After being appointed, the designated President presents himself in front of the Parliament for the vote of approval. After the President has been confirmed in his office, the Member States determine the members of the Commission conjointly with the President. The whole college then presents itself in front of the European Parliament for the vote of approval.

This form of investiture by the Parliament existed in the past, but only in 2004 was the attention of the European public drawn for the first time to the European Parliament's right of confirmation. In autumn 2004, the designated President of the Commission was openly threatened with rejection of his team, which led him to postpone the vote of approval. The European Parliament had in particular disapproved of the strongly conservative, Catholic Italian candidate and also voiced criticism of the Hungarian, Latvian and Dutch candidates. After two changes in the appointments and two further changes to the areas of responsibility, the new Commission was approved by the Parliament after a delay of two months.

Although the Commission members are proposed by their Member States, the Council and the Parliament must confirm the future Commissioners in their office. After taking up office, the Commission members can no longer be led by national and party political interests because they have to safeguard the independence of the Commission and are obliged to act in accordance with the European Union as a whole. When holding office, the Commission members may not seek or accept any instructions from a government or any other body. The Member States themselves are obliged to ensure that this independence is maintained and may not attempt to influence the Commission when it is fulfilling its tasks.

The President and Vice-Presidents

In the EU's past, the main stress was on the collegial nature of the body. The President was more a *primus inter pares* and, despite their being individually responsible for a particular section, all of the Commissioners also in a way had overall responsibility for the policies of the EU.

The college as a whole always took decisions by a majority of its members' votes (Article 219). Although this is not always the case, nowadays, in addition to the college's responsibility, the President has greater political responsibility. According to Article 217, he exercises political control, determines the internal structure and can also reallocate responsibilities between Commissioners and, in agreement with these, appoint Vice-Presidents. In the current Commission under Barroso there are five Vice-Presidents:

1. The first Vice-President, Margot Wallström from Sweden, is in charge of communications and inter-institutional relations. Her principal task relates to better communication with the media and the public on the Commission's policies, a task in which she needs the support of her colleagues. She is also in particular responsible for co-ordinating the Commission's policies with the strengthened European Parliament.
2. The German Vice-President, Günther Verheugen, is responsible for corporate and industrial policy.
3. The third Vice-President of the Commission is the Frenchman Jacques Barrot. His area of responsibility is transport policy.
4. The fourth Vice-President, Siim Kallas, is from Estonia. His areas of responsibility are administrative tasks, audit and anti-fraud. (Fraud in particular is becoming an issue of increasing importance.)
5. The fifth Vice-President of the Commission is the former Italian foreign minister Franco Frattini. As Commissioner, he is responsible for the growing and ever more important areas of justice, freedom and security.

In the rather egalitarian Commission of the past the title of 'Vice-President' was largely honorary in nature. In the President's absence, the highest-ranking Vice-President chaired the college. However, a new wind is blowing through the new Commission. President Barroso endeavoured to run his Commission in a more hierarchical manner and give individual Vice-Presidents more political weight by putting them in charge of Commissioners' working groups. In a body now made up of 27 Commissioners this stronger hierarchical team appears to be a thing of necessity. It is the only way to guarantee the Commission's efficiency.

DISTRIBUTION OF TASKS AMONG COMMISSION MEMBERS (2004–2009)

In each Commission there are areas of responsibility with greater and lesser political importance. As a result, the political weight within the

Commission is naturally very unevenly distributed. When the Commission is being reappointed, every five years, a lively tug-of-war takes place behind the scenes so that each country can obtain the most important area of responsibility for 'its' Commissioner. In this respect, there exist old national preferences among the Member States, but these cannot always be satisfied.

The President frequently appoints in important areas Commissioners who are beginning a second term of office and who, due to their previous activity, bring special knowledge of the EU and political experience with regard to the machinery of the European Commission.

This process proved to be more difficult where the new Commission was concerned, because, following the accession of the 10 new Member States, 10 new members had to be included. Furthermore, the five 'big' members – Germany, France, Italy, Great Britain and Spain – lost their old right to nominate two Commissioners. After the accession of Romania and Bulgaria a further two Commissioners were added. This is why this comprehensive table of all 27 Commissioners and their responsibilities includes only a few faces from the old Commission:

The two Vice-Presidents, Wallström and Verheugen, as well as the Luxembourgian Commissioner, Viviane Reding, who is responsible for Information Society and Media, were members of the previous Commission. The Spaniard Almunia is neither a proper Commissioner from the old team around Romano Prodi nor a wholly new Commissioner because he replaced another Spaniard, Pedro Solbes, who left office prematurely during the last months of the Prodi Commission. The same applies to Jacques Barrot, who replaced Michel Barnier at the end of the Prodi Commission.

The most important areas of responsibility in the Commission are agricultural policy, regional policy, foreign trade, the single market, enlargement and competition policy. These are followed in second rank by environmental policy, foreign policy, development aid and budgetary policy.

DECISION-MAKING BY THE COMMISSION MEMBERS

The Commission usually meets every Wednesday. The closed meetings are chaired by the President in the meeting room of the Commission's

Berlaymont building, which was reopened in winter 2004 after being thoroughly renovated. This building houses the General Secretariat of the Commission, the legal service and the press relations service. All of the Commissioners and their closest colleagues, known as the Cabinets, also have their office in the Berlaymont.

Three basic decision-making procedures are available to the Commission:

1. First, decisions can be taken within the context of the weekly meetings of the whole college of the Commission. Decisions of political importance in particular come about in this way. A vote then takes place among the Commissioners, whereby a simple majority of the votes is the crucial factor.
2. Second, in written procedure, a proposal is submitted to the college in written form without a meeting taking place. When a deadline set by the Commissioner responsible for the area in question has passed, the decision is considered as accepted if no Commissioner has raised an objection to it. If an objection is raised, the proposal must be discussed and voted on within the college. Written procedures mainly concern matters related to everyday administrative business.
3. Third, there is the empowerment procedure, which is the most frequently used decision-making procedure of the Commission. In this case, as a result of a decision of the Commission, individual Commissioners are authorized to sign, in other words, to take decisions, on behalf of the Commission in their area of responsibility. This procedure is the main source of a type of sectional responsibility on the part of the Commissioners. Decisions in the agricultural sector and in relation to anti-dumping procedures are mostly taken using the empowerment procedure. The collegial principle is safeguarded here too, due to the fact that individual Commissioners from other sections can always challenge decisions taken in this manner.

THE CABINETS

With a form of decision-making that adheres to the collegial principle, it is clear that a Commissioner needs to have a broad overview of all EU policy areas when preparing the meetings of Commissioners and

Table 2.1 Members of the Barroso Commission (2004–2009)

Commission member	Area of responsibility[1]	Nationality
José Manuel Barroso	President	Portuguese
Margot Wallström	Vice-President – Institutional Relations and Communications Strategy	Swedish
Günther Verheugen	Vice-President – Enterprise and Industry	German
Jacques Barrot	Vice-President – Transport	French
Siim Kallas	Vice-President – Administration, Audit and Anti-Fraud	Estonian
Franco Frattini	Vice-President – Justice, Freedom and Security	Italian
Viviane Reding	Information Society and Media	Luxembourgian
Stavros Dimas	Environment	Greek
Joaquín Almunia	Economic and Monetary Affairs	Spanish
Danuta Hübner	Regional Policy	Polish
Joe Borg	Fisheries and Maritime Affairs	Maltese
Dalia Grybauskaite	Financial Planning and Budget	Lithuanian
Janez Potočnik	Research and Technological Development	Slovenian
Ján Figel'	Vocational and General Education and Culture	Slovakian
Leonard Orban	Multilingualism	Romanian
Markos Kyprianou	Health	Cypriot
Meglena Kuneva	Consumer Protection	Bulgarian
Olli Rehn	Enlargement	Finnish
Louis Michel	Development and Humanitarian Aid	Belgian
László Kovács	Taxation and Customs Union	Hungarian
Neelie Kroes	Competition	Dutch
Mariann Fischer-Boel	Agriculture and Rural Development	Danish
Benita Ferrero-Waldner	External Relations and European Neighbourhood Policy	Austrian
Charlie McCreevy	Internal Market and Services	Irish
Vladimir Špidla	Employment, Social Affairs and Equal Opportunities	Czech
Peter Mandelson	Trade	British
Andris Piebalgs	Energy	Latvian

[1] Table in accordance with the sequence of protocol.

in relation to daily political business. The Directorates General, which are answerable to the Commissioners, are not capable of this because they are active in only one area of responsibility, such as environmental policy or agricultural policy. This is why there is an intermediate organ – the Cabinets.

Similar to a ministerial office with officials working directly with the minister, the Cabinet members on the one hand form the link between the Directorate General and the Commissioner and, on the other, between one Commissioner and the other Commissioners.

The number of staff working in a Cabinet varies and is laid down by the Commission at the beginning of its term of office. There are currently six to seven 'A' posts in each Cabinet (in other words, positions within the EU institutions that correspond to the higher civil service). The President's Cabinet has three additional posts.

Due to the highly important political role they fulfil, staff in such a Cabinet are frequently selected because they have been working in the Commissioners' environment up until that point. People with special skills and abilities in the Commissioner's area of responsibility are also often sought. According to the valid code of conduct for Cabinets, no more than half of the members of staff should have the same nationality as the Commissioner. In addition, either the Head of Conduct or his or her deputy should have a different nationality. In the interests of promoting women, it was decided that at least two of the six Cabinet members must be female. Such a Commissioner's Cabinet is run by a Head of Cabinet and a Deputy Head of Cabinet.

The Cabinet Heads decide together with the Commissioner the way in which the work is allocated within the Cabinet. Due to the distinctive collegial principle, the six to seven individuals usually have tasks allocated vertically and horizontally. In this case, vertical means that the different areas of responsibility for which the Commissioner is directly responsible are each assigned to one Cabinet member. For example, if a Commissioner is responsible for enlargement, the countries covered by the enlargement policy are assigned specific Cabinet members.

Horizontal responsibilities, on the other hand, cover all of the Commission's areas of responsibility. Due to the collegial principle, it is incumbent upon one specific member of each Cabinet to keep the Commissioner up to date regarding the most important developments within a particular policy area and to prepare him or her for the discussions within the college.

The Cabinet analyses the proposals, which are often hundreds of pages long, for the Commissioners and develops the most important core policy elements from them. The Cabinets also play an important role when policies are being communicated to the outside world. Among other things, they write speeches for the Commissioners or revise texts of speeches written by the divisions for the Commissioner.

A good Cabinet can enable a Commissioner who is not very well versed in policy to shine, while a bad Cabinet deprives Commissioners of the opportunity to make their name in relation to EU policy in general as well as in their area of responsibility.

Preliminary negotiations on political compromises related to decisions to be put to the Commission thus mainly take place at Cabinet level. This usually happens during two meetings that take place on the Monday and Tuesday before the Wednesday meeting of the college. During these two meetings, the collegial meeting for the current week is prepared down to the tiniest detail so that as many points of contention as possible between the Commissioners can be cleared out of the way. During the Monday meeting, all the Cabinet members from all 27 Cabinets responsible for the special area discuss a proposal for a decision. In this respect, the relevant staff member from the office of the Commissioner with responsibility for the area in question presents the case. Before the college meets, the Heads of Cabinet then have their weekly meeting in order to clarify as much as possible as many contentious issues as they can.

There is no doubt that, without the Cabinets, the Commissioners would be almost incapable of performing their political role. The Cabinets are the backbone of the commission college. However, political importance within the Commission is directly linked to the collegial principle. The more influence the Commissioners exert on areas for which they are not directly responsible, the greater the need to negotiate between the Cabinets.

At present it is not possible to foresee to what extent this trend will continue or further develop. Much also depends on the political successes of the President and the present Commission as a whole. Due to the standing they have acquired over time, individual Commissioners and Heads of Cabinet can also exert greater influence within the Commission. The same applies to the Directorates General in their areas of responsibility.

3

Directorates General and Services: the administrative structure of the Commission

THE EUROPEAN COMMISSION AS AN AUTHORITY

The administrative structure of the Commission

On the one hand, the European Commission is the collegial organ of the 27 Commission members (*see* Chapter 2). On the other, the Directorates General and Services make up the Commission as an authority. The administrative apparatus, well over 20,000 people strong, is divided into sectoral Directorates General and horizontal Services with cross-cutting roles. As a rule, each of the 27 Commission members is responsible for one or several of the Directorates General or Services.

The Commission's Directorates General and Services are structured according to function. Each of them is responsible for one or several policies or duties and employs officials, temporary staff and national experts. Around half of the Directorates General and Services are comparable to national ministries and deal with specific areas of Community policy (e.g. external relations, agriculture, the single market, social affairs, trade and regional policy).

The other Services – the French term *services* is most frequently used to describe them – operate horizontally. They are primarily responsible for the co-ordination, coherence and effectiveness of the Commission's work and for the different aspects of internal management of the Commission. The General Secretariat is particularly important; it guarantees an efficient internal workflow, the smooth running of the collegial decision-making process and good relations with the other institutions of the EU. The Legal Service is equally significant; it is responsible for providing legal advice internally, checks all of the Commission's texts from a legal point of view and ensures that the content of all text versions is the same in all of the Community languages. The Directorates General for Interpreting and Translation translate texts into each of the 23 official languages and facilitate understanding at multilingual conferences through simultaneous interpreting. The Commission's employees are divided up among the Directorates General and other Services in the following way:

The internal structure of the Commission's divisions corresponds to the classic pyramid diagram. At its top is a Director General, who is supported by one or several Deputy Directors General. In addition, one or several assistants are available to the Directors General. The Directorates General are divided up into several 'directorates' – comparable perhaps to departments in some national ministries – and finally into 'units'. The directorates are identified by capital letters, the units by Arabic numerals. The titles of the officials running these units correspond to this structure:

- Director General[i];
- Director;
- Head of Unit.

The operational level within the administrative structure of the Commission is the unit (French: *unité*). All decisions are implemented

[i] In September 2005, a rotational decision will be taken with regard to the filling of the posts of Director General and Deputy Director General. This means that, by January 2006, staffing of the highest administrative posts in the European Commission will have changed fundamentally. For this reason the names of the Directors General and their Deputies are mentioned in the individual chapters, but not in the schematic illustrations (organigrams) for the Services.

Table 3.1 The administrative structure of the European Commission

27 members of the Commission	
The President of the Commission **Five Vice-Presidents** **22 members of the Commission**	
Cabinets of the Commission members	
General Services • Secretariat-General • Legal Service • Official Publications Office • European Anti-Fraud Office • European Recruitment Office • Eurostat	**Internal Services** • DG Personnel and Administration • Internal Audit Service • Bureau of European Policy Advisers • Joint Interpreting and Conferencing Service • DG Data Processing • Office for Administration and Payment of Individual Entitlements • Infrastructures and Logistics Office, Brussels • Infrastructures and Logistics Office, Luxembourg
The Policy Areas • DG Employment, Social Affairs and Equal Opportunities • DG Education and Culture • DG Internal Market and Services • DG Fisheries and Maritime Affairs • DG Research • Joint Research Centre • DG Health and Consumer Protection • DG Information Society • DG Justice, Freedom and Security • DG Agriculture and Rural Development • DG Regional Policy • DG Taxation and Customs Union • DG Environment • DG Enterprise and Industry • DG Transport and Energy • DG Competition • DG Economic and Financial Affairs • DG Budget • DG Communications	**External Relations** • Humanitarian Aid Office ECHO • DG External Relations • DG Development • DG Enlargement • EuropeAid – Cooperation Office • Trade

Table 3.2 Division of staff between the Directorates General and Services

Directorates General/Services	Officials
Cabinets	406
Secretariat-General	443
Legal Service	300
DG Communications	405
Bureau of European Policy Advisers	19
DG Economic and Financial Affairs	403
DG Enterprise and Industry	646
DG Competition	535
DG Employment and Social Affairs	496
DG Agriculture	815
DG Energy and Transport	806
DG Environment	440
DG Research	1,121
Joint Research Centre	1,590
DG Information Society	752
DG Fisheries	252
DG Internal Market and Services	335
DG Regional Policy	436
DG Taxation and Customs Union	319
DG Education and Culture	535
DG Health and Consumer Protection	549
DG Justice, Freedom and Security	241
DG External Relations	701
DG Trade	385
DG Development	266
DG Enlargement	202
EuropeAid – Office for Co-operation	734
Humanitarian Aid Office	137
Eurostat	528
DG Personnel and Administration	664
DG Data Processing	335
DG Budget	396
Internal Audit Service	72
European Anti-Fraud Office	259
DG Interpreting	588
DG Translation	1,857
Official Publications Office	485
Infrastructures and Logistics Office, Brussels	466
Paymaster's Office	257
Infrastructures and Logistics Office, Luxembourg	188
Recruitment Office	85
Unified External Service	798
Total	**21,247**

Source: European Commission, 2004

there. If an issue affects different divisions, a directing head of unit (*chef de file*) is appointed. He is responsible for the dossier, contacts the other affected Services (*services associés*) and consults with them. The head of unit in charge asks other units to make a statement; inter-service meetings frequently take place. The Secretariat General of the Commission ensures that the internal procedural regulations and deadlines are complied with and fulfils important co-ordinating tasks. The Legal Service must be consulted in every case. If the relevant units cannot come to a joint decision on a dossier, there is an attempt to reach agreement at Cabinet level, either during the weekly Cabinet meetings or during the special Cabinet meetings.

Unlike most other administrative bodies, the Commission is subject to near-permanent restructuring. The type of work done by the Commission demands and encourages continuous rethinking with regard to the existing structural forms. Conceptual and structural tasks are of greater importance than in national authorities because there are no pre-existing models for the drafting of EU policy. The latest political changes are frequently expressed in new types of assignments for which no adequate administrative structures are available. In these cases, task forces are formed: these are special working groups within the Commission, which, for example, became active during the negotiations on accession. Since the Council of Ministers naturally does not approve an unlimited number of new positions for the Commission, staff must be released for new areas of activity by restructuring and adjusting priorities.

The seat of the European Commission

In 1992, the European Council in Edinburgh made a decision on the headquarters of the EU institutions. The Commission has its head office in Brussels. In 2004, 15,535 officials and temporary staff were working there. Individual divisions (e.g. the Eurostat Statistical Office) and parts of individual Directorates General and Services (e.g. the Translation Service) are based in secondary headquarters in Luxembourg. In 2004, 2,776 people were employed there. In addition, several hundred members of the Commission's staff work in the 129 Delegations of the Commission in third-party countries.

In Brussels itself, the Directorates General and Services are divided among a considerable number of administrative buildings. After years of renovation work, the Berlaymont building on the lively Rue de la Loi has once again become the Commission's main base. Due to asbestos-related problems, it had to be vacated in 1991 and lost its role as the headquarters of the Commission in Brussels. The new Berlaymont, officially opened by the former President of the European Commission, Romano Prodi, during celebrations held on 21 October 2004, once again unites the college of Commissioners with their Cabinets under one roof. The members of the Prodi Commission and their staff had moved into the buildings occupied by their Directorates General and Services.

OFFICIALS AND STAFF OF THE EUROPEAN COMMISSION

Staff regulations and administrative reform of the Commission

In October 2004, the European Commission employed 21,247 officials and temporary staff, by far the highest number of staff in any institution of the European Union. (Including the decentralized agencies, staff numbers exceeded 25,000.) Taken together, about 37,000 employees in all worked in the European institutions in 2004. There were 4,897 in the European Parliament, 3,148 in the European Council and 1,644 in the European Court of Justice. Eurosceptics have frequently voiced the criticism that the European Commission is a bureaucratic monster: this seems dubious considering that the Commission works on such crucial policy areas as economic and competition policy for nearly half a billion EU citizens, but employs fewer officials than the administrative body of a medium-sized city.

Employees of the European Commission must be citizens of an EU Member State and in a position to work in a multilingual and multicultural environment outside their country of origin. They must be capable of working in several foreign languages on a daily basis, in both spoken and written form. (English, French and German are all working languages of the Commission. For decades, French dominated in meetings and texts but, since the 1990s – in particular following the accession of Sweden and Finland – English has been gaining ground. The accession of eight Central and Eastern European countries as well as Cyprus and Malta has further consolidated this development.)

According to Article 1 of the European Staff Regulations, an official is someone who 'has been appointed to a permanent position in one of the bodies of the Community through an act of that body's appointing authority in accordance with the provisions of the staff regulations'. The staff regulations regulate the individual and collective rights and duties that officials enjoy and fulfil. For example, in contrast to German civil servants, European officials have the right to strike. According to Article 11 of the Staff Regulations, 'in the execution of his office and in his behaviour, an official must be guided exclusively by the interests of the Communities; he or she may not request or receive instructions from any government, authority, organization or person outside of this body.' However, officials working in the Commission naturally retain their nationality and maintain a special bond with their country of origin. Although there are no regulations on quotas concerning the employment of European officials, the staff regulations stress the necessity to achieve the greatest possible balance between the EU nationalities. By 2010, more than 4,000 officials from the new EU Member States will have been integrated into the apparatus of the Commission. The nationalities of the official working in the Commission in October 2004 were divided up as shown in Table 3.3.

In addition to the regular officials who, according to the staff regulations, are to fulfil the core tasks of the Commission, the Commission also employs a number of temporary staff members (*agents temporaires*) and 'national experts'. Temporary staff members are mostly but not exclusively active in the area of research and development. They also help to alleviate staff shortages, carry out exceptional and temporary tasks and support the cabinets. National experts from the EU Member States and the accession countries, who may work in Brussels for a maximum of four years, provide the Commission with a closer bond to the national administrations and a specialized knowledge base. In addition, due to the presence of the national experts, the Member States have the opportunity to shape particularly important and sensitive subject areas.

In 1962, staff regulations were created for the European officials by an act of the Council. These staff regulations have changed in many ways over the years. In response to a corruption scandal and crisis in 1999 and the subsequent resignation of the EU Commission under its President, Jacques Santer, the most comprehensive reform of the staff regulations occurred at the turn of the millennium. The Prodi Commission introduced the reform process in January 2000 with a 'White Paper on administrative reform'. In October 2001, the

Table 3.3 Officials and temporary staff working in the Commission according to Member State

Member State	Officials
Austria	436
Belgium	4,929
Czech Republic	47
Cyprus	9
Germany	2,036
Denmark	535
Spain	1,786
Estonia	32
France	2,478
Finland	604
Great Britain	1,458
Greece	932
Hungary	57
Italy	2,640
Ireland	553
Luxembourg	313
Latvia	32
Lithuania	36
Malta	22
Netherlands	746
Portugal	775
Poland	76
Sweden	609
Slovak Republic	44
Other countries	0
Total	**21,247**

Source: European Commission, 2004

new regulations, which focus on the promotion of efficiency and transparency were adopted. The core components of the most recent administrative reforms, which have explicitly set themselves the goal of creating an 'administrative body for half a billion citizens' are as follows: a rigorous and transparent form of performance appraisal, promotion based on performance instead of years of service, and the improvement of working conditions. The Commission has been implementing the measures to these ends since 2002; in some areas (e.g. regarding career and salary structures), transitional regulations will apply in the coming years.

Recruitment

As part of the comprehensive administrative reforms, the regulations affecting the recruitment procedure, the careers system and salaries were amended quite significantly. According to Article 27 of the staff regulations, European officials must 'satisfy the highest demands with regard to ability, performance and integrity' and 'must be selected from as broad as possible a geographical basis among the nationals of the Member States'. An age limit of 45 existing since 1998 was abolished as part of the administrative reforms. The European Parliament and the European Ombudsman in particular no longer considered the general exclusion of older workers to be justifiable because of the precarious situation on the labour market as well as the Charter of Fundamental Rights of the European Union. This means that age, as well as gender, skin colour and religion, cannot be used as a reason for unequal treatment.

If a post is to be filled in the European Commission or in another organ of the EU, a check is first made to see whether a transfer or a promotion is possible within the organ in question, an internal selection procedure may be carried out, or an official may be recruited from another institution. If it is not possible to fill the post in one of these ways, a general selection procedure is initiated. This selection procedure – called the *concours* in French – can also be used to form a reserve for future recruitment. When higher-ranking officials (e.g. Directors General) are being recruited, this procedure is not followed in most cases because the filling of such positions depends above all on political considerations.

Selection procedures must be publicized at least two months before the interviews are scheduled to take place, in the *Official Journal of the European Communities*. (They are sometimes also published in the jobs sections of trans-regional newspapers or in the specialist press.) These advertisements provide information on both the requirements and the conditions for admission, and contain the prescribed application form. The demands made on the successful applicants are high. In addition to a basic knowledge of one of the official languages, sufficient knowledge of at least one additional official language is required. Naturally, the applicants must also have an excellent knowledge of the European Union in order to be successful during the extremely difficult general selection procedure. Furthermore, there are special subject-specific posts that require specialist knowledge and extensive professional experience. As a rule, the selection procedures involve written and oral examinations which each applicant must complete successfully. The examining committee then draws up a list of applicants who fulfil the requirements for the advertised positions. Each of the Commission's divisions uses this list when filling its vacant positions. The number of names on this list of suitable persons always exceeds the number of positions available and is valid for a limited period of time. Even if an applicant is successful during the *concours*, he or she is not guaranteed a position.

The most important changes to the recruitment procedure for the European institutions initiated as part of the administrative reforms concern increased inter-institutional co-operation, which is co-ordinated by the European Personnel Selection Office (EPSO). The office, which began work on 1 January 2003, is an inter-institutional recruitment authority that promotes transparency, standardization and equal treatment during the selection procedure, and tests recruitment practices in order to better harmonize staff requirements and applicants' profiles.

To give potential applicants a taste of the work done by the EU, the Commission offers two internships a year lasting for a period of five months. The internships – called *stages* in French – begin on 1 March (closing date for applications: 1 September of the previous year) and 1 October (closing date for applications: 1 March of the same year) of each year. The participants, some of whom receive remuneration, usually carry out the tasks of young officials in administration, i.e. they compile information and documents, organize working groups, public hearings and meetings, write reports and answer queries, and revise the language contained in texts.

The Commission receives over 7,000 applications for each internship period, whereas only 600 places have to be filled. The basic precondition for participation is a completed university education or proof that an applicant has successfully studied for at least eight semesters. The participants come from all over the world, although most of them are from the Member States and the candidate countries. A commission of experts makes a pre-selection of the applications and includes about 2,500 applicants in what is known as a 'blue book'. The Directorates General and individual units then make their final selection from this document.

Careers

Before the administrative reforms came into force, a distinction was made between four career groups (A to D), which were divided into different salary groups. To enter any of these groups, applicants first had to provide evidence of a specific level of education (a university degree or a higher school-leaving certificate). The current necessity for staff to fulfil an increasing number of tasks and the blurring of the differences between positions caused by developments in information technology led to fundamental changes in this system, which were completed as part of the process of administrative reform. The four types of career were merged into two function groups and 16 salary groups. The former 'C' and 'B' officials now became assistants (AST officials). Classified as part of salary groups 1–11, they are mainly active in supportive positions. 'A' officials became administrators (AD officials). They occupy salary groups 5–16, draw up and implement EU law, and are used for scientific and consultative purposes.

While the old career and salary system practically guaranteed salary increases for employees with the most years of service, the new system is increasingly based on performance, motivation and the employee's willingness to take responsibility. Promotions and salary increases no longer happen automatically, but are based on an assessment of the officials' behaviour, his performance and competence. These assessments occur annually and are carried out in the form of a discussion with an official's immediate superior. It has also become easier for an assistant to rise to the position of administrator. Following a period of further training, an assessment and preparation for the demands of the higher function group, such a move, which was rare as part of the old system, is facilitated. Since value is generally placed on continuous career development, there is increasing support for efforts to obtain further training. The budget for professional training was increased and the average number of days on which such training may take place was being extended from 2.5 to 10.

Salaries

In a time of increasing globalization, the European Commission finds itself in strong competition with other international organizations and companies for the best workers on the labour market, and it

Table 3.4 Function and salary groups

Function Group AD, active as ('administrator')		Function group AST, active as ('assistant')	
Director General	AD 16	–	
Director General/Director	AD 15	–	
AD Director/ Head of unit/ Advisor/ Head linguistic expert, Head legal expert, Head scientific expert	AD 14	–	
AD Head of unit/ Advisor Head linguistic expert, Head legal expert, Head scientific expert	AD 13	–	
AD Head of unit/ Principal translator, Principal interpreter, Principal legal expert, Principal scientific expert	AD 12	–	
AD Head of unit/ Principal translator, Principal interpreter, Principal legal expert, Principal scientific expert	AD 11	AST 11	Personal assistant, Administrative assistant, Technical assistant
AD Head of unit/ Senior translator, Senior interpreter, senior legal expert, Senior scientific expert	AD 10	AST 10	Personal assistant, Administrative assistant, Technical assistant

Table 3.4 *(continued)*

Function Group AD, active as ('administrator')			Function group AST, active as ('assistant')
AD Head of unit/ Senior translator, Senior interpreter, senior legal expert, Senior scientific expert	AD 9	AST 9	Personal assistant, Administrative assistant, Technical assistant
AD Translator, interpreter, legal expert, scientific expert	AD 8	AST 8	Principal clerical officer Senior documentalist Senior technician
AD Translator, interpreter, legal expert, scientific expert	AD 7	AST 7	Principal clerical officer Senior documentalist Senior technician
AD Translator occupying initial post Interpreter occupying initial post, Legal expert occupying initial post, Scientific expert occupying initial post	AD 6	AST 6	Clerical officer Documentalist Technician
AD Translator occupying initial post Interpreter occupying initial post, Legal expert occupying initial post, Scientific expert occupying initial post	AD 5	AST 5	Clerical officer Documentalist Technician
	–	AST 4	Clerical officer occupying initial post, Documentalist occupying initial post, Technician occupying initial post

Table 3.4 Function and salary groups *(continued)*

Function Group AD, active as ('administrator')		Function group AST, active as ('assistant')	
	–	AST 3	
			Clerical officer occupying initial post, Documentalist occupying initial post, Technician occupying initial post, Parliamentary usher
	–	AST 2	
			Secretarial assistant, Technical assistant, Parliamentary usher
	–	AST 1	
			Secretarial assistant, Technical assistant, Parliamentary usher

Source: European Commission, 2004

therefore has to offer attractive salaries in order to acquire highly qualified employees. This is why officials' salaries were fixed at a high rate from the very beginning and are thus significantly higher than those typically earned by officials in the Member States. Despite the most recent and partially successful attempts to rationalize European employment regulations and the salary system, this issue is regularly taken up in the media and not always in the most objective manner. The gap in salaries between European and national officials is often criticized and politicized. However, it should be pointed out that the salary levels for EU institutions are comparable with the salaries paid by the EU Member States to officials active in the diplomatic service in foreign countries. Salaries paid in other international institutions also largely correspond to the salary levels for European Union officials.

Obviously, the European Commission alone does not decide on the salaries to which its officials are entitled. The European Council fixes basic salaries which apply for several years and the regular adjustments applied to the officials' salaries. The latter, however, are proposed by the European Commission.

As part of the administrative reforms, the following three aspects of the salary system were changed in accordance with the reforms to the careers system:

- The existing salary level was retained, but adapted to the new careers system. More attention is now paid to the officials' performance and competence than to their years of service. Officials who perform well have the opportunity to climb higher on the salary ladder as their career progresses. However, no significant change was made to the overall volume of salary payments, which means that officials do not earn less today than they did in the past. However, all newcomers are placed on a lower salary level than was previously the case.
- The development in salaries was tied to that of salaries in the public service in the European Member States so that time-consuming annual negotiations can be avoided.
- Third, the allowance system was greatly simplified. (Allowances typically paid to officials of the European Commission include the household allowance, the allowance for dependent children, the education allowance, the expatriation allowance, an allowance for an annual journey to the official's country of origin and the reimbursement of relocation expenses.)

The officials' basic monthly salary is paid in accordance with their salary level and their number of years of service. The monthly basic salaries are fixed in accordance with Table 3.5 overleaf.

Naturally, EU officials also pay tax; the highest tax rate is 45 per cent. Private health insurance is deducted from the monthly salary. The normal retirement age for EU officials is 60; however, they are free to retire between 50 and 65 years of age. A European official acquires a claim to a pension after completing at least 10 years of service; after completing 35 years of service, officials are entitled to the highest possible pension totalling 70 per cent of their last basic salary. In order to qualify for a pension, officials are obliged to contribute a portion of their gross salary.

Table 3.5 Basic monthly salary for EU officials in 2004, in euros

Salary group	Length of service level				
	1	2	3	4	5
16	14,822.26	15,445.74	16,094.79	–	–
15	13,100.93	13,651.45	14,225.11	14,620.87	14,822.86
14	11,579.04	12,065.60	12,572.62	12,922.41	13,100.93
13	10,233.93	10,663.98	11,112.09	11,421.25	11,597.04
12	9,045.09	9,425.17	9,821.23	10,094.47	10,233.93
11	7,994.35	8,330.28	8,680.33	8,921.83	9,045.09
10	7,065.67	7,362.57	7,671.96	7,885.41	7,994.35
9	6,244.87	6,507.29	6,780.73	6,969.38	7,065.67
8	5,519.42	5,751.35	5,993.03	6,159.77	6,244.87
7	4,878.24	5,083.24	5,296.84	5,444.21	5,519.42
6	4,311.55	4,492.73	4,681.52	4,811.77	4,878.24
5	3,810.69	3,970.82	4,137.68	4,252.80	4,311.55
4	3,368.02	3,509.54	3,657.02	3,758.76	3,810.69
3	2,976.76	3,101.85	3,232.19	3,322.12	3,368.02
2	2,630.96	2741.52	2,856.72	2,956.20	2,976.76
1	2,325.33	2,423.04	2,524.86	2,595.11	2,630.96

4

The policies

DIRECTORATE GENERAL FOR EMPLOYMENT, SOCIAL AFFAIRS AND EQUAL OPPORTUNITIES – DG EMPL

http://ec.europa.eu/dgs/employment_social/index_en.htm

The Directorate General for Employment, Social Affairs and Equal Opportunities has become one of the strategic Services of the European Commission since the European Council approved the so-called Lisbon Agenda on 23 and 24 March 2000 in order to consolidate employment, growth and social cohesion as the components of a knowledge-based economy.

By this time it had become clear that the high rate of unemployment observed in almost all of the EU Member States had to be tackled jointly. Due to the challenge posed by a globalized world economy increasingly based on knowledge, and due to the fact that new competitors on the world market were overtaking the EU countries, the EU believed that joint reflection on the future of its economic, social and employment policy was necessary.

The Directorate General for EMPL, which is headed by the Czech Commissioner Vladimir Spidla, wants and needs to co-operate closely with authorities at local, regional and national level as well as with businesses and employers. In this respect, the aim is to come up with concrete measures to solve individual problems related to social and employment policy in order to create more employment in Europe. The co-operation between individual Member States and the relevant authorities is as important as the taking of measures at EU level aimed at solving existing problems at European level.

In order to do justice to these challenges the DG has divided up its work into three general policy areas:

- social affairs;
- employment affairs; and
- equal opportunities.

The 'Social Agenda' newly published on 9 February 2005 by the Commission and its Directorate General for Employment, Social Affairs and Equal Opportunities is a response to the challenge of the Lisbon Strategy to modernize the social model in Europe. The new Social Agenda, which for the next five years has set itself the goals of creating more employment in Europe, combating the increasing poverty in Europe and promoting equal opportunities, is to help all citizens to benefit from the economic growth in Europe.

This programme is a continuation and an updated version of the political and legal developments of earlier years. Overall economic development and the accession of new Member States with different social and employment policies (e.g. Spain, Greece and Portugal) forced the EU to initiate common regulations for the growing European labour market in the areas of health and safety in the workplace and a dialogue with and between the social partners.

Legal measures affecting health and safety in the workplace, improved working conditions and the integration of excluded persons into the labour market, and whose purpose is to create equality of opportunity between men and women, are implemented as part of the co-decision procedure by a qualified majority of the Council and following a hearing by the Economic and Social Committee and the Committee of the Regions. Measures affecting social security and social protection for employees in their employment contracts are implemented by a unanimous decision of the Council.

Policy areas and division of work

The Directorate General for Employment divides its tasks up among eight directorates and is headed by the German Director General

Table 4.1 Organizational chart, DG Employment, Social Affairs and Equal Opportunities

Deputy Director General			
Directorate A Employment strategy and definition and co-ordination of ESF policy **A.1** Employment analysis **A.2** Employment strategy **A.3** Labour administration **A.4** Co-ordination of the ESF strategy and local development of employment	**Directorate B** Monitoring the employment situation and social integration in the Member States as well as interventions by the European Social Fund I **B.1** Italy, Malta and Romania **B.2** France, Belgium and Slovak Republic **B.3** Sweden, Finland and Estonia **B.4** Community initiatives	**Directorate C** Monitoring the employment situation and social integration in the Member States as well as interventions by the European Social Fund II **C.1** Germany, Austria and Slovenia **C.2** Denmark and Poland **C.3** Spain and Lithuania **C.4** Article 6 of the ESF and ECSC	**Directorate D** Adaptability, social dialogue and social rights **D.1** Cross-sector social dialogue, labour relations, adaptation to change **D.2** Labour law and organization of labour **D.3** Anti-discrimination and relations with civil society **D.4** Safety and health protection in the workplace
Directorate E Social protection and social integration **E.1** Analysis of the social and demographic situation **E.2** Social protection and social integration; policy co-ordination **E.3** Free movement of employees and co-ordination of the systems of social security **E.4** Social protection: pensions and health	**Directorate F** Resources **F.1** Personnel and administration **F.2** Budget and financial co-ordination **F.3** Auditing of the ESF **F.4** Information technology and workflows **F.5** Ex-post controlling of expenditure by those directly responsible for administration	**Directorate G** Cross-cutting issues and international questions **G.1** Equal treatment of men and women **G.2** Enlargement and international issues **G.3** Integration of handicapped people **G.4** Communication and editing **G.5** Evaluation	**Directorate H** Monitoring the employment situation and social integration in the Member States as well as interventions by the European Social Fund III **H.1** Greece, Cyprus and Bulgaria **H.2** Netherlands, Hungary and Croatia **H.3** Ireland, United Kingdom and Latvia **H.4** Portugal, Czech Republic and Luxembourg

Nikolaus van der Pas. Directorate F deals with all of the DG's administrative tasks, e.g. personnel-related issues and IT.

Directorate A: Employment strategy as well as definitions and co-ordination of the ESF policy

The aim of Directorate A is to develop policies that promote the creation of jobs in the EU Member States and to combat unemployment through improved access to the labour market.

In this respect, Unit A.1 carries out analyses in order to improve the expertise and knowledge base related to the ways in which the labour market works. Here, trends in employment are analysed within the context of the general structural changes in the Member States.

Unit A.2 supports the Member States in relation to completing co-ordination of their employment strategies. This work is supplemented by Unit A.3, which is responsible for contacts with the employment authorities in each of the Member States.

Directorates B, C and H: Monitoring the employment situation and social integration in the Member States and interventions by the European Social Fund

An important part of the Lisbon Strategy involves co-ordination of the individual employment policies of the Member States and agreeing on common goals in order to combat unemployment. A common European employment strategy is thus to be created at last. To this end, the European Commission has at its disposal an important financial instrument, the European Social Fund (ESF), in order to translate its strategic employment policy goals into concrete measures.

The ESF supports measures for the prevention and combating of unemployment, the development of human resources and social integration on the labour market in order to promote a high level of employment, the equal treatment of men and women, sustained development, and social and economic cohesion in the EU.

The ESF offers different types of aid as well as different programmes that develop people's 'employability' skills.

The European Employment Services (EURES), the European portal for professional mobility, is an additional instrument whose purpose is to promote co-operation between each of the EU countries and their employment authorities, trade unions, labour organizations and local and regional bodies. It is a network of co-operation that provides information, advice and recruitment/placement at European level for all interested EU citizens who want to benefit from the laws on the free movement of persons and mobility.

Further information on the EURES can be found on the internet at: http://europa.eu.int/eures/home.jsp?lang=de&langChanged=true.

Directorates B, C and II are divided up into units responsible for up to three countries. Each unit carefully monitors the employment situation in each of the countries and decides jointly with the national and local authorities on the use of funds from the European Social Fund.

In this respect, Directorate B has the main task of monitoring the national plans for employment and integration in Italy, Malta and Romania (B.1), in Belgium, France and Slovakia (B.2), as well as in Sweden, Finland and Estonia (B.3), and in managing the European Social Fund in these countries. Unit B.4 has the special task of planning and providing support during implementation of the 17 programmes that make up the Community Initiative, known as EQUAL. This initiative, which is being financed by funds from the ESF, is to guarantee that discrimination and inequalities existing in the world of work and when people are seeking work are combated.

Three Units in Directorate C deal with Germany, Austria and Slovenia (C.1), Denmark and Poland (C.2), and Spain and Italy (C.3). Unit C.4 was created in order to fulfil two special tasks. On the one hand, it deals with implementation of the measures contained in Article 6 of the ESF, which includes requests for the submission of proposals and individual project management. The Article 6 measures promote the development of new, future-oriented policies and support programmes by exploring new content-related and structural approaches in the area of employment (including vocational training and industrial adaptation). On the other hand, this Unit manages the types of state aid granted under the ECSC Treaty and implements social measures in the area of mining.

Directorate H has the same country-related tasks as Directorates B and C. It is responsible for the following countries: Greece, Cyprus and Bulgaria (H.1), the Netherlands, Hungary and Croatia (H.2), Ireland, the United Kingdom and Latvia (H.3), and Portugal, the Czech Republic and Luxembourg (H.4).

Directorate D: Adaptability, social dialogue and social rights

Directorate D deals with the social dialogue between employers and employees. Unit D.1 specializes in cross-sector social dialogue and the dialogue within the branches of industry going through changes. Furthermore, it is in charge of relations with the European Foundation for the Improvement of Living and Working Conditions, with offices in Dublin, Ireland. Unit D.2 deals with labour law and the organization of labour. These areas include both amendments to laws in a changing work environment as well as improving the position of employees, and involves a debate on their social rights. The unit also co-ordinates the creation of a general monitoring system for the 17 directives in the area of labour law and their implementation in the Member States.

D.3 works on the problem area of anti-discrimination and relations with civil society. In this respect, this unit also monitors implementation of the anti-discrimination directive and, together with the Directorate General for Justice, Security and Freedom, is responsible for establishing the new agency of fundamental rights.

Unit D.4 deals with safety and health protection in the workplace and, in this connection, maintains close links with the European Agency for Safety and Health at Work, with offices in Bilbao, Spain. Furthermore, it is responsible for contacts with the World Health Organization (WHO), the International Labour Organization (ILO) and third-party countries.

Directorate E: Social protection and social integration

It is incumbent on this directorate to improve social protection for all of the people of Europe and to encourage social integration. In this respect, Unit E.1 develops analyses of the social and demographic situation in the EU by awarding studies – for example, to academics carrying out research in this area – as well as by influencing the shaping of the 16 framework programmes for research and technological development, within whose context studies related to social policy are also carried out.

As part of the EU programmes, Unit E.2 deals with combating social exclusion by means of analyses and by co-ordinating the national plans of action in these areas. In addition, the unit is, among other things, responsible for implementing the Community's programme of action aimed at combating social exclusion and evaluating co-ordination in the areas of social protection and social integration. Unit E.3 deals with the free movement of employees within the EU and the necessary harmonization of the social security systems accompanying this process. E.4 is responsible for co-ordinating the Member States' policies in the area of pensions and health insurance institutions.

Directorate G: Cross-cutting issues and international questions

Within this directorate, Unit G.1 deals with equal treatment for men and women. This also includes one of the Community's own programmes of action in this area. G.2 deals with all external aspects of the EU's employment policy and related issues, in particular the issue of how these policies are to be applied to the enlargement countries. G.3 pays particular attention to the special social problems experienced by the disabled.

G.4 is in charge of communicating the aims of the EU employment policy to the other agents involved in this area. G.5 evaluates the policies and processes in the Directorate General.

European Foundation for the Improvement of Living and Working conditions (EUROFOUND)

http://www.eurofound.europa.eu/

The goal of this foundation, which was established in 1975 by the European Council, is to promote better living and working conditions in the European Union. Its task is to collate information, analyses and research on living and working conditions in the EU and to share and discuss them with governments and other decision-makers, as well as with trade unions, employers and all the other social partners in all 27 EU countries. In this respect, it focuses on the following issues:

- employment and working conditions;
- work–life balance;
- industrial relations and partnerships; and
- social cohesion.

European Agency for Safety and Health at Work (OSHA)
http://osha.europa.eu/

This European agency was established with the purpose of taking initiatives in order to make the workplace in Europe safer, healthier and more productive. So far, it has drawn 'attention to the risks of excessive noise at work and researched and highlighted issues related to the connection between safety and health protection. Furthermore, the agency organizes conferences in order to discuss these issues with all the parties involved as part of an exchange and in order to contribute to a better and safer labour policy using new approaches.

DIRECTORATE GENERAL FOR EDUCATION AND CULTURE – DG EAC
http://ec.europa.eu/dgs/education_culture/index_en.html

The Directorate General for Education and Culture (EAC) is headed by the Slovakian Commissioner Ján Figel' and the Romanian Commissioner Leonard Orban. It deals with general education and vocational training, culture and issues related to youth, languages, sport and civil society.

The tasks fulfilled by the Directorate General are divided up into three main areas of focus. First of all, it is striving to build a 'Europe of knowledge'. The knowledge-based society is to be the foundation for permanent growth, and improved and sufficient employment, as well as for solidarity and cohesion among the citizens of Europe. The creation of a global model area for education and training is to be the main contribution to this goal. This ambitious goal for the current decade was announced in March 2000 in Lisbon by the European Council. Second, the DG EAC is contributing to the development of a European cultural area, which involves safeguarding and recognizing the cultural wealth of Europe. Last, the Directorate General wants to include all European citizens in the process of unifying Europe. Citizens, and young people in particular, are to play an active role in the European project, thereby promoting understanding, tolerance, and a sense of belonging and openness within the EU.

As provided for in the Community Treaty (Article 149), the main goals of the European Commission in the area of general education are:

Table 4.2 Organizational chart, DG Education and Culture

Directorate A	Directorate B	Directorate C	Directorate D	Directorate E
Life-long learning: Policy of general education and vocational training	Life-long learning: General education and vocational training, programmes and measures	Culture and communication	Youth, sport and relations with the citizens	Resource
A.1 Co-ordination of the policy of life-long learning	**B.1** Co-ordination of the programmes for life-long learning	**C.1** Culture	**D.1** Youth: policy	**E.1** Human resources
A.2 Schooling and higher education	**B.2** Financial audit	**C.2** Communication and information	**D.2** Youth: programmes	**E.2** Budget planning and co-ordination, reporting
A.3 Vocational and adult education and training	**B.3** Comenius, Grundtvig	**C.3** Dissemination and analyses of findings	**D.3** Sport	**E.3** Finances and controls
A.4 Innovation and transversal policy	**B.4** Erasmus, Jean Monnet	**C.4** Central Library Youth, sport and relations with the citizens	**D.4** Civil society: partnerships and visits Resources	**E.4** Data processing
A.5 Policy of multilingualism	**B.5** Leonardo da Vinci			**E.5** Document management and logistical support
A.6 Analyses, statistics and indicators	**B.6** Tempus, Erasmus Mundus			

- improved dissemination of languages;
- the promotion of youth exchanges;
- greater mobility of teachers and students;
- close co-operation between educational institutions; and
- a lively exchange of experiences within the context of the different education systems.

The following are provided for (Article 150) in the area of vocational training:

- improved adaptability in relation to changes in industrial processes;
- improved initial training and further training;
- effective co-operation between teaching establishments and companies;
- greater mobility;
- a lively exchange of information and experiences.

The European Commission has for many years organized various programmes and initiatives (e.g. the Erasmus and Leonardo da Vinci programmes, the European Credit Transfer System and the E-Learning action plan) in order to achieve these goals. The EU particularly wants to encourage the participation of young people in the democratic life of Europe.

In the area of culture, the EU has set itself the goals of disseminating European culture and history, safeguarding and protecting the European cultural heritage, non-commercial cultural exchanges and the promotion of artistic and literary works (*see* Article 151 of the Community Treaty). Through initiatives such as the Culture 2000 programme, the selection of the European Cities of Culture, directives on the trade in cultural possessions and the programme for the twinning of cities, the European Commission is translating the aforementioned initiatives into reality.

The areas of education and culture acquired a legal basis only in the Treaty of Maastricht, signed in 1992. The EU is to support, co-ordinate and supplement the educational and cultural policies of the Member States; the harmonization of national laws is prohibited.

Policy areas and division of work

The current Director General of the DG EAC is Odile Quintin from France. Directorates A to D deal with the different aspects of the above-mentioned areas (*see* below). Directorate E is responsible for internal processes such as personnel management, budget co-ordination and data processing.

Directorate A: Life-long learning – Policy of general education and vocational training

Directorate A of the Directorate General deals with the thematic bases of general education and vocational training. The concept of life-long learning is important when the core aspects of the policy are being drafted. Life-long learning – a central component of the Lisbon Strategy – aims not only to increase competitiveness and employment, but also to promote social integration, active citizenship and the personal development of the individual. The European Commission defines life-long learning as 'all learning activity undertaken throughout life, with the aim of improving knowledge, skills and competence, within a personal, civic, social and/or employment-related context'.

Unit A.1 deals with general co-ordination of the policy of life-long learning, which is made up of different policy focuses. Units A.2 and A.3 are responsible for measures in schooling and higher education as well as in vocational and adult education and training. In both areas the European Commission's main goals are to increase the standard of education, make access to education easier and open up general education and vocational training to Europe and the world. A.2 and A.3 develop measures to make these goals a reality.

Unit A.4 is in charge of developing innovative measures in the area of general education and vocational training. Furthermore, it co-ordinates cross-cutting issues, for example in the areas of research, social integration, the information society and mobility. Unit A.5 is responsible for the policy on multilingualism and drafts measures that clarify the benefits of language knowledge to European citizens, improve foreign-language courses and create a language-friendly environment in Europe. Finally, Unit A.6 draws up analyses, statistics and indicators, and evaluates them, thereby facilitating the subsequent checking and development of effective measures.

Directorate B: Life-long learning – General education and vocational training, policies and programmes

Directorate B of the DG EAC manages the practical side of the policy of life-long learning. It organizes the specific programmes that the European Commission uses to promote general education and vocational training, and implements these. Unit B.1 co-ordinates the measures and Unit B.2 carries out the financial audit for the programmes run by the Directorate.

B.3 runs the Comenius and Grundtvig programmes. Comenius is targeted towards the first phase of education, from nursery school to secondary school, and supports partnerships between schools and projects for the training and further education of teaching staff. Grundtvig supports all aspects of adult education, such as trans-national co-operation projects between educational institutions and initiatives aimed at improving teacher training. Unit B.4 is responsible for the Erasmus and Jean Monnet programmes. Erasmus is a European university project that encompasses exchange programmes for students and teachers, the joint development of teaching plans and a harmonized European system for the consideration, transferral and accumulation of students' performances (European Credit Transfer System, or ECTS). The Jean Monnet programme promotes research and educational projects dealing with European integration.

Leonard da Vinci, the European programme for the promotion of vocational training, promotes trans-national projects in order to support mobility and innovation and to improve the quality of training. Unit B.5 is in charge of this programme. Last, B.6 deals with the Tempus and Erasmus Mundus programmes. The aim of these programmes is to promote co-operation with third-party countries in the areas of university education and vocational training.

Directorate C: Culture and communication

Directorate C deals with European and international cultural policy. Unit C.1 is in charge of European cultural policy and cultural programmes. The programmes from the late 1990s (Kaleidoscope, Ariane and Raphael) were replaced at the beginning of the new millennium by the general Culture 2000 action programme. Culture 2000 supports cultural initiatives and events that are organized on a trans-national basis and that are devoted to music, the theatre, the plastic arts or literature among others.

Unit C.2 deals with the European Commission's communication and information policy, although naturally DG Communication is responsible for the majority of this policy. Unit C.3 deals with the dissemination and assessment of the results of opinion polls; in other words, it sounds out currents of opinion in Europe. Unit C.4 is responsible for the European Commission's Central Library. This contains important publications on subjects related to European integration, European and national documents and legislation, and publications from other international organizations, as well as a large number of newspapers and journals. The library is open to external visitors from 10am to 5pm, Monday to Thursday, and from 10am to 1.30pm on Fridays.

Directorate D: Youth, sport and relations with citizens

Unit D of the Directorate General deals with the target group of youth and the subject of sport. Unit D.1 formulates the European Commission's general youth policy. In this respect, the role played by young people as European integration progresses is being revaluated on a continuous basis. The inclusion of young people in public life, and the consideration of their interests in all policy areas, are the unit's most important policy guidelines used as a reference by Unit D.1. The concrete measures are administered in Unit D.2. One example is the YOUTH programme. Here, financial aid is used to support a range of exchange programmes and voluntary projects in which young people from 31 European countries can take part.

Unit D.3 drafts the European Commission's sports policy. The European Commission co-operates with national and international sports bodies, organizations and associations, and initiates projects for the promotion of sport and health awareness, such as the European Year of Education through Sport 2004. Finally, Unit D.4 endeavours to encourage activities among European citizens. The European Commission supports action projects and seminars proposed by non-governmental organizations (NGOs), associations and clubs that are particularly interesting from a European point of view and that encourage participation by citizens. Unit D.4 also functions as the European Commission's Visitor Service.

European Centre for the Development of Vocational Training (CEDEFOP) *http://www.cedefop.europa.eu/*

The European Centre for the Development of Vocational Training was established in 1975 and, since 1995, has had its offices in the Greek city of Thessalonica. Its Head is Aviana Bulgarelli. It works on developing and improving vocational training measures throughout Europe. In its capacity as a specialist and decentralized agency, it provides technical and scientific know-how and promotes co-operation between different European partners in the area of vocational training. The CEDEFOP gathers, analyses and disseminates information, sponsors innovative and trans-national research and provides a forum for the exchange of opinions. Until 2006, the most important goals of the agency were:

- better access to vocational training;
- greater mobility;
- increasing the esteem in which learning is held; and
- supporting educational and training networks and partnerships in the enlarged union.

European Training Foundation (ETF)
http://www.etf.europa.eu/

Headed by the British Director, Muriel Dunbar, the European Training Foundation (ETF), with offices in Turin, carries out work that is not dissimilar to that done by the CEDEFOP. However, the geographical focus of the ETF is on the applicant countries – South Eastern and Eastern Europe, Central Asia and the Mediterranean area. The foundation also has the status of an autonomous agency and works for the European institutions, in particular for the European Commission. Through exchanges of know-how, the ETF helps people develop their professional skills. By doing so, it aims above all to contribute to competitiveness, employment and mobility in modern economies. In the EU's partner countries, it supports sustained socio-economic development by promoting vocational training systems. EU programmes such as PHARE, CARDS, Tacis and MEDA facilitate the implementation of reforms in this area. The foundation establishes priorities for the reorganization of vocational and further education and training, and drafts, monitors and evaluates projects in co-operation with agents in the partner countries in order to push reforms forward.

The ETF also provides technical support during the implementation of the European Commission's Tempus programme.

DIRECTORATE GENERAL FOR INTERNAL MARKET AND SERVICES – DG MARKET

http://ec.europa.eu/dgs/internal_market/index_en.htm

The EU Internal Market is one of the main successes of the European Union. Enormous growth-related potential is opening up, particularly for companies, including small and medium-sized businesses, which can sell their goods on the whole EU Internal Market of more than 450 million inhabitants, instead of only in their home countries.

The Internal Market, although it is simple in concept, is extremely complicated in a legal sense. Although it has been safeguarded from a legal point of view since 1993, it has to be defended every day. The central concepts of the Internal Market are what are known as the four freedoms, and the basic principle of non-discrimination against EU citizens. The four freedoms are the freedom of movement of goods (Articles 23–31 of the EC Treaty), services (Articles 39–60 of the EC Treaty), capital (Articles 43–48 and 56–60 of the EC Treaty), and persons (Articles 39–42 of the EC Treaty).

Policy areas and division of work

Headed by the German Director General Jörgen Holmquist, the Directorate General for the Internal Market and Services in the European Commission deals with three of these four freedoms (all of them except the freedom of movement of persons). The Directorate General consists of eight Directorates. Directorate A is responsible for planning, management and communication.

Directorate B: Fundamental issues

Directorate B deals with fundamental issues, in other words with the way in which the Internal Market operates (B.1), and with improving legislation. Several aspects are taken into consideration with regard to this central issue, namely evaluating the laws and the legal status as

Table 4.3 Organizational chart, DG Internal Market and Services

Deputy Director General			
Directorate A Planning, management and communication **A.1** Personnel and funds management **A.2** Programming and planning **A.3** Information chronology and document management **A.4** Internal and external communication	**Directorate B** Basic issues **B.1** How the Single Market operates **B.2** Improving legislation: Estimating consequences and evaluation **B.3** Improving legislation: Legal aspects **B.4** Single Market: External aspects	**Directorate C** Awarding of tenders **C.1** Economic and international aspects; electronic awarding of tenders **C.2** Drafting and application of tender laws I **C.3** Drafting and application of tender laws II	**Directorate D** Knowledge-based economy **D.1** Copyright and knowledge-based sectors **D.2** Industrial property **D.3** Regulated professions
Directorate E Services **E.1** Services I **E.2** Services II **E.3** Services III **E.4** Postal Services	**Directorate F** Free movement of capital, corporate law, corporate management **F.1** Free movement of capital and financial integration **F.2** Corporate law, corporate management and financial crime **F.3** Accounting and auditing	**Directorate G** Financial services and financial markets **G.1** Financial services **G.2** Infrastructure of financial markets **G.3** Securities markets **G.4** Asset management	**Directorate H** Financial institutions **H.1** Banks and financial conglomerates **H.2** Insurance and pensions **H.3** Transactions with private customers, consumer policy and payment systems

well as assessing the consequences of existing or planned laws (B.2 and B.3). To prevent unwanted side effects being caused by laws in third-party countries, any analysis of the Internal Market and its operation always takes into account the way in which new regulations might affect the EU's trade partners in third-party countries. For example, new regulations requiring companies to register in a particular way in order to operate within the Internal Market could affect certain companies in third-party countries and restrict their activities. It is the task of Unit B.4 to recognize such problems before they occur.

Directorate C: Awarding of tenders

The award of public tenders is an important aspect of the Internal Market. After all, public tenders with an estimated volume of 1,500 billion euros are awarded within the EU every year. Directorate C deals mainly with ensuring that companies from all the Member States have a real chance to apply where the awarding of all public tenders in each of the Member States is concerned. Since the laws on awarding tenders and the practice of awarding tenders have developed in different ways in all of the Member States, the EU has issued a series of directives and acts relating to such procedures. These measures aim to bring the practice of awarding tenders into line throughout Europe, and to guarantee that information on public tenders is published and disseminated. In this way, everyone participating on the Single Market has the same opportunity to take part in these tenders.

Directorate D: Knowledge-based economy

An increasing amount of the work done within the EU has its origins in knowledge-based branches of the economy, in other words in fields of activity that are using research and science as the basis of their economic success. The more copyright and industrial property play a role here, the closer these branches are monitored by Directorate D. The different units (D.1 for copyright and knowledge-based branches, D.2 for industrial property and D.3 for regulated professions) check that the regulations in the EU and in the Member States agree and whether the whole body of legislation is suitable enough to protect activities within these branches and to increase their economic success. Directives and acts are also developed in these directorates to guarantee uniform protection of patents, brands and designs.

Directorate E: Services

Services are acquiring an increasingly higher standing within the EU. While industry used to be the EU's core branch of business, most of its workforce is now employed in service companies, and 60–70 per cent of the EU's real net output also comes from the service sector. The laws needed for this workforce are ordered according to branch, recorded in Directorate E and processed (E.1, E.2, E.3). One service branch (postal services) has its own unit (E.4), due to its complex nature and its special legal status in many Member States. After tough political negotiations, the Postal Directive 2002/39/EC approved a new legal basis on 10 June 2002. Its purpose was to push forward the process involving the gradual and controlled opening up of the market, thereby increasing competition in this traditionally protected area. As a result, more competition should occur between different postal service providers.

Directorate F: Free movement of capital, corporate law and corporate management

In common with any other highly developed free-market economy, the EU Internal Market would be inconceivable without the free movement of capital. Without it, the efficient use of financial resources in the Internal Market would not be possible and the best businesspeople would not receive the financial resources they need to fulfil their most important tasks: the creation of value and the provision of jobs. Unit F.1 for the free movement of capital and financial integration, located within Directorate F, deals with this issue. Its principal task is to shape EU law in such a way that a businessperson in Finland, for example, could obtain a loan just as easily from a Portuguese or a German bank as from a Finnish bank.

However, to make the Internal Market a reality, standardization of corporate law and business management law is also necessary. If the laws governing the ways in which companies operate differ too much, this can be disadvantageous when competition within the EU is occurring on a daily basis. Unit F.2 deals with all related issues. In addition to corporate law and corporate management, it also deals with financial crime. Closely related to these issues, but also broader, are issues related to accounting and auditing, which are dealt with by Unit F.3.

Directorate G: Financial services and financial markets

The facilitation of free movement of capital within the Internal Market is also the task of Directorate G, next door, which deals with financial services and financial markets. Here, the staff deal with areas such as banking services and the granting of loans (G.1). They also deal with the infrastructure of financial markets (G.2), in other words with their structure and international links, as well as with securities markets (G.3). Internationalization with regard to the possibilities of individual citizens owning securities is also being promoted as a result of the EU's regulatory activities. This means that today it is no longer a legal or practical problem for small shareholders in the EU to own securities from different countries.

Directorate H: Financial institutions

Directorate H deals with this issue and works on aspects of financial institutions, in other words bank and financial conglomerates, and how they deal with the principle of the free movement of capital (F.1). An important issue for the individual EU citizen in this respect is free choice of insurance and freedom of movement in relation to pensions (e.g. when a private pension insurance contract is being concluded in a country other than the person's country of birth, or the country where that person would like to spend the 'autumn' of his or her life). The regulations in this area are the responsibility of Unit H.2.

Private customers are still frequently at a disadvantage from a legal point of view in relation to large banks and corporate groups, and Unit H.3 is in charge of dealing with transactions with private customers, consumer policy and payment systems. The individual EU citizen now benefits from a decisive advantage when withdrawing cash and paying with a credit card within the euro zone because, since 1 July 2002, the same charges for withdrawing cash have applied throughout the EU. If an EU citizen on holiday in a country other than his or her own withdraws cash with a cash card, his or her bank may not charge one cent more than it would on a transaction made at home. Unit H.3 played a significant role in the development of the corresponding EU legislation on trans-national payments.

Community Plant Variety Office (CPVO)

http://www.cpvo.europa.eu/

The task of the Community Plant Variety Office, which was established in 1995 and has its offices in Angers, France, is to implement the Community Act on Community Plant Variety Rights. One representative from each Member State sits on the institute's administrative board, which is chaired by an Office President appointed by the Council of Ministers. The CPVO consists of the Technical Unit, the Financial and Administrative Unit and the Legal Unit.

An application for the protection of a plant variety can be made to the national authorities or directly to the CPVO. When the legal inspection has been completed, a technical inspection takes place; depending on the variety, this can last up to one year for ornamental plants and as long as six years for certain species of fruit trees.

When all the conditions have been fulfilled, the CPVO grants the Community plant variety rights for a period of time – usually 25 years, or up to a maximum of 30 years for wine, potatoes and trees. The Community Plant Variety Office finances itself through income in the form of different charges.

Office of the European Union for Trademarks and Designs (OAMI) *http://www.oami.europa.eu*

The task of the Office of the European Union for Trademarks and Designs (OAMI), whose offices are located in Alicante, Spain, is to register Community brands and Community designs so that they are protected by law throughout the EU.

The free movement of goods and services in the Internal Market requires a Community trademark for the protection of brands. This provides a standard, Europe-wide and exclusive protection right for all economic actors within the EU. In this way, brand names of all types afforded this form of protection cannot be used by unauthorized persons within the EU. Applications for registration may be submitted to the national authorities for industrial property or directly to the Office of the European Union for Trademarks and Designs. All brands existing within the different Member States can be protected throughout the whole EU if an application is made to the OAMI. No obstacles then exist with regard to their being exported or licensed.

Every natural and every legal person can become the owner of a Community trademark if the brand is not already being used as part of the free movement of goods. This form of protection is valid for 10 years and can be extended by the owner for an unlimited period of time.

DIRECTORATE GENERAL FOR FISHERIES AND MARITIME AFFAIRS – DG FISH

http://ec.europa.eu/dgs/fisheries/index_en.htm

The Directorate General for Fisheries – DG FISH – is responsible for drawing up and implementing the European Union's Common Fisheries Policy (CFP). The aim of this policy is to organize the preservation, management and use of living maritime resources, and the processing and marketing of products obtained from fishing and aquaculture. The first joint regulations in the area of fisheries policy were drawn up in 1970. Since then, increases in productivity, a stabilization of the market, and maintenance of the supply and provision of products to the consumer at a reasonable price have been the most important objectives of the CFP. The safeguarding of sustained fishing methods within and outside Community waters is of particular importance. Since the first joint regulations, the CFP has been significantly expanded and now takes the economic, social and biological effects of fishing into account. A fundamental reform of the CFP that came into force on 1 January 2003 put even greater emphasis on guaranteeing the conservation of the fish stocks, protecting the maritime environment and safeguarding the economic efficiency of the European fishing fleets.

Fishing and aquaculture play an important role in relation to employment in many areas. (For example, 64,700 people were employed in the fisheries sector in Spain in 2001.) This is why, as in the area of agriculture, conflicts of interest frequently have to be resolved when resources are being allocated from the EU budget.

The Common Fisheries Policy can be divided up into four main areas:

- First of all, it deals with issues related to the conservation of stocks. Total allowable catches (TAC) are established on the basis of studies and shared out among the EU Member States. Measures are also taken for the protection of immature fish.

Table 4.4 Organizational chart, DG Fisheries and Maritime Affairs

Directorate A	**Directorate B**	**Directorate C**	**Directorate D**	**Directorate E**
Conservation	External policy and markets	Structural policy	Control and enforcement	Resources and relations with stakeholders
A.1 Conservation management **A.2** Fleet management **A.3** Environment and health **A.4** Research and scientific analysis	**B.1** International policy and maritime law **B.2** International and regional agreements **B.3** Bilateral agreements **B.4** Joint market organization and trade	**C.1** General aspects of structural policy **C.2** Germany, Belgium, Netherlands, Great Britain, Ireland, Poland, Estonia, Latvia, Lithuania, Sweden, Denmark, Finland **C.3** Greece, Spain, France, Portugal, Italy, Cyprus, Malta **C.4** Luxembourg, Austria, Czech Republic, Slovenia, Slovakia; aquaculture, fish processing, marketing	**D.1** Monitoring and licences **D.2** Maritime Supervisory Authority **D.3** Legal issues	**E.1** Budget, public procurement and control **E.2** Inter-institutional relations, dialogue with the sector; information and communication **E.3** Human resources, IT, document management, logistics **E.4** Economic analysis

- Second, supporting the fisheries sector plays an important role in the European Union's structural policy. In order for it to be able to meet the demands of the modern world, the EU grants subsidies for intensive market research and for the modernization of fishing fleets, but also for the reduction of improper fishing practices.
- Third, the CFP aims to create a common fisheries market within the Community and to co-ordinate the interests of both producers and consumers. This area is being enlarged by the phased opening of the European fisheries market to the global market.
- Fourth, the Common Fisheries Policy encompasses negotiations on bilateral and multilateral fisheries agreements and representation of the Community's interests within international organizations and regional fisheries associations.

According to the Community Treaty, it is the European Commission's task to propose laws for the shaping of the fisheries policy and to enforce these. Members of the European Parliament are only heard in the area of fisheries policy, but they can express their views on the proposed drafts. The European Council then decides on laws and directives.

Policy areas and division of work

The Directorate General for Fisheries is headed by the Maltese Fisheries Commissioner Joe Borg. The Director General of the DG FISH is Fokion Fotiadis and the Taskforce for Maritime Affairs is directly answerable to him. This taskforce deals with working out a joint position on issues related to maritime and coastal resources not directly connected to the area of fisheries. These include, among other things, management of maritime traffic, use of maritime resources, contributing to sustained maritime development and co-ordination of the organizations that usually deal with maritime affairs. The Taskforce for Maritime Affairs seeks opinions, analyses future challenges and possible developments, and makes policy proposals based on this information. Directorate F mainly deals with internal tasks. Its four units deal, among other things, with the budget, relations with institutions, industry and interest groups, the communication and information policy, personnel and documentation management and business analyses.

Directorate A: Conservation of stocks

Since the 1990s in particular, it has become obvious that stocks must be protected from over-fishing. Directorate A of the DG Fisheries is responsible for conservation of stocks and the environment. Unit A.1 deals with stock management. The first priority is to set total allowable catches so that only the amount of fish is taken from the stock that does not endanger the continued existence of the species. Furthermore, technical measures for limiting catches of immature fish, unwanted fish and marine mammals are being drafted, e.g. on the use of minimum mesh sizes and selective fishing gear as well as closed areas and seasons. Fleet management is the task of Unit E.2. It draws up proposals for reducing the Community fleet and developing it from a technical point of view. Multi-Annual Guidance Programmes (MAGPs) set targets for fleet reduction and define steps to be taken in order to bring fleet capacities into line with existing stocks.

Unit A.3 deals with health and the environment. It examines the often negative environmental consequences of fishing and the factors that influence fishing and aquaculture (e.g. water pollution caused by tourism and traffic). Its task is to guarantee sustained management of the maritime environment and to ensure that environmental issues are taken into consideration when policy decisions are being taken. The fourth unit is responsible for research and scientific analysis as part of the DG FISH's remit.

Directorate B: External policy and markets

The fisheries policy is not limited to the coastal zones of the EU, but takes into consideration fishing in all the seas of the world.

Directorate B deals with this international or external policy. The first of the four units is responsible for international fisheries policy (e.g. within the United Nations or the Organization for Economic Co-operation and Development); here, assistance is provided in relation to agreements on international maritime law such as the United Nations Convention on Law of the Sea, signed in 1982. Unit B.2 deals with international and regional fisheries agreements. These are often handled via the Regional Fisheries Organizations (RFO).[i] Unit B.3 is in charge

---

[i] The Regional Fisheries Organizations are established by means of international agreements and form a framework within which governmental representatives negotiate on high stocks of sea fish and trans-national stocks, i.e. including stocks outside of the EU. The EU is currently a contractual partner in 11 Regional Fisheries Organizations.

of the bilateral fisheries agreements that the EU concludes with third-party countries to safeguard access by the Community fleet to the waters of the relevant countries. The European Commission negotiates these agreements on behalf of the Community.

Unit B.4 deals with structuring the Community markets for the products obtained from fishing and aquaculture. In this respect, the most important instruments are common marketing standards, producers' organizations, a system of price support for minimum prices and clear regulations on trade with third-party countries.

Directorate C: Structural policy

Like agricultural policy, fisheries policy is part of the EU's structural policy. In accordance with the policy of economic and social cohesion, the maintenance and further development of fisheries management is being pursued, especially in regions with poor structures. For example, the creation of protected harbour areas, the improvement of harbour facilities and the restructuring of fishing fleets are taking place in a targeted manner. The general aspects of this structural policy – e.g. co-ordination with other European structural funds measures – as well as policy structure measures in relation to enlargement of the EU are dealt with by Unit C.1. The other units within the directorate deal with geographical areas. C.2 is responsible for Germany, Belgium, the Netherlands, Great Britain, Ireland, Poland and the Baltic and Scandinavian countries; C.3 is responsible for France, Portugal, Spain, Italy, Greece, Malta and Cyprus; C.4 is responsible for Austria, Hungary, the Czech Republic, Slovakia, Slovenia and Luxembourg. The directorate is also in charge of structural measures in the areas of fish processing, aquaculture and marketing.

Directorate D: Control and enforcement

To prevent fraud and to guarantee efficient and transparent fisheries management, Directorate D monitors compliance with legislation. Unit D.1 deals with the licences that, since 1995, are required by all ships within the Community area and all EU ships outside of the Community waters. Unit D.2 is in charge of the Fisheries Agency established within the Commission in 1983. The Member States themselves are responsible for implementing measures and imposing sanctions; in this respect, the 27 EU inspectors draft rules for supervision, provide support and monitor the national inspectors when they are fulfilling their tasks, and draw up related reports for the European Commission. However, unlike in the past, the EU inspectors are now authorized to examine and report on activities without informing the EU Member State in question beforehand. The EU Fisheries Agency's main controlling tasks include registration of catches, inspections made by the North-West Atlantic Fisheries Organization as part of the Regional Organizations for the Fisheries in the North-West Atlantic and the monitoring of fishing using drift nets. Unit D.3 deals with procedures related to infringement of agreements and with other legal aspects of the fisheries policy.

European Fisheries Control Agency (EUFA)

On 28 April 2004, the European Commission proposed the setting-up of a European Fisheries Control Agency.)[ii] This Community institution, which has a juridical personality and is currently in the planning stage, will have its offices in Vigo (Spain) and employ around 50 staff. Its aim will be to co-ordinate the Member States' fishing controls and measures for their implementation. It will hold the Member States liable for compliance with existing regulations in relation to Community waters, help them to fulfil their obligations in relation to regional fisheries organizations and agreements with third-party countries, train fisheries inspectors, award joint supply contracts within the framework of control activities and develop new control procedures for fisheries. Around 5 million euros are being provided for the equipping of the agency, which, at the time of going to press, had not yet started operations. Most of these funds are provided from the Community budget.

DIRECTORATE GENERAL FOR RESEARCH AND TECHNOLOGICAL DEVELOPMENT – DG RTD

http://ec.europa.eu/dgs/research/index_en.html

According to Article 163 of the Community Treaty, it is the declared

[ii] Proposal for a Regulation of the Council on the establishment of a European Fisheries Control Agency and for an amendment to Regulation (EC) No. 2847/93 on the introduction of a control system for the Common Fisheries Policy COM (2004) 289.

Table 4.5 Organizational chart, DG Research and Technological Development

Deputy Director General				
Directorate A Co-ordination of Community activities	**Directorate B** Structural aspects of the European Research Area	**Directorate C** Science and society	**Directorate D** Human factor, mobility and Marie Curie activities	**Directorate E** Biotechnologies, agriculture and food
A.1 Framework programme; inter-institutional relations **A.2** Support during implementation of research programmes **A.3** Legal and cross-cutting issues **A.4** Planning, programming, evaluation **A.5** Analysis of the effects of Community measures	**B.1** Future scientific and technological requirements; basic research **B.2** Improving co-operation in the area of research and the European knowledge base **B.3** Building up scientific and technological capacities: Research infrastructures **B.4** Administration and finance	**C.1** Strategic and policy aspects **C.2** Consultation on scientific policy **C.3** Ethics and science **C.4** Women and science **C.5** Information and communication **C.6** Education and science	**D.1** Strategic and policy aspects **D.2** Institutional grants **D.3** Research and training networks **D.4** Supporting top-class scientific work **D.5** Individual grants **D.6** Administration and finance	**E.1** Strategic and policy aspects **E.2** Food quality **E.3** Safety in food production **E.4** Administration and finance

Table 4.5 *(continued)*

Directorate F Health	**Directorate G** Industrial technologies	**Directorate H** Transport	**Directorate I** Environment	**Directorate J** Energy
F.1 Strategic and policy aspects **F.2** Serious illnesses **F.3** Diseases caused by poverty **F.4** Basic genomic research **F.5** Biotechnology and applied genomics **F.6** Administration and finance	**G.1** Strategic and policy aspects **G.2** Products, processes and structural forms **G.3** Materials **G.4** Nano-sciences and nano-technologies **G.5** Coal and steel research fund **G.6** Administration and finance	**H.1** Strategic and policy aspects **H.2** Inland and sea transport **H.3** Air transport **H.4** Administration and finance	**I.1** Research policy issues and sustained development **I.2** Environmental technology and pollution prevention **I.3** Management of natural resources and services **I.4** Environment and climate system **I.5** Administration and finance	**J.1** Strategic and policy aspects **J.2** Energy production and distribution systems **J.3** New and renewable sources of energy **J.4** Nuclear fission and protection against radiation **J.5** Joint fusion research **J.6** Association treaties on fusion **J.7** Administration and finance

Directorate K	**Directorate M**	**Directorate N**	**Directorate R**
Research in the social sciences and humanities; futures research	Investment in research and links with other policies	International scientific co-operation	Resources
K.1 Strategic and policy aspects **K.2** Scientific and technological futures research **K.3** Futures research in the social sciences and humanities **K.4** Administration and finance	**M.1** Policy aspects, private investments, relations with the European Investment Bank (EIB) **M.2** Open co-ordination of the research policy **M.3** Aspects of competition, structural policies **M.4** Research and small- and medium-sized business **M.5** Administration and finance	**N.1** Policy issues related to international scientific co-operation **N.2** Co-operation activities within the Community **N.3** Multilateral co-operation activities **N.4** Administration and finance	**R.1** Personnel policy and equal opportunities **R.2** Budget and financial service **R.3** Further education and internal information **R.4** IT administration office **R.5** Work environment: infrastructure, logistics and room allocation **R.6** Co-ordination and integration of the internal control systems

objective of the European research policy 'to strengthen the scientific and technological bases of Community industry and encourage it to become more competitive at the international level, while promoting all the research activities deemed necessary by virtue of other chapters of this Treaty'. The European Research Area (ERA) is considered particularly important. The project approved by the European Council in Lisbon in March 2000 is to create the foundations for a common knowledge and technology policy – comparable to an 'Internal Market for Research' – and integrate the scientific and technological capacities of the Member States. To realize these policy objectives, the European Union is taking a series of measures:

- implementing research programmes;
- supporting co-operation between business, research centres and universities;
- promoting co-operation with third-party countries and international organizations;
- disseminating and evaluating findings from activities in the area of joint research and technological developments;
- promoting training for and the mobility of EU researchers.

Headed by the Slovenian Commissioner, Janez Potočnik, the European Commission's Directorate General for Research and Technological Development (RTD) is responsible for working out, co-ordinating and implementing the European research policy and is contributing to a growing interest and improved understanding of the role played by science and research in today's society.

The European Union and the Member States have to co-ordinate all their activities to guarantee coherence between the national policies and the policies of the Community. However, the European Union has no independent powers, but instead plays a co-ordinating role and promotes co-operation without trying to bring Member States into line. The focal point of the EU's research policy activities is the co-financing of the framework research programme and various individual programmes. The multi-annual framework programme is proposed by the European Commission and approved by the European Parliament and European Council using the co-decision procedure. It is implemented using specific programmes that are open to both private and public research institutions.

The objective of the framework programme running between 2002 and 2006, for which 17.5 billion euros were made available, was to contribute to the creation of the European Research Programme. For reasons of efficiency, the programme concentrated on seven areas considered particularly important in today's knowledge-based economic and social system.

The content-related priorities of the Sixth Framework Programme area are as follows:

- bio-sciences, genomics and biotechnologies for use in the health sector;
- technologies and the information society;
- nano-technologies and nano-sciences, knowledge-based, multifunctional materials, new production procedures and systems;
- air and space travel;
- food quality and safety;
- sustained development, global changes and eco-systems;
- the cross-cutting issue of citizens and the state in the knowledge-based society.

Policy areas and division of work

The Directorate General for Research consists of 14 directorates and is headed by the Spaniard José Manuel Silva Rodríguez. Directorate R is responsible for administration and internal processes. The remaining directorates deal with research-related issues. They either work on a specific area of research or issues that affect the shaping of the general European research policy.

Directorate A: Co-ordination of joint activities

Directorate A in the Directorate General for Research co-ordinates Community activities in the area of research and technological development both internally and with the policy of the Member States. As part of the Sixth Framework Programme, the directorate is responsible for policy-oriented research that supports the development and implementation of Community measures, for example in the area of agricultural, fisheries, environmental and health policy. The directorate's first unit (A.1) deals with the co-ordination of the framework programmes and the shaping of relations with the other EU institutions. Unit A.2 provides support in the implementation of the research programmes, while Unit A.3 deals with legal issues (e.g. the regulations for participation in research programmes). Units A.4 and A.5 plan and assess the Community's measures.

Directorate B: Structural aspects of the European Research Area

Directorate B strives to consolidate the European Research Area through structural improvements. In this way the European Commission aims, among other things, to expand Europe's scientific and technological capacities and consolidate co-operation in the area of research in Europe (B.2 and B.3). The Sixth Framework Programme pays special attention to improved co-ordination and co-operation regarding research efforts in Europe. Initiatives in this area include the networking and opening up of regional and national research projects through the ERA-NET Programme and the creation of an integrated information system to facilitate the exchange of information via research activities and programmes.

Directorate C: Science and society

Directorate C deals with basic issues concerning the relationship between societal factors and scientific work. In addition to advice on scientific policy (C.2), the focus here is on issues such as ethics and science (C.3), and women and science (C.4). In this respect, the European Commission draws up ethical standards for the research projects to be supported and monitors compliance with these standards. The cloning of human embryos, transgenic animals and the development of new gene tests are among the areas dealt with here. Furthermore, the European Commission promotes equality of opportunity for and participation by women in all scientific disciplines by integrating more and more women into European science networks and, for example, supporting female scientists in the area of industrial research. C.6 deals with the relationship between science and education in Europe.

Directorate D: Human factor, mobility and Marie Curie activities

Directorate D is responsible for personnel issues in research and for the networking of research and education systems. In this respect, the directorate awards grants for the furthering of research (D.2 and D.5), and tries to establish research networks (D.3). Grants are available to individuals (e.g. students, professors) and institutions (e.g. universities, research institutes). There are additional programmes of financial support for top-class scientific work (D.4). As part of the Sixth Framework Programme, the Marie Curie Activities constitute a particular focal point of the directorate's work. The aim of the project is to promote the education and mobility of European research staff by facilitating participation by researchers of all ages – both from the EU and third-party countries – in programmes of further education and exchange programmes.

Directorate E: Biotechnologies, agriculture and food

Directorate E deals with issues related to biotechnology in the areas of agriculture and food. It is responsible for general policy and strategic issues in these areas and promotes improved quality of foods (E.2) and greater safety in food production (E.3). In this area, the European Commission supports research initiatives related to developing healthier, safer, more variable and more environmentally-friendly production methods and processes, and finding remedies for food-related illnesses and allergies.

Directorate F: Health

Directorate F of the Directorate General for Research promotes research activities in relation to health. It deals with the general problem of serious diseases (F.2) – in particular with the sub-area of cancer – as well as with diseases and epidemics caused by poverty (F.3). In addition to basic genomic research (F.4), the European Commission promotes research in the areas of medical biotechnologies and applied genomics (F.5). A sum of 2.25 billion euros has been provided under the Sixth Framework Programme for projects in the areas of the biosciences, genomics and biotechnology. It is hoped that more intensive research efforts in these areas and advances in the decoding of human and animal genetic material will benefit public health, for example in the fight against cancer and children's illnesses, as well as against diseases caused by old age and poverty, and that these more intensive research efforts will increase the competitiveness of the European biotechnology industry.

Directorate G – Industrial technologies

All aspects of industrial research are dealt with in Directorate G. In addition to research projects on production processes (G.2) and materials (G.3), research programmes in the areas of coal and steel (G.5) and nano-science and nano-technology in particular are being sponsored. Nano-technological research is an important part of the

Sixth Framework Programme. The European Commission is hoping for speedy development of this form of technology, which in the future is to be applied in the areas of transport, energy, electronics and biomedicine.

Directorate H: Transport

Directorate H is in charge of research initiatives in the area of transport. In this area, the main distinction is made between inland and sea transport (H.2) and air transport (H.3). Research projects in the area of air travel generally concentrate on improving Europe's competitiveness in the production of passenger aircraft, engines and equipment, reducing the negative effects of air traffic on the environment and expanding the capacities and safety of the air travel system. For years, the EU has been providing evidence of originality, technological and scientific competence and economic efficiency in the area of air travel. Airbus accounts for half of the orders for aircraft in the world, while the European Space Programme Ariane has a 50 per cent share in the international satellite market.

Directorate I: Environment

Directorate I deals with research in the area of the environment. It sponsors research projects related to the prevention of pollution (I.2), management of natural resources (I.3) and the relationship between environmental issues and climate systems (I.4). The focal points of the Sixth Framework Programme are economical and renewable energy technologies, and safe and environmentally-friendly transport systems, as well as a better understanding of global changes, eco-systems and biodiversity.

Directorate J: Energy

Directorate J promotes research in the areas of energy production and distribution (J.2). Research initiatives in the areas of new and renewable energy sources (J.3) and nuclear energy are particularly important. Projects related to nuclear fission (J.4) are also being sponsored, as are programmes in the area of nuclear fusion (J.5). During the course of the Sixth Framework Programme, which ran from 2002 to 2006, research projects on controlled thermonuclear fusion, the handling of radioactive waste and protection against radiation were implemented; a total of 1.23 billion euros were made available for these projects.

Directorate K: Humanities and social sciences and futures research

Directorate K is principally responsible for the future coherence of the European research policy. It examines the EU's research and innovation policy, and adapts it to future challenges and changes (K.2). In addition, it ensures the practical nature of the European research policy and promotes the development and implementation of other Community measures, for example with regard to the agricultural, fisheries, transport and health policy. Furthermore, Directorate K is responsible for research in the humanities and social sciences, in particular in the areas of economic development, the movement of persons, population trends and gender roles (K.3).

Directorate M: Investments in research and links with other policies

Directorate M deals with private investment, cultivates relations with the European Investment Bank (M.1), contributes to the co-ordination of the European research policy (M.2) and weighs up the most significant effects of European research activities on European regional and structural policy (M.3). Furthermore, it is responsible for the relationship between research policy and small- and medium-sized businesses in Europe (M.4). Since small- and medium-sized businesses play a fundamental role in European competitiveness, the creation of jobs and the development of new technologies, their interests are taken into special consideration in the Sixth Framework Programme. At least 15 per cent of the budget is provided for small- and medium-sized businesses. The main aim here is to consolidate research capacities.

Directorate N: International scientific co-operation

Directorate N is in charge of co-ordinating international scientific co-operation. N.1 deals with the general aspects of this issue. Furthermore, N.2 promotes the Community's research sector's efforts in the area of co-operation, while N.3 orchestrates multilateral co-operation in the area of research. The European Commission either co-operates with third-party countries within the context of the seven thematic areas contained in the framework programme, or it creates specific international research projects with different groups of countries. The budget for co-operation in the area of international research totals 315 million euros in the Sixth Framework Programme, which ran from 2002 until 2006.

Joint Research Centre *http://jrc.ec.europa.eu/*

The Joint Research Centre (JRC) supports both the European institutions and the Member States in the drafting and implementation of European laws and directives through scientific advice and technical know-how. It is a centre of reference and knowledge for the European Union. Unlike the European Commission's Directorate General for Research, which provides financial support for research programmes for which applications have been made, the Joint Research Centre implements research projects in different areas. As an Office of the European Commission, it acts independently of private and national interests and promotes the general interests of the EU Member States.

Broad sections of the European public, in particular companies, are benefiting from the work conducted by the Joint Research Centre:

- By providing access to research infrastructures and networks, it plays a significant role in making a European Research Area (ERA) a reality. The objective of the ERA is to make the European Union a competitive and dynamic, knowledge-based economy.
- Through co-operation in the area of research and the provision of findings from research and research institutions, the JRC supports European industry (e.g. in the harmonization of industrial standards and the preparation of international trade talks) and thereby promotes economic growth and the creation of jobs.
- The research centre makes a significant contribution to the smooth development of the EU enlargement process by co-operating with universities, research organizations, industry and the political institutions in the candidate countries and the new Member States.
- The JRC promotes the safety, health and well-being of European citizens by developing, for example, more efficient food controls, new techniques for water reprocessing and new methods of atomic energy production.

Table 4.6 Organizational chart, Joint Research Centre

		Deputy Director General		
Directorate A Institutional and scientific relations	**Directorate B** Programme and resource management	**Directorate C** Ispra site Directorate	**Directorate D** Institute for Reference Materials and Measurements	**Directorate E** Institute for Transuranium Elements
A.1 Secretariat of the administrative board **A.2** Scientific cooperation and management of technologies **A.3** Enlargement **A.4** Public relations work **A.5** Operational support **A.6** Relations with Parliament, Council and Member States	**B.1** Personnel **B.2** Budget and resource planning **B.3** Analytical accounting and finances **B.4** Work programme **B.5** Evaluation **B.6** Planning, monitoring of progress and internal controls **B.7** Further training	**C.1** Nuclear decommissioning and waste facilities management **C.2** Occupational health and safety **C.3** Social services **C.4** Site maintenance and operational support **C.5** Informatics, networks and library **C.6** Management support **C.7** Logistics **C.8** Site development	**D.1** Operational support **D.2** Reference materials **D.3** Infrastructure and management **D.4** Isotope measurements **D.5** Neutron physics **D.6** Informatics and electronics **D.7** Institute development and programme management **D.8** Food safety and quality	**E.1** Operational support **E.2** Hot cell technology **E.3** Materials **E.4** Nuclear fuels **E.5** Nuclear chemistry **E.6** Actinides research **E.7** Nuclear safety and infrastructure management **E.8** Safety of nuclear laboratories

Table 4.6 *(continued)*

Directorate F	**Directorate G**	**Directorate H**	**Directorate I**	**Directorate J**
Institute for Energy	Institute for the Protection and the Security of the Citizen	Institute for Environment and Sustainability	Institute for Health and Consumer Protection	Institute for Prospective Technological Studies
F.1 Operational support	**G.1** Operational support	**H.1** Operational support	**I.1** Operational support	**J.1** Operational support
F.2 Cleaner energies	**G.2** External security	**H.2** Climate change	**I.2** Validation of alternative biomedical testing methods	**J.2** Sustained development in industry, energy production and transport
F.3 High flux reactors	**G.3** Agricultural and fisheries policy	**H.3** Global vegetation monitoring	**I.3** Toxicology and chemical substances	**J.3** Consolidation of the European Research Area (ERA)
F.4 Technical and scientific support for the TACIS- and PHARE-financed programmes	**G.4** Risk analysis	**H.4** Emissions and health	**I.4** Biomedical substances and systems	**J.4** Information and communication technologies
F.5 Scientific and technical programmes	**G.5** European Laboratory for Structural Assessment (ELSA)	**H.5** Inland waters, seas and coastal regions	**I.5** Biotechnology and genetically modified organisms	**J.5** Sustained development in agriculture, food and health
	G.6 Sensors, radio technology and internet safety	**H.6** Land management and natural hazards		
	G.7 Nuclear safeguards	**H.7** Land use		
	G.8 Statistical support to antifraud	**H.8** Renewable energies		

The Joint Research Centre is financed mainly from the EU budget. The thematic focus of the JRC's multi-annual research programme is approved by the European Council.

The JRC's work programme, which is strongly geared towards the Directorate General's current research programme, sets clearly defined goals that correspond to the requirements of the European consumer.

The priorities set by the Council for the period from 2003 to 2006 were:

- food, chemicals and health (212 million euros);
- environment and sustainability (286 million euros);
- nuclear issues (290 million euros);
- cross-cutting issues that create a connection between society and technological and scientific research, for example the development of future technological prospects and the development of answers to questions of public safety and the fight against fraud (262 million euros).

The JRC has achieved great success in recent years. For example, it has developed a Europe-wide system for comparing air quality and created an electronic data archive as part of a European initiative on the use of multimedia in training.

Policy areas and division of work

The Joint Research Centre consists of seven separate research institutes with offices in five countries – Belgium, the Netherlands, Germany, Italy and Spain. The three institutes with offices in Ispra (Italy) are co-ordinated by a separate Directorate based in Ispra itself. Two Directorates dealing with overlapping issues form a part of the JRC based in Brussels. The first of these Directorates is responsible for inter-institutional and scientific relations (Directorate A), while the second is in charge of programme and resource management (Directorate B). The units in Directorate B, located in Brussels and Ispra, are responsible for personnel, the budget and control. They also create the JRC's multi-annual work programmes and work on improving operational methods and organizational structures. The Director General of the research centre is the German Roland Schenkel; the responsible Commission member is the Slovenian Janez Potočnik, who is in charge of science and research.

Directorate A: Institutional and scientific relations

The main tasks of the Brussels-based Directorate A concern overlapping issues and management. Unit A.1 contains the secretariat of the administrative board that is made up of one high-ranking representative from each Member State. The purpose of the administrative board is to support the Director General in his work and to maintain the dialogue with the Member States. A.2 is responsible for issues related to intellectual property and the promotion of scientific co-operation. Unit A.3 examines the ways in which European policy measures can better respond to the scientific and technological requirements of EU enlargement. The fourth unit deals with public relations work. Unit A.5 provides operational support, while Unit A.6 co-ordinates contacts with the Parliament and Council as well as national authorities and organizations.

Directorate C: Ispra Site Directorate

Directorate C is in charge of the three research institutes in Ispra (the Institute for the Protection and the Security of the Citizen, the Institute for Environment and Sustainability and the Institute for Health and Consumer Protection). Unit C.1 manages the programme for nuclear decommissioning and waste disposal facilities that the JRC no longer requires for its work. It guarantees that this project is implemented in a safe, efficient and punctual manner. Units C.2 to C.8 fulfil managerial tasks. Among other things, they deal with occupational safety, maintenance of the research facilities, legal, financial and logistical issues, and communication.

Directorate D: Institute for Reference Materials and Measurements

The task of the Institute for Reference Materials and Measurements (IRMM), located in Geel, Belgium, is to develop a standardized and reliable system for biological, chemical, biotechnical and nuclear measurements to support EU measures (e.g. in the policy areas of health, consumer protection, agriculture and industry). Unit D.2 produces high-quality chemical, biological, clinical and industrial reference materials that are used to support the implementation of EU directives in the areas of food quality, food safety, consumer and industrial products, the environment and health. Unit D.4 deals with isotope measurements. Unit D.5 deals with neutron physics. It supplies European safety authorities and industry with information used to assess the safety of nuclear facilities. Finally, Unit D.6 carries out chemical, physical and biological investigations in the area of food safety and food quality. It develops, harmonizes and certifies analytical methods, controls the occurrence of biological and chemical substances in foods and animal feed, and collates this information.

Directorate E: Institute for Transuranium Elements

Directorate E, the Institute for Transuranium Elements (ITE), located in Karlsruhe, Germany, aims to protect the European citizen from dangers arising from the handling and storing of high-grade radioactive substances. Units E.2 to E.8 carry out research into specific sub-areas of nuclear energy. E.2 deals with issues of hot cell technology. Among other things, the unit seeks ways of increasing the effectiveness of nuclear power in nuclear power plants. Unit E.3 carries out research into materials, Unit E.4 deals with research into nuclear fuels, Unit E.5 analyses different aspects of nuclear chemistry, and Unit E.6 contains a state-of-the-art laboratory for actinides research. Unit E.7 guarantees the safety of the ITU's staff and the local population and environment, and maintains the infrastructure of the nuclear facility. Unit E.8 is responsible for the safety of nuclear laboratories.

Directorate F: Institute for Energy

The Institute for Energy, located in Petten in the Netherlands, was founded in 1962 and today contains four scientific units and two units with supportive roles. The research facility contributes to the conception, development, implementation and monitoring of Community laws in the energy sector. In this respect, safety and environmental sustainability play a particularly important role.

Unit F.1 deals with location management. Unit F.6 provides scientific and technical support. Unit F.2 carries out research into the development of cleaner energies, for example into the reduction of pollutants and greenhouse gas emissions. Unit F.3 uses a high flux reactor for research in the area of medicine, nuclear safety and waste management. Waste analysis and risk assessments in the area of nuclear energy are carried out in the fourth unit. For instance, the unit supports the Europe-wide harmonization of safety criteria for nuclear facilities. Unit F.5 provides scientific and technical support for the TACIS- and

PHARE-financed programmes that promote environmental protection and nuclear safety in the accession countries and the Eastern European and Central Asian states.

Directorate G: Institute for the Protection and the Security of the Citizen

The Institute for the Protection and the Security of the Citizen, which constitutes Directorate G of the Joint Research Centre, carries out its work in Ispra, Italy. The institute supports EU measures for protecting the European citizen from economic and technological dangers. Unit G.1 fulfils general managerial tasks, while Units G.2 to G.9 are research units.

Unit G.2 provides scientific and technical support in areas such as conflict prevention, development aid, migration and the fight against terrorism for the European Commission's Directorate General for External Relations. Unit G.3 supports the relevant Directorates General in the development and implementation of the Common Agricultural and Fisheries Policy, while Unit G.4 carries out risk analysis in order to improve prevention and crisis intervention when natural catastrophes or accidents occur. Unit G.5 contains the European Laboratory for Structural Assessment (ELSA), which inspects the vulnerability of buildings in the case of natural catastrophes or deliberate attacks. Unit G.6 deals with sensors, radio technology and internet safety, while Unit G.7 carries out risk analysis in the area of energy, transport and food safety. Unit G.8 takes part in monitoring nuclear safety, including the checking of contracts and agreements. Unit G.9 develops statistical procedures and applies them in the fight against fraud.

Directorate H: Institute for Environment and Sustainability

Directorate H of the Joint Research Centre, the Institute for Environment and Sustainability (IES), was founded in 2001 and has its offices in Ispra, Italy. In addition to Unit H.1, which deals with administrative issues, the institute contains seven scientific units that also support the preparation and implementation of EU measures in specific areas.

Unit H.2 carries out research into the biological, chemical and physical processes involved in climate change. Unit H.3 monitors changes in global vegetation, which are taken into consideration when multilateral environmental agreements are being developed and when environmental issues are being included in the development policy. Unit H.4 deals with the connection between emissions, air pollution and health, while Unit H.5 deals with the state of inland waters, seas and coastal areas. Unit H.6 carries out research into the connections between industrial, municipal and agricultural waste management and soil and groundwater pollution. Last, Units H.8 and H.9 are responsible for the development of agriculture and land use, as well as for carrying out research into renewable energy sources.

Directorate I: Institute for Health and Consumer Protection

The Institute for Health and Consumer Protection (IHCP), which was founded in 1998, is Directorate I of the Joint Research Centre's Directorate General and the third research facility with offices in Ispra, Italy. In addition to the administrative unit, the IHCP contains five scientific units. Unit I. 2 deals with the development and scientific endorsement of alternative test procedures in the area of biomedicine, which are to replace experiments carried out on animals in laboratories. Unit I.3 checks whether existing and new types of chemicals and toxic substances represent a danger for human health or the environment, and makes proposals for the classification, labelling and registering of new substances. New biomedical substances and systems (e.g. the application of nuclear technology in the area of medicine) are dealt with in Unit I.4. Unit I.5 carries out research into the harmful effects of physical and chemical substances on people (e.g. problems caused by chemicals, radiation and noise). Unit I.6 is responsible for biotechnology and for dealing with genetically modified organisms (GMO).

Directorate J: Institute for Prospective Technological Studies

The Institute for Prospective Technological Studies (IPST), located in Seville, Spain, is the seventh research institute and Directorate J of the Joint Research Centre. The institute monitors and analyses scientific and technological developments, their effects on societal and economic issues and the policy-related conclusions that can be drawn from them. Unit J.2 carries out research into sustainable developments in industry, energy production and transport, while Unit J.5 monitors developments in agriculture, food and health, and takes these into consideration when creating sustainable policy measures. Unit J.3 supports the European Commission in the consolidation of the European Research Area (ERA) by analysing the relevance and effectiveness of research activities at the European, national and regional levels. Finally, Unit J.4 monitors new trends and possibilities in the area of information and communications technology.

DIRECTORATE GENERAL FOR HEALTH AND CONSUMER PROTECTION – DG SANCO

http://ec.europa.eu/dgs/health_consumer/index_en.htm

The Directorate General for Health and Consumer Protection is headed by two commissioners, namely the Cypriot Commissioner Markos Kyprianou, who is responsible for Health, and the Bulgarian Commissioner Meglena Kuneva, who is responsible for Consumer Protection policy areas. The EU's health policy is based on Article 152 of the EC Treaty, which obliges the Community to guarantee a high degree of health protection when all Community policies are being drafted. The aim of the Community's activities is to add to the Member States' policies in this area and to help improve the health of EU citizens, prevent human diseases and combat the causes endangering human health.

The EU's consumer policy is based on Article 153 of the EU Treaty, which obliges the Community to achieve a high level of consumer protection in order to protect the health and safety of consumers within the EU, but also to protect the economic interests of consumers by informing them of their rights and helping them to set up organizations to defend their interests.

The aim of the Directorate General is thus to make safe foods produced and sold in the EU and consumer goods, to shape the Internal Market for the well-being and protection of consumers, and to protect and improve the health of EU citizens. In order to be able to fulfil these tasks, the DG combines three policy areas that deal with food safety, consumer affairs and public health.

Table 4.7 Organizational chart, DG Health and Consumer Protection

Deputy Director General		
Directorate A General issues **A.1** Co-ordination and inter-institutional relations **A.2** Legal issues **A.3** Financial resources and financial controls **A.4** Information: Systems and publications **A.5** Personnel	**Directorate B** Consumer affairs **B.1** Analysis and development of consumer policy; relations with consumer organizations; international issues **B.2** Dishonest trading practices and various laws for the area of consumer protection **B.3** Product and service safety **B.4** Protection of the consumer's legal, economic and other interests **B.5** Enforcement and legal protection	**Directorate C** Public health and risk assessment **C.1** Programme management **C.2** Health information **C.3** Health risks **C.4** Health factors **C.5** Health policy strategy **C.6** Health policy measures **C.7** Risk assessment
Directorate D Food safety, production and distribution chain **D.1** Animal feed **D.2** Biological risks **D.3** Chemical substances, impurities and pesticides **D.4** Legislation in the area of food and biotechnology **D.5** Relations with the European Food Safety Authority; early warning system	**Directorate E** Food safety, plant protection, animal health and animal welfare, international issues **E.1** Plant protection **E.2** Animal health, animal welfare and animal production **E.3** Issues related to international food, veterinary and plant protection **E.4** Bilateral relations	**Directorate F** Food and Veterinary Office **F.1** Country profiles, co-ordination and supervision **F.2** Food obtained from animals: Mammals **F.3** Food obtained from animals: Birds and fish **F.4** Food obtained from plants, plant protection, processing and production **F.5** Feeds, import controls and residues **F.6** Quality, planning and development

Policy areas and division of work

Robert Madeline, the Director General, is in charge of around 800 staff who are highly specialized in their fields (e.g. doctors, vets, food scientists, agricultural experts, economists, natural scientists and scholars in the humanities). Their tasks are divided up among six directorates, including Directorate A, which is responsible for general administration and also for co-ordination of legal issues within the directorate and for relations with other EU institutions.

Directorate B: Consumer issues

EU consumer policy and the fostering of consumer rights is the necessary opposite pole to the free movement of goods and services. Only these can make the European Internal Market complete for the benefit of consumers.

This is why Unit B.1 is responsible for the analysis and development of consumer policy. It deals with relations with consumer organizations and international issues. The European Commission is trying to consolidate the role played by consumer organizations in the Internal Market through its contacts with these organizations so that they can improve their ability to act throughout Europe. Among other issues, Unit B.2 deals with dishonest trading practices and various other laws in the area of consumer protection. Dishonest trading practices are subject to a broad range of interpretations in the Member States, which is why activities have to be consolidated in this area.

Unit B.3 is responsible for legal regulations in the area of product and service safety in Europe. Through the New Approach Directives, producers and service providers are ascribed a high degree of responsibility for product safety, which is framed by a strong European product liability law. (More information on this subject is available on the internet at www.newapproach.org.) Unit B.4 deals in a general manner with the protection of consumers' legal, economic and other interests, while Unit B.5 deals with issues related to law enforcement and legal protection.

Directorate C: Public health and risk assessment

Directorate C deals with public health and risk assessment. In this respect, Unit C.1 has sole responsibility for management of the programmes in this area. One of these programmes is the anti-smoking campaign known as HELP; its aim is to draw the attention of EU citizens, in particular teenagers, to the health risks involved in smoking.

Unit C.2 is in charge of analysing and collating health information and it also has the administrative task of compiling health data and analyses from throughout the EU. In addition, the neighbouring units, C.3 and C.4, work on assessing and analysing health risks and health factors in the EU. To the fore is the protection of the population against pandemics such as the wave of influenza that has been public knowledge for a long time, and occurs at regular intervals; at the same time, new policy reactions for new types of dangers are being developed. By building up and operating common structures for speedy reactions to crises, the European Commission is aiming to prepare the EU for, for example, bio-terrorism or new, dangerous tropical diseases.

Unit C.5 deals with the EU's health policy strategy, while Unit C.6 is in charge of health policy measures in general. This includes the EU's attempt to increase co-operation by the Member States with regard to improving the effectiveness and efficiency of the health systems. Unit C.7 works on Europe-wide standards for risk assessment of various dangers, which threaten the health of EU citizens; these include infectious and non-infectious diseases such as tuberculosis, measles and influenza.

Directorates D and E: Food safety, production and distribution chains, plant protection, animal health, animal welfare and international issues

The EU is one of the largest producers and consumers of food in the world. Most of the products produced in the EU are exported, while most of the products consumed in the same area are imported. This is why the European Commission has to take factors both internal and external to the EU into consideration where food safety and the safety of the production and distribution chains are concerned, and include them as part of policy planning. These issues are the daily bread of Directorates D and E.

Units D.1 and D.2 deal with animal feed and the biological risks associated with food safety. An increasing amount of attention has in recent years been paid to the issue of animal feed after many scientists claimed that the controversial feeding of animal remains to cattle was at least partially responsible for the BSE crisis.

Chemical substances can also place a burden on the food chain and threaten human health. To reduce risks such as dioxin contamination in chicken meat, Unit D.3 deals with chemical substances, contaminants and pesticides, while Unit D.4 is in charge of legislation in the area of food and biotechnology. In the area of biotechnology, the EU is particularly sensitive with regard to genetically modified food and the consequences of this for food safety.

Relations with the European Food Safety Authority, which was founded in 2002 and has its offices in Parma, Italy, are looked after by Unit D.5. This unit is also responsible for co-ordinating the European Early Warning System for threats to food safety, which was set up to inform all Member States at an early stage about serious health hazards.

Unit E.1 deals with issues of plant protection, while Unit E.2 deals with animal health, animal welfare and animal production in general. Phytosanitary and veterinary inspection regulations for animals and plants issued by the EU, which are used for food processing in the EU, are a subject of great economic and political importance in the Community. These regulations have tremendously significant direct effects on arable farming and cattle breeding in the Member States, and also on links in the whole supply chain such as cattle transporters and slaughterhouses.

Unit E.3 is responsible for all issues related to international food – from Argentine beef consumed in the EU to the soy sauces imported from Japan that are sold in local supermarkets – dealing with veterinary and plant protection and with relations with multilateral organizations. The neighbouring Unit E.4 fosters important bilateral relations, for example co-operation with significant food trading partners such as the USA.

Directorate F: Food and Veterinary Office

EU-wide co-ordination of quality controls by the food and veterinary authorities is required so that the many types of EU regulations can be implemented. After food-related crises in Europe such as BSE, foot-and-mouth disease and avian flu, health controls for animals and plants carried out from the very start have become a high priority so that, when they are introduced on to the Internal Market as food products, they do not constitute a danger for the consumer (from the producer to the consumer). This is why the directorate ensures that all measures taken by the Member States are implemented throughout the EU.

Directorate F deals with this issue and also creates country profiles. Units F.2 and F.3 both deal with food obtained from animals, F.2 with mammals and F.3 with birds and fish. Unit F.4 is responsible for food obtained from plants, plant protection, processing and distribution, the nerve centre of the Directorate General, while Unit F.5 is in charge of feed, import controls and residues obtained from substances in feeds and food. Unit F.6 deals with quality, planning and development.

European Food Safety Authority (EFSA)
http://efsa.europa.eu/

The food-related scandals of the 1990s , including BSE and dioxin, seriously undermined consumer confidence in the safety of the food chain. This led to the decision to establish a new agency that was given the task of independently and objectively advising on issues of food safety related to the food chain. The main aim of the European Food Safety Authority (EFSA) is 'to contribute to a high degree of health protection for consumers in the area of food safety, so that their trust can be rebuilt and maintained'. The legal basis for the EFSA is provided for by Regulation (EC) No. 178 of 28 January 2002.

The EFSA provides scientific advice on all issues in connection with food safety, including animal health and animal welfare as well as plant health and issues of nutrition. The EFSA's risk assessments provide a sound scientific basis for the representatives of EU institutions with political accountability (i.e. the European Commission, the European Parliament and the Council) for the establishing of the policy, legislative and regulatory measures that are required to guarantee a high level of consumer protection in relation to food safety.

European Centre for Disease Protection and Control (ECDC) ***http://www.ecdc.europa.eu/***

The European Centre for Disease Prevention and Control is a new EU agency that was created in order to strengthen Europe's defences against infectious diseases such as SARS, influenza and HIV/AIDS.

At the present time, infectious diseases can spread throughout the world like wildfire. The ECDC was founded in 2004 to improve co-operation between the disease control agencies in the different Member States. The ECDC is still in its infancy and, in partnership with national health authorities throughout Europe, will improve the surveillance of diseases and develop early warning systems. The agency's offices are located in Stockholm, Sweden.

DIRECTORATE GENERAL FOR INFORMATION SOCIETY AND MEDIA – DG INFSO

http://ec.europa.eu/dgs/information_society/index_en.htm

The information society is a reality within the European Union, where each citizen recognizes the way in which the speedy dissemination of information has changed his or her private and professional life. A large of amount of the business done within the EU now relies on activities supported by media from the information society.

The political activities in this area of the EU, and primarily of the European Commission, are multifarious. Recent years have seen the creation of a significant number of regulations used as a basis for the electronic media in the EU, for example the Directive on Access to New Media, the Directives on Licensing Networks and Services in Electronic Media, the Directive on General Services and User Rights with regard to such Networks and the Directive on Competition in the Markets for Electronic Communication Services. The European Commission naturally has to be familiar with and follow the fast-moving developments in all of these areas.

Policy areas and division of work

A single Directorate General, headed by the Director General Fabio Colasanti, deals with the Information Society and the Media. In addition to a large number of special advisers based in this Directorate General, the Directorate General consists of 10 directorates. Directorate R deals with personnel and financial matters as well as with internal IT requirements. Among other things, Directorate S deals with the planning and co-ordination of all policy areas, the legal aspects of policy development and inter-institutional relations.

Directorate A: Audiovisual area, media and internet

Directorate A deals with all matters related to audiovisual media and the internet, including copyright in the digital environment (A.1) and legal issues related to the internet and network security (A.3). All the issues affecting actors other than the EU are dealt with in Unit A.4 for international relations. Unit A.2 is responsible for the EU Media Programme. The Media Plus Programme, for which 400 million euros were made available, covered the period from 2001 to 2006. With this programme the EU promoted European film and television productions and improved related distribution and publicity as well as sponsoring film festivals.

Directorate B: Electronic communications policy

Directorate B deals with electronic communications media in general. Its Unit B.1 is in charge of policy development, while Units B.2 and B.3 work on implementing regulations in this area. All issues related to the radio spectrum policy in the Member States are dealt with by Unit B.4. Since implementation of EU policy, as is the case with most policies, is completed by the Member States, an individual unit, A.5, monitors the activities of the EU countries in this area.

Directorate C: Lisbon Strategy and policies for the information society

The EU's Lisbon Strategy is a programme whose purpose is reform of the whole EU economy. In accordance with this strategy, the EU is to become the biggest knowledge-based economic area in the world by 2010. Electronic media and the internet play an important role in this strategy, which is why Directorate C has sole responsibility for this area. In July 2005, under the title '2010 – A European Information Society for Growth and Employment', the European Commission approved a strategic policy framework calling on all EU institutions and Member States to inject new life into the Lisbon process.

Within Directorate C, Unit C has overall responsibility for this area. The stimulus required in relation to technological developments for such a broad strategy is provided by Unit C.2, while Unit C.3 deals with evaluation of the policy.

Table 4.8 Organizational chart, DG Information Society and Media

		Deputy Director General		
Directorate R Resources	**Directorate S** General affairs	**Directorate A** Audiovisual, media, internet	**Directorate B** Electronic communications policy	**Directorate C** Lisbon Strategy and policies for the information society
R.1 Personnel **R.2** Budget and finance **R.3** Information system development and support **R.4** Information systems development and support	**S.1** Planning and co-ordination **S.2** Management support **S.3** Inter-institutional relations **S.4** Legal aspects	**A.1** Audiovisual and media policies, digital rights, Taskforce for Co-ordination of Media affairs **A.2** MEDIA Programme and media competence **A.3** Internet, network and information security **A.4** International relations	**B.1** Policy development **B.2** Implementation of regulatory framework I **B.3** Implementation of regulatory framework II **B.4** Radio spectrum policy **B.5** Procedures related to national regulatory measures	**C.1** Lisbon Strategy and eEurope **C.2** Strategy for ICT research and development **C.3** Evaluation and monitoring **C.4** Operative procedures related to the Information Society Technologies programme

Directorate D	Directorate E	Directorate F	Directorate G	Directorate H
Network and communications technologies	Content	New technologies and infrastructures	Components and systems	
D.1 Communications technologies	**E.1** Interfaces	**F.1** Future technologies	**G.1** Nano-electronics and photonics	**H.1** ICT for health
D.2 Networked audiovisual systems	**E.2** Knowledge and content technologies	**F.2** Grid technologies	**G.2** Microsystems and nano-systems	**H.2** Electronic administrative services
D.3 Software technologies	**E.3** Learning and cultural heritage	**F.3** Research infrastructures	**G.3** Embedded systems	**H.3** eInclusion
D.4 ICT for trust and security	**E.4** Information market	**F.4** New work environments	**G.4** ICT for transport	**H.4** eTEN
D.5 Networking of companies through ICT	**E.5** Cognition	**F.5** Administration and finance	**G.5** ICT for environment	**H.5** Administration and finance
D.6 Administration and finance	**E.6** eContent and safer internet		**G.6** Administration and finance	
	E.7 Administration and finance			

Directorate D: Network and communications technologies

Directorate D deals with individual aspects of networks and communications technologies (D.1). Unit D.2 deals with networked audiovisual systems, while Unit D.3 is in charge of software development. Unit D.4 is responsible for the ways in which eBusiness and information technology systems as a whole can be made more secure so that users can gain confidence in relation to these systems and use them. Unit D.5 deals with increased networking between companies through information and communications technology, while Unit D.6 deals with administration and finance.

Directorate E: Content

All of Directorate E, which is located in Luxembourg, deals with the financial aspects of information technology as well with the types of content that can be provided for or sold to citizens and users in the information society. The directorate is divided up into six units. Unit E.1 deals with technological interfaces, Unit E.2 with knowledge and content technologies, and Unit E.3 with issues such as how the new technologies can be successfully used for learning and passing on the cultural heritage of the EU. Unit E.4 deals with the development and regulation of the information market, Unit E.5 with cognition, Unit E.6 with issues of internet security, and Unit E.7 with administration and finance.

Directorate F: New technologies and infrastructures

Since new technologies and the way they are used are constantly changing, Directorate F tries to follow developments of technologies and infrastructures in their infancy.

Directorate G: Components and systems

While the whole application is seen as a new form of technology, it usually consists of individual technical innovations. Directorate G is responsible for developing a policy for promoting use of individual components and systems for overall technological progress. This is why Unit G.1 deals, for example, with nano-electronics and photonics, Unit G.2 with microsystems and nano-systems, and Units G.3 and G.4 with developments in information and communications technologies in the areas of transport and environment.

Directorate H: Information and communications technologies for citizens and companies

The concept of an eEurope relates mainly to increasing participation by citizens and companies in society and politics. Directorate H is responsible for policy developments in this area. For example, Unit H.2 (eGovernment) monitors the attempts made by many national, regional and communal bodies in the EU to reduce the administrative expenses for citizens and companies through the use of specific offers on the internet and to develop new forms of participation such as online citizens' forums.

A social approach is being pursued by Unit H.3 which, in the form of eInclusion, is managing a programme with which the EU wants to promote groups existing at the edge of the information society. Groups that typically do not take part, or only take part to a certain extent, in the information society include the elderly, the disabled and socially disadvantaged persons who cannot afford access to technologies.

European Network and Internet Security Agency (ENISA) *http://www.enisa.europa.eu/*

The aim of this agency, which was established in March 2004, is to contribute to the achieving of a high degree of network and information security so that consumers, citizens and companies within a functioning market can interact without any reservations. The aim of the agency is to become a centre of expertise for the European Commission, the Member States and business and to use this expertise in the development of new policies and Community laws. In order to do so, it gathers data and carries out analyses on security-related problems in the EU and new types of risks, and promotes risk analysis and methods of risk management. Public–private partnerships are also to be developed in order to draw attention to this problem. The agency is run by a director, an administrative board and a permanent stakeholders' group. This group consists of representatives from affected groups such as the IT industry, consumer protection groups and experts from universities active in this area. The group advises the agency's director.

DIRECTORATE GENERAL FOR JUSTICE, FREEDOM AND SECURITY – DG JLS

http://ec.europa.eu/dgs/justice_home/index_en.htm

The Italian Commissioner Franco Frattini is in charge of policy in the Directorate General for Justice, Freedom and Security, which takes its short form, 'JLS', from the French Justice, Liberté et Sécurité.

With the creation of the Internal Market within the European Union and the ending of border controls between all Schengen states, all citizens of the EU are in contact and can interact with each other to an extent never previously possible. The Schengen Agreement facilitates the free movement of people without border controls in all EU Member States except Great Britain and Ireland, which are not full members of the Schengen Agreement, and all participating Member States, which can end their border controls only after a long period of transition. The Schengen Agreement has been EU law since 1999. The free movement of people across borders also includes Norway and Iceland, although these countries are not EU Member States. With such a degree of freedom to travel, the goal of the EU must be to guarantee as much safety and legal protection as possible for EU citizens throughout the whole European Union. The current basic EU Treaty states that the EU is to be further developed as an area of freedom, security and law (Article 2 of the EU Treaty in its version following the entry into force of the Treaty of Nice). In order to take the sensitivity of Member States in individual areas into consideration, the EU's powers have been divided up among two of the three pillars. This means that policies related to asylum issues, securing the external borders and immigration are components of the first pillar, while issues of juridical co-operation in civil and criminal matters, police work, the fight against the trade in drugs, weapons and human beings as well as against organized crime and the fight against terrorism are included in the third pillar. The EU's plans of action in the area of justice, security and the law have thus always to take the conditions existing in the different institutions into consideration where division of these powers is concerned.

Through implementation of the programme approved by the European Council in Tampere, Finland, the EU has already made significant progress in the creation of this unified judicial area. Implementation of this programme was completed in 2004. In order to make further progress in this area, an additional, multi-annual, comprehensive work programme, known as the Hague Programme, was approved by the European Council in the Hague on 5 November 2004 for the period from 2005 to 2010.

The most important aims of this programme are the strengthening of EU citizenship, development of the common policy for asylum, movements of migrants and borders, as well as the fight against illegal immigration. In this connection endeavours are being made in relation to closer political co-operation with the immigrants' countries of origin and transit countries as well as in relation to further developing the common visa policy. All nationals of non-EU countries living in the Member States were also included in the programme. In the fight against terrorism, the Hague Programme aims in particular to increase the exchange of information between Member States, while the combating of organized crime is to be improved through better co-operation between police forces.

Since the Treaty of Nice entered into force, there have been different legal bases in the policy areas in this field. Depending on the date of the regulation and the specific policy area, when a vote is being taken in the Council either a qualified majority or unanimity applies. The European Parliament is only consultative in relation to making legislation in this respect. The initiatives for new EU laws can come from both the European Commission and a Member State.

Policy areas and division of work

The Directorate General for Justice, Freedom and Security is headed by Fabio Colasanti from Italy. The Directorate General, which is one of the new offices of the European Commission, consists of four directorates and employs 320 officials.

Directorate A: General affairs

Directorate A for general affairs consists of five units. Unit A.1 deals with strategic policy planning, policy evaluation and relations with the other institutions. Unit A.2 deals with relations with third-party countries and issues of enlargement. This includes, for example, the particularly critical issue of the removal of border controls with the new Member States under the Schengen Agreement and the issue of relations with the EU's neighbouring states, e.g. Ukraine. Unit A.3 deals with the directorate's technical equipment, staff and logistical processes, while Unit A.4 is in charge of the budget. Unit A.5 is responsible for information on this EU policy area and communications with EU citizens. A small, local security office is directly attached to Directorate A.

Directorate B: Immigration, asylum and border controls

The main focus here is on the harmonization and simplification of asylum procedures within the EU. Since the reform of the EU Treaty in Amsterdam, introduction of a standardized asylum system has been one of the EU's most important goals, although this is considered a difficult undertaking due to the different traditions and legal systems in the Member States. For Germany, one of the main destinations for immigrants, it is especially important that asylum policy within the EU be regulated in a standardized and fair manner.

The Directorate General for law manages the ARGO Programme in this policy area. The ARGO Programme, which is the successor to the Odysseus Programme, supports the improvement of administrative

Table 4.9 Organizational chart, Justice, Freedom and Security

Deputy Director General			
Directorate A General affairs	**Directorate B** Immigration, asylum and borders	**Directorate C** Civil justice, citizens' rights and citizenship	**Directorate D** Policy co-ordination
A.1 Strategy planning, evaluation and institutional affairs **A.2** External relations and enlargement **A.3** Personnel, information technology and logistics **A.4** Finance and control **A.5** Information and communication	**B.1** Borders and visas **B.2** Immigration and asylum **B.3** Large IT systems **B.4** Financial solidarity in the areas of immigration, asylum and borders	**C.1** Civil justice **C.2** Co-ordination of the fight against drugs **C.3** Citizenship and citizens' rights **C.4** Financial support in the areas of civil justice, citizens' rights and citizenship **C.5** Data protection	**D.1** Fight against terrorism, trafficking and exploitation of human beings: Law enforcement co-operation **D.2** Fight against economic, financial and computer crime **D.3** Criminal justice **D.4** Financial support (AGIS programme) and prevention of general crime

co-operation between the 27 Member States in the areas of external borders, visas, asylum and immigration.

Within the relevant Directorate, Unit B.1 deals with borders and visas, while Unit B.2 is in charge of immigration and asylum. Unit B.3 deals with the large computer networks, systems and databases operated by the Member States in this area.

Unit B.4 deals with financial solidarity in the area of asylum, immigration and borders because, due to their geographical location, some Member States obviously have more work to do in relation to securing their borders than others (e.g. Poland, with its border within the EU, which is long compared to Luxembourg's border).

Directorate C: Civil justice, basic rights and EU citizenship

Directorate C deals with the issue of civil justice, basic rights and EU citizenship. Some rights have already been fully developed within the EU, for example the right of all EU citizens to settle in any of the Member States in order to work there. Other rights need to be consolidated, for example the right of all people to have access to justice. In this respect, Unit C.1 deals with civil laws in the Member States. As described above, one of the long-term aims of the Hague Programme is for civil actions to be able to take place beyond borders and for judgements made in different Member States to be mutually recognized and applied.

Unit C.2 deals with co-ordination of the anti-drugs policy. Unit C.3 is responsible for citizens' rights and basic rights and their application in the Member States. Unit C.4 is in charge of the financial support for co-operation in the area of justice, law and citizens' rights.

Directorate D: Internal security and criminal justice

Another fundamental right is the right to protection against all sorts of criminality in all the Member States. In this respect, the goal is above all to improve networking between the law enforcement authorities in the Member States, via pan-Union agencies such as EUROPOL and the working group of European police chiefs. The creation of a European Police College is also a goal of the EU. Furthermore, the European Commission is developing and managing several programmes whose aim is to improve co-operation between the police forces of the Member States; the OISON Programme aims to improve co-operation between law enforcement authorities; STOP II to combat the trade in human beings in Europe; the Falcone Programme to train and further educate people who fight organized crime; and OCTOPUS to combat corruption in Central and Eastern Europe. As part of these action plans the EU takes the fight against drug-related crime and drug consumption very seriously.

Unit D.1 is in charge of the fight against terrorism, human trafficking and the exploitation of human beings, and guarantees increased co-operation in the enforcement of laws. Unit D.2 fights against economic and financial crime and cyber crime. The latter includes crimes committed with the help of the internet (e.g. spying in order to obtain online account data or passwords).

Unit D.3 deals with criminal justice in Europe, while Unit D.4 is responsible for financial support and the prevention of crimes. This includes management of the AGIS programme, whose purpose is to improve co-operation between police, customs and judicial authorities in all 27 Member States.

European Monitoring Centre for Drugs and Drug Addiction (EMCDDA) *http://www.emcdda.europa.eu/*

This monitoring centre, which began work in 1995, has its official offices in Lisbon. The work of the centre, which was set up by the European Commission, is to collate and process 'objective, reliable and comparable information' on drugs and drug addiction in Europe for the relevant Services of the European Commission, the European Union and national authorities. The aim of accumulating this information is to obtain an overview of the nature of the problem and how it develops with regard to drug consumption and drug addiction in Europe, and to propose corresponding means and policy proposals for solving these problems. The monitoring centre for drugs is the main driving force behind the EU Action Plan on Drugs approved by the European Council in December 2005.

Close co-operation with national authorities and experts is one of the centre's most important areas of work. The European Monitoring Centre for Drugs and Drug Addiction also seeks to establish close links with international bodies and their programmes, such as the United Nations International Drug Control Programme, the World Health Organization, the Pompidou Group in the European Council, the World Customs Organization, the International Criminal Police Organization (Interpol) and the European Police Office (Europol).

European Monitoring Centre for Racism and Xenophobia (EUMC) *http://www.eumc.europa.eu/*

This centre, with offices in Vienna, Austria, is headed by the German Director Beate Winkler and began its work as a European institution in 1998. The purpose of setting up the European Monitoring Centre for Racism and Xenophobia (EUMC) is to provide objective, reliable and comparable information and data for the Community and the Member States on xenophobia, racism and anti-Semitism in Europe. The aim is to find out the causes of xenophobia and to provide corresponding means and initiatives for decision-makers at European level.

The European Racism and Xenophobia Information Network (RAXEN) is an important component of this institution. The network is to be used for gathering information and data at national and EU level. To this end, the EU has concluded agreements with 15 national contact points, which, in close co-operation with the EUMC, gather, co-ordinate and disseminate country- and EU-specific information. Following a proposal made by the European Commission in June 2005, the EUMC's mission and staff were expanded, while the EUMC was transformed into the European Fundamental Rights Agency, which became operative on 1 January 2007.

European Police Office – EUROPOL
http://www.europol.europa.eu/

The European Police Office, which was founded in 1992, has its offices in the Dutch capital The Hague, and is headed by its German Director Max-Peter Ratzel. Europol defines itself as a law enforcement organization and gathers, stores, compares, analyses, evaluates and, if necessary, transfers data on different crimes. Europol is answerable to the European Council and its body dealing with justice and home affairs, which is made up of the interior ministers from each of the EU countries. The aim of Europol is to organize close and efficient co-operation between the EU Member States in the prevention and combating of criminality, such as the drugs trade, the illegal trade in vehicles, the trafficking of adults and children, counterfeiting, the trade in radioactive and nuclear substances, and terrorism. A large number of Europol's officials are envoys from national authorities, for example from national police services.

European Police College – CEPOL *http://www.cepol.europa.eu/*

The offices of the General Secretariat of the European Police Academy (CEPOL), which was created in 2000 as the result of a decision of the European Council, are located in Hampshire, England. The mission of the CEPOL is to provide support in the training, further training and education of high-ranking officials in the police forces of the Member States. The aim is to consolidate knowledge of the police systems and police structures in each of the Member States.

DIRECTORATE GENERAL FOR AGRICULTURE AND RURAL DEVELOPMENT – DG AGRI

http://ec.europa.eu/dgs/agriculture/index_en.htm

The Directorate General for Agriculture (DG AGRI) is under the political control of the Danish Commissioner, Mariann Fischer Boel, and

Table 4.10 Organizational chart, DG Agriculture and Rural Affairs

Deputy Director General			
Directorate A.I International affairs I **A.I.1** World Health Organization (WHO), Organization for Economic Co-operation and Development (OECD), United States, Canada **A.I.2** Europe and new independent states, Africa, Asia, Oceania, Afro-Caribbean-Pacific (ACP) states, Least-Developed Countries (LDC), General Preferential System (GPS)	**Directorate A.II** International affairs II **A.II.1** Latin America, Mediterranean countries, Gulf states, Arabian Peninsula, South-Eastern Europe, Western Balkans **A.II.2** Enlargement, European Neighbourhood Policy	**Directorate B** Inter-institutional relations **B.1** Internal and external communication **B.2** Document management, security, personal data **B.3** Relations with the other Community organs and non-governmental organizations (NGOs)	**Directorate C I** Economics of agricultural markets and common market organizations **C.1** Arable crops, sugar, fibre plants, feeds **C.2** Olive oil, horticultural products **C.3** Wine, alcohol, tobacco, seeds, hops **C.4** Animal products

Table 4.10 *(continued)*

Directorate D Direct aid, market policy measures, sales-related measures	**Directorate E.1** Programmes for rural development	**Directorate E.II** Programmes for rural development	**Directorate F** Cross-cutting aspects of rural development
D.1 Direct aid **D.2** Implementation of market policy measures **D.3** Market policy instruments **D.4** Sales-related measures and contributions to information-related measures	**E.I.1** Belgium, France, Luxembourg, Netherlands **E.I.2** Cyprus, Greece, Ireland, Great Britain **E.I.3** Denmark, Lithuania, Poland **E.I.4** Hungary, Italy, Malta	**E.II.1** Czech Republic, Portugal, Slovakia, Spain **E.II.2** Estonia, Finland, Latvia, Sweden **E.II.3** Austria, Germany, Slovenia **E.II.4** Special Accession Programme for Agriculture and Rural Development (SAPARD)	**F.1** Quality policy for agricultural products **F.2** Environment and forests **F.3** Financial co-ordination of measures **F.4** Coherence of measures
Directorate G Economic analyses and evaluation	**Directorate H** Agricultural legislation	**Directorate I** Resource management	**Directorate J** Audit of agricultural expenditure
G.1 Analyses and overall concept **G.2** Quantitative analyses, forecast, statistics **G.3** Analysis of situation in agricultural enterprises **G.4** Evaluation of measures for agriculture **G.5** Analysis of agricultural trade policy	**H.1** Agricultural laws, simplification **H.2** Competitive conditions **H.3** Monitoring of application of agricultural laws, infringements, complaints **H.4** Co-ordination of procedures, joint secretariat of administrative committees	**I.1** Budget management **I.2** Support and central financial controls **I.3** Data processing **I.4** Management of European Agriculture Guidance and Guarantee Fund (EAGGF) **I.5** Personnel and administration **I.6** Measures-related management, relations with European Court of Auditors	**J.1** Co-ordination of horizontal issues related to rendering of accounts **J.2** Audit of expenditure on market policy measures **J.3** Audit of direct aid **J.4** Audit of expenditure on rural development **J.5** Financial audit

employs around 100 staff. It is one of the most powerful Directorates General because the EU has more influence in the areas of agriculture and rural development than in any other policy area. Since the negotiations on the Treaty of Rome (1957), an important focus has been on agriculture. Memories of the food shortages after the Second World War were still fresh in people's minds at the time, and agriculture therefore became a key element of the policy of European unification. It remains so today. Following the accession of the 10 new Member States in May 2004, there are now around 11 million farmers in Europe.

Articles 32 to 38 of the Community Treaty form the legal bases for the single agricultural policy. According to Article 33, the European agricultural policy has the following aims:

- increasing the productivity of the agricultural sector through the furthering of technical progress, rationalization of agricultural production and the best possible use of production factors, in particular the workforce;
- in this way to guarantee an appropriate living for the agricultural population, in particular by raising the per capita income of persons employed in the agricultural sector;
- to stabilize the markets;
- to safeguard the supply;
- to ensure that consumers are supplied at reasonable prices.

In order to achieve these goals, common market organizations (CMOs) were created for almost all agricultural products; their regulations ensure that obstacles to the trade in agricultural products within the EU are removed and the same instruments and market mechanisms are applied. Furthermore, the CMOs maintain common customs barriers in relation to third-party countries. The EU's agricultural products take precedence where marketing is concerned and have price advantages compared to imported products. In addition, steps frequently taken include price regulations, product aid, storage measures in the case of over-production, subsidies for agricultural exports and joint endeavours in the area of vocational education, training and research. Expenditure under the Common Agricultural Policy (CAP) is taken from the Community budget. In 2005, the agricultural budget made up almost half of the total EU budget – 49.11 billion euros from an overall budget of 105.23 billion euros.

The demands made on the European agricultural policy have changed and broadened in recent years and decades. In addition to the traditional aims of the agricultural policy, the Directorate General for Agriculture must ensure the following:

- that the European agricultural sector increases its competitiveness so that it can continue to subsist on the global market;
- that greater attention is paid to the issues of the environment and animal welfare as well as to aspects of consumer protection and health;
- further development of the rural area and the formation of efficient local communities which can create and maintain jobs in the agricultural sector and in all other areas;
- simplification of agricultural laws, and greater transparency and accessibility in their provisions and regulations.

As part of Agenda 2000 and the reform of the CAP approved by the EU's ministers for agriculture on 26 July 2003, important measures for the realization of these goals were taken and the support mechanisms of the Community's agricultural sector were fundamentally changed.

The main task of the Directorate General for Agriculture is the management and proper implementation of the Common Agricultural Policy. In addition, the European Commission uses its right to take initiatives and make proposals for the continued simplification and improvement of European agricultural laws. The DG AGRI also deals with co-operation and co-ordination with other relevant policy areas (e.g. trade, health and consumer protection, regional policy and the environment) and is responsible for use of the EU's financial resources.

The European Parliament has a right of consultation regarding the agricultural policy, i.e. it can discuss proposals during a plenary sitting and in the presence of the relevant member of the European Commission. The Council then decides on laws and directives by qualified majority.

Policy areas and division of work

The Directorate General for Agriculture and Rural Development, headed by the Director, Jean-Luc Demarty from France, is divided up into 12 directorates. Directorate B is responsible for the communication policy, document management, security and relations with other Community organs and non-governmental organizations. Directorates I and J are in charge of funds management and auditing agricultural expenditure. The six units in Directorate I deal in particular with management of budgetary funds and funds used for the European Agriculture Guidance and Guarantee Fund (EAGGF), data processing, personnel issues and relations with the European Court of Auditors. The five units of Directorate J deal with the rendering of the accounts and auditing of the expenditure on market policy measures, direct aid and rural development. Nine additional directorates work on thematic aspects of the agricultural policy and are explained in greater detail below.

Directorate A.I: International affairs (in particular multilateral negotiations)

Directorate A.I is responsible for international aspects of the European agricultural policy. Unit A.I.1 of the directorate deals with relations with the World Health Organization (WHO) and the Organization for Economic Co-operation and Development (OECD) since agricultural policy is very important in the area of world trade. The World Trade Organization (WTO) Ministerial Conference held in Cancún, Mexico, in September 2003 failed above all due to unsolvable conflicts of interest in the area of agriculture. The liberalization of world trade and, in particular, the reduction in agricultural subsidies and import duties, were resolutely demanded by developing countries, but rejected, in the requested form, by the USA and the European Union. Unit A.I.1 also manages bilateral agricultural policy relations with the United States and Canada.

Unit A.I.2 maintains relations with a series of states and groups of countries, namely most of Europe, and the newly independent states, Africa (with the exception of the Mediterranean area), Asia, Oceania and the Afro-Caribbean-Pacific (ACP) states. In addition, it deals with problems related to agricultural policy in the least-developed countries (LDCs) and manages the General Preference System (GPS) for agricultural products. Last, Directorate A.I.2 maintains contacts with the United Nations Food and Agriculture Organization (FAO) and deals with the Convention on Food Aid signed in London in 1999.

Directorate A.II: International affairs (in particular enlargement)

Unit A.II.1 deals with agricultural policy relations with the countries of Latin America, the Mediterranean area, South-Eastern Europe and the Western Balkans as well as with the Gulf states and the Arabian Peninsula.

A second focus of the work done by Directorate A.II is the connection between agriculture and enlargement (Unit A.II.2). In the run-up to enlargement in May 2004, considerations related to the agricultural policy were particularly important because the agricultural sectors in the accession countries still make up an unusually high share of the national economy as a whole. The most important goals were the harmonization of the accession countries' legislation with the *acquis communautaire* (the total body of European Union law accumulated thus far), a fundamental liberalization of the sector and the modernization and development of agriculture and rural areas in the accession countries. These goals were achieved above all by using the pre-accession instrument for agriculture known as the Special Accession Programme for Agriculture and Rural Development (SAPARD). Unit A.II.2 is also responsible for the agricultural aspects of the European Neighbourhood Policy.

Directorate C: Economics of agricultural markets (and common market organizations)

Directorate C deals with the economic issues arising as a result of the organization of the agricultural markets. In order to manage production and stabilize the markets, it creates specific production and sales regimes, i.e. through production quotas, lowest-price guarantees, etc – the common market organizations – for individual products. EU farmers and international producers who want to import goods into the EU must comply with these regimes. This work is divided up among four units within Directorate C, each of which is responsible for specific agricultural products. Unit C.1 deals with arable crops, sugar, fibre plants and feeds, Unit C.2 with olive oil and horticultural products, Unit C.3 with wine, alcohol, tobacco, seeds and hops, and Unit C.4 with animal products.

Directorate D: Direct support, market measures and promotion

Directorate D is responsible for implementing the political and financial measures used to organize and regulate the European agricultural market. Unit D.1 is responsible for management of direct aid to which agricultural enterprises are entitled in the form of income subsidies. In return, agricultural enterprises must comply with certain obligations (e.g. in the area of the environment, animal welfare and occupational safety). As part of the agricultural reforms agreed in 2003, from 2005 direct aid in most regions of the EU, and in particular for larger businesses, is to be reduced step by step and detached from the volume of production.

Unit D.2 is responsible for the daily implementation of concrete market measures in the affected agricultural sectors. These take the form of export subsidies, production quotas, import quotas and import duties. Unit D.3 is responsible for the general laws on market instruments. Unit D.4 is responsible for information and promotion programmes which stress the benefits of Community products with regard to quality, hygiene, safety, animal welfare and environmental protection, and which therefore aim to increase the sales of EU products in both the Internal Market and abroad.

Directorate E.1: Rural development programmes

Directorates E.I and E.II are involved in the development of European rural areas. Various programmes are being developed in this respect. There are regulations on early retirement for farmers over 55 years of age which, if taken advantage of, can lead to a change in the designated land use for non-agricultural purposes (e.g. to foster natural reserves). In addition, farmers can apply environmentally friendly and animal-friendly production procedures to obtain financial aid. Furthermore, there are financial incentives to encourage afforestation and regulations favouring disadvantaged regions. The modernization and diversification of agricultural enterprises is being promoted through investment (e.g. in processing and marketing systems), the installation of young farmers and support for forestry and vocational education and training.

Each of the units in Directorate E is responsible for certain EU states. Unit E.I.1 deals with Belgium, France, Luxembourg and the Netherlands; Unit E.I.2 is responsible for Cyprus, Greece, Ireland and the United Kingdom; Denmark, Lithuania and Poland are dealt with after by Unit E.I.3; Hungary, Italy and Malta are the responsibility of Unit E.I.4.

Directorate E.II: Rural development programmes II

The first three units in Directorate E.II are also arranged according to country. Unit E.II.1 deals with the Czech Republic, Portugal, Slovakia and Spain; Unit E.II.2 looks after Estonia, Finland, Latvia and Sweden; Austria, Germany and Slovenia are the responsibility of Unit E.II.3. Unit E.II.4 is responsible for general management of the Special Accession Programme for Agriculture and Rural Development (SAPARD), which supports targeted measures for the promotion of agriculture and the development of rural areas in the Central and Eastern European countries. Important goals include, for example, diversification of economic activities in rural areas and the protection and maintenance of the rural heritage.

Directorate F: Horizontal aspects of rural development

The cross-cutting issues dealt with by Directorate F include the quality policy for European agricultural products. In 1992, the European Commission developed a system for protecting and enhancing the status of agricultural products with a special tradition, quality or origin. These measures, which protect the rights of the producer and provide appropriate information for the consumer, are managed in Unit F.1. Unit F.2 deals with the inclusion of environmental issues in the rural development policies and with the drafting of laws designed to guarantee the maintenance and sustained development of European forests. For example, in 2004, as a reaction to an increasing number of eco-businesses and the rapid increase in consumer demand, the European Commission approved a 'European Action Plan for Ecological Agriculture and Ecologically Produced Products'. Its aim was to promote the further development of ecological agriculture in the EU through specific measures. Unit F.3 is responsible for financial co-ordination of the measures for development of rural areas, while Unit F.4 examines these measures for the coherence and checks whether agricultural policy measures are in accordance with existing Community law, the provisions of the Common Agricultural Policy (CAP) and the other Community policies.

Directorate G: Economic analyses, perspectives and evaluation

Directorate G fulfils a cross-sectional and basic task, since its five units analyse the development of the EU's agricultural policy. Unit G.1 draws up general analyses and overall concepts, Unit G.2 deals with quantitative analysis, forecasts and statistics, while Units G.3, G.4 and G.5 evaluate and assess the situation in agricultural enterprises, agricultural measures and the agricultural trade policy. The aim of the evaluations and assessments is to provide information on the effectiveness of agricultural policy measures. They make a decisive contribution to the drafting and adaptation of laws in the CAP.

Directorate H: Agricultural legislation

Directorate H contains the DG Agriculture's legal units. Unit H.1 deals with agricultural laws and their simplification. Unit H.2 deals with the connection between the European agricultural and competition policy. As in other economic areas, it is the task of the European Commission to avoid market distortion and monopolies. However, at the same time, it must guarantee that the application of competition regulations does not contradict the aims of the common market organizations or the agricultural sector in general. Unit H.3 monitors the correct application of the agricultural laws, punishes infringements and receives complaints. Unit H.4 co-ordinates legal procedures and contains the secretariat of administrative committees, which is made up of representatives of the Member States and which expresses opinions on agricultural measures proposed by the European Commission.

DIRECTORATE GENERAL FOR REGIONAL POLICY – DG REGIO

http://ec.europa.eu/dgs/regional_policy/index_en.htm

The Directorate General for Regional Policy has to manage the second-largest share of expenditure provided by the EU. It deals with the EU's regional and cohesion fund that makes up most of the overall structural fund, which, at 32.4 billion euros a year, constitutes around one-third of the annual budget.

Table 4.11 Organizational chart, DG Regional Policy

		Deputy Director General		
Directorate A Resources **A.1** Strategic programme planning, relations with European Parliament, Committee of the Regions and Economic and Social Committee **A.2** Human resources and further education **A.3** Budget and financial management **A.4** Informatics	**Directorate B** Drafting and reform of cohesion policy, co-ordination, solidarity fund and the most remote regions **B.1** Co-ordination, solidarity fund **B.2** Drafting and analysis, enlargement negotiations **B.3** Legal issues, procedures and relations with the committees	**Directorate C** Thematic development, effects and evaluation **C.1** Thematic development and effects **C.2** Evaluation and complementarity **C.3** Innovative measures	**Directorate D** Territorial co-operation, municipal and innovative measures **D.1** Territorial co-operation **D.2** Municipal measures **D.3** Co-ordination of issues connected to the most remote regions	**Directorate E** Programmes and projects in Denmark, Germany, Latvia, Lithuania, Austria, Sweden, Slovakia and Great Britain **E.1** Germany **E.2** Latvia and Great Britain **E.3** Denmark, Lithuania and Sweden **E.4** Austria and Slovakia
Directorate F Programmes and projects in Belgium, Estonia, Finland, Ireland, Luxembourg, Spain and the Czech Republic **F.1** Spain **F.2** Belgium, Luxembourg and Czech Republic **F.3** Estonia, Finland and Ireland	**Directorate G** Programmes and projects in Greece, Italy, Malta, the Netherlands, Hungary and Cyprus **G.1** Italy and Malta **G.2** Greece **G.3** Netherlands, Hungary and Cyprus	**Directorate H** Programmes and projects in France, Poland, Portugal, Slovenia **H.1** Poland **H.2** Portugal and Slovenia **H.3** France **H.4** Instrument for Structural Policies for Pre-Accession (ISPA)	**Directorate I** Audit **I.1** Co-ordination of the audit, relations with the European Court of Auditors and European Anti-Fraud Office (OLAF) **I.2** Control and audit of European Fund for Regional Development (EFRE) **I.3** Control and audit of the cohesion fund and ISPA	

The European Fund for Regional Development (EFRE) was established in 1975 to reconcile the discernible differences in development then existing between the EU regions, both between the Member States and within individual Member States. By sponsoring specific projects, the aim of the fund is to support the development of the economy in certain regions.

The aims of the fund should really be viewed in the context of all structural funds, which divide up all European regions into specific target regions in accordance with specific statistical features. There are three target regions. Target 1 regions have a per capita gross domestic product (GDP) of less than 75 per cent of the EU average and have the characteristics of underdeveloped regions. They include regions with low population density located in Sweden, Finland and Austria as well as the most remote regions, such as several islands (the Azores or the Canaries) and the French overseas territories. Only target regions defined in this way can submit projects in order to obtain sponsorship through the regional fund. If, as is often the case, their agricultural sector is highly inefficient and unproductive, they can also receive help from the rural development fund managed by the Directorate General for Agriculture or, if it is a question of coastal areas with fisheries, from the financial instrument for fisheries management for which the Directorate General for Fisheries and Maritime Affairs is responsible.

Target 2 regions are regions experiencing socio-economic changes in the industrial and services sectors, rural regions where development is on the decline, problem areas within cities and crisis regions dependent on fishing. In principle, target 3 involves support for the adaptation and modernization of the education, training and employment systems and policies in all the regions not included under target 1.

In addition to the regional fund, the cohesion fund was set up in the middle of the 1990s. This is based on the concept that an Internal Market and political union also require economic and political cohesion. This cohesion fund is used to sponsor projects in the areas of transport and the environment in the poorer countries of the EU. Projects related to the Trans-European Network are benefiting from this fund.

Unlike the regional fund, the yardstick used to award funds from the cohesion fund is that the per capita GDP of a country must be less than 90 per cent of the EU average. When the cohesion fund was being set up, this definition covered Greece, Spain, Portugal and Ireland. However, both the regional fund and the cohesion fund are co-financed funds, which means that the Member States cannot use them by themselves, but must use them in conjunction with funds from their own budgets.

Furthermore, the Directorate General for Regional Policy also manages the Community initiatives established in accordance with the principles of regional policy:

- The INTERREG Programme promotes cross-border, trans-national and interregional co-operation within the EU. One successful example of this is the regional co-operation between the triangle of countries constituted by Austria, Slovakia and Hungary. The INTERREG Programme is being successfully continued for the third time, which is why the most recent programme is called INTERREG III.
- The specific aim of the URBAN II Initiative is to revive the economy and social life of cities and suburbs going through a social or economic crisis.

Both the regional fund and the cohesion are being affected by a serious statistical effect caused by the enlargement of the EU by 12 countries. Since almost all of the new countries, with the exception of Cyprus and Malta, are relatively poor, they have reduced the per capita GDP of the EU from a purely statistical point of view. This means that a large number of the regions previously defined as poor now automatically lie above the per capita average for the EU and therefore no longer qualify for support from the regional fund. The same thing is happening in relation to the cohesion fund because, after enlargement, the new countries are located below the 60 per cent per capita GDP mark due to this statistical effect. However, transitional measures have been planned for some of these regions, while additional transitional measures where financing is concerned are planned in order to cushion the effects of the changes so that some of the poorest regions in the old 15 Member States do not find themselves without support from the funds overnight. Discussions are in full swing as to which programming and financial instruments are to be used in the future to promote cohesion between the poorest and richest regions, without losing sight of the differences within the old Member States.

Policy areas and division of work

These issues and their inclusion in policy programmes are dealt with in the Directorate General for Regional Policy, whose Director General is Dirk Ahner from Germany. As is the case in the other Directorates

General, one directorate (Directorate A) is responsible for the general resources of the Directorate General and for relations with the European Parliament and the other institutions.

Directorate B: Drafting and reform of cohesion policy, fund co-ordination and the most remote regions

Unit B.1 deals with co-ordination and manages the solidarity fund, which was set up in order to help regions within the EU affected by catastrophes (e.g. floods or other natural disasters). Unit B.2 within the directorate deals with the drafting and analysis of policy requirements and is responsible for talks on enlargement in this area. Unit B.3 deals with legal matters and procedures, and relations with the committees.

Directorate C: Thematic development, effects and evaluation

Directorate C is a sort of cross-sectional directorate because it develops the thematic aspects of all the funds and analyses the effects of reforms (Unit C.1). Evaluations are carried out in Unit C.2, where the funds' 'complementarity' in particular is analysed (in other words, the extent to which the Member States have provided funds from their own budgets to co-finance projects). Unit C.3 tries to develop innovative measures.

Directorate D: Territorial co-operation, municipal and innovative measures

Directorate D is responsible for territorial co-operation between different regions (Unit D.1). The task of Unit D.2 on the other hand is to monitor and develop measures in the area of municipal policy. These relate to the aforementioned URBAN II Programme in particular, which is tailor-made for the needs of large cities. The most remote regions of the EU, such as some Spanish and Portuguese islands in the Mediterranean Sea and the Atlantic Ocean, as well as the French overseas territories, have special problems in many areas, whether it be links with the mother countries, trade routes, access to markets, education and training or access to medical care. Unit C.3 tries to co-ordinate all these issues and to promote possible solutions through concrete policy programmes.

Directorates E, F, G and H: Programmes and projects in the 27 Member States

Directorates E, F, G and H are responsible for implementing the funds, programmes and initiatives mentioned above, and also deal with programmes and project analysis for certain countries.

In Directorate E, Unit E.1 is responsible for Germany, while Unit E.4 is responsible for Austria and Slovakia. Units E.2 and E.3 on the other hand deal with Latvia and Great Britain as well as Denmark, Lithuania and Sweden. In Directorate F, Spain is looked after in Unit F.1, Belgium, Luxembourg and the Czech Republic are dealt with in Unit F.2 and Unit F.3 looks after Estonia, Finland and Ireland. In Directorate G, Unit G.1 is responsible for the management of programmes in Italy and Malta, Unit G.2 for programmes in Greece and Unit G.3 for programmes in the Netherlands, Hungary and Cyprus.

Directorate H is responsible for programmes in Poland (Unit H.1), Portugal and Slovenia (Unit H.2) and France (Unit H.3), and also manages the special structural instrument for the pre-accession strategy. The aim of this instrument, which stands the candidate countries in good stead, is to prepare them for management of monies from the cohesion fund by advance sponsoring of programmes in the areas of transport and the environment.

Directorate I: Audit

Directorate I is another cross-sectional directorate which, given the large amount of managed fund that come from the EU budget, deals with the rendering of accounts and auditing for the whole Directorate General.

Unit I.1 co-ordinates the rendering of all accounts and deals with relations with the European Court of Auditors and the European Anti-Fraud Office (OLAF). Both of these institutions have become increasingly important in the area of EU budget management because, due to the small number of staff it employs, the EU plans and manages the awarding of funds at the highest level, but leaves actual implementation to the Member States. In order to prevent misuse of funds at this level, the EU always involves the European Anti-Fraud Office (OLAF) in cases of doubt and always discusses matters with the European Court of Auditors. Unit I.2 is in particular in charge of the rendering of accounts in relation to the European Fund for Regional Development (EFRE), while Unit I.3 is responsible for controls and the rendering of accounts in relation to the cohesion fund and the Instrument for Structural Policies for Pre-Accession (ISPA).

DIRECTORATE GENERAL FOR TAXATION AND CUSTOMS UNION – DG TAXUD

http://ec.europa.eu/dgs/taxation_customs/index_en.htm

Since the European Community was designed for customs union from the very beginning, customs is one of the EU's main policy areas. This area is wholly communitized and also significant because customs revenue was and still is one of the original forms of revenue for the Community. The co-ordination and monitoring of customs administration by the Member States, which apply EU law originating in this area, is thus now the most important task in this area for the Directorate General. Customs union differs from a basic free trade zone due to the fact that the participating states can not only carry on trade among themselves without any restrictions, but can also levy the same customs duties on foreign trade in relation to third-party countries.

Policy areas and division of work

The Director General with responsibility for the Directorate General for Taxation and Customs Union is Robert Verrue from France. The Directorate General consists of five directorates, two of which deal with customs union and two with tax matters. The EU's tasks in relation to the area of customs union are laid down in Articles 25 to 31 of the EC Treaty. In contrast, its powers in the area of taxation policy are based on Articles 90 to 93 of the EC Treaty.

Directorate A: Co-ordination and programmes

This directorate and its three units (Unit A.1 for inter-institutional relations, internal co-ordination and strategic planning, Unit A.2 for information, further education and programme management, and Unit A.3 for data processing) deals with the Directorate General's general tasks such as relations with the other institutions of the EU and strategic planning. The few programmes run by the Directorate General are also managed here. For example, the current Customs 2007

Table 4.12 Organizational chart, DG Taxation and Customs Union

Directorate A Co-ordination and programmes	**Directorate B** International affairs and tariff-related issues	**Directorate C** Customs policy	**Directorate D** Indirect taxes and tax management	**Directorate E** Analyses and tax policies
A.1 Inter-institutional relations, internal co-ordination, strategic planning **A.2** Information, further education **A.3** Data processing	**B.1** International affairs and technical assistance **B.2** Strategic, political and economic forecasts, evaluation **B.3** Harmonised System (HS) Convention, combined nomenclature, tariff classification **B.4** Economic aspects of customs, relief from customs duties, Integrated Tariff of the European Communities (TARIC), most remote regions	**C.1** Customs policy and customs controls **C.2** Rules of origin **C.3** Customs law and controls related to application of Community law **C.4** Transit procedure, tariff suspensions, safety of distribution chain	**D.1** Value added tax (VAT) and other types of sales tax **D.2** Consumer taxes and taxes in the areas of transport, the environment and energy **D.3** Controls related to application of Community law and state aid/indirect taxes **D.4** Administrative co-operation and combating tax evasion	**E.1** Analyses and co-ordination of tax policies **E.2** Laws in the area of direct taxes **E.3** Controls related to application of Community law and state aid/direct taxes **E.4** Economic aspects of taxation

Programme whose purpose is to establish new standards in the area of co-operation for the whole EU of the 27. Its aim is to create several information exchange systems between the national administrative bodies, to finance training seminars for customs officials and experts, to facilitate employee exchanges and to produce a comprehensive electronic system that businesses in the EU can use to enter a paper-free customs environment.

Directorate B: International affairs and tariff-related issues

Since the customs union is a reality within the EU and taxation issues still only play an important role in related policy formulations, a significant number of the tasks of the Directorate General are fulfilled in Directorate B, which deals with international affairs and tariff-related issues. In this respect, the EU customs tariff is naturally being referred to, which is levied when goods are being imported into the Community.

Unit B.1 deals with international affairs and technical assistance. This concerns third-party states in particular that carry on trade with the EU and receive technical support from the EU. Unit B.2 generally deals with strategy and political and economic forecasts.

Unit B.3 deals with the complex and extremely detailed agreements that regulate down to the smallest detail how all goods are to be classified (combined nomenclature). As a result of this form of nomenclature, the same sort of tariffs are to be levied by the Member States on computer mouse pads or flat screens imported into the EU so that importers in Portugal do not apply different conditions from those applied in Finland.

In this respect, economic aspects naturally have to be taken into consideration. The issue of tariff exemption for specific goods based on international agreements and their economic effects are monitored by the officials in this directorate, for example by Unit B.3. Among other things, this Unit is responsible for setting the customs tariffs for all retail goods imported into the EU (using the Integrated Tariff of the European Communities, or TARIC). The related database indicates to anyone seeking advice in this area that, for example, 'Reception apparatus for television, whether or not incorporating radio-broadcast receivers or sound or video recording or reproducing apparatus; video monitors and video projectors operating by means of a flat panel display (for example, a liquid crystal device), capable of displaying digital information generated by an automatic data-processing machine' have been assigned the TARIC number 8528300500. Using import data and the country of origin, all EU citizens can ascertain how much customs duties they must pay for such an appliance when importing it into the EU.

Directorate C: Customs policy

In order that all the finely developed policies and concepts take effect, Directorate C deals with their application and implementation. Unit C.1 deals with customs policy and the practice of customs controls. A single unit, C.2, deals with the EU's complex rules of origin. These rules regulate in detail when a specific product can be considered to have been produced in a specific country. This issue is extremely important for both importers and exporters because nowadays final production of many products is preceded by the production of primary products in different countries. If the suppliers of machine parts that were finally assembled in a EU country are based in several non-EU countries, the rules of origin must be applied to find out what customs tariff applies. Unit C.3 deals with customs law and commissions monitoring of the application of Community law in the Member States.

Last, Unit C.4 deals with administrative processes in the area of customs administration, namely the transit procedure for goods, the existing procedure used for tariff suspensions and the safety of the distribution chain. The EU's computer-assisted transit procedure is a system of concessions that facilitates trade within the EU. The main priority of this system of concessions is to facilitate the temporary non-levying of tariffs, charges and valued added tax to be charged on goods sent to a third-party country or imported from a third-party country while the goods are being transported. The temporary non-levying of tariffs and charges applies until the goods leave the customs zone in question, are subject to a different customs rule or until the tariffs and charges are paid and the goods can move freely.[iii]

Problems can arise when this system, which is vital for trade within the EU, is being used, and Unit C.4 attempts to solve such problems. For example, attempts at moneymaking through manipulation of the available data are always being discovered, which can constitute the offence of customs fraud or tax evasion.

[iii] Report of the Committee of Inquiry into the Community Transit Procedure. Rapporteur: Mr Edward Kellett-Bowman. Document of the European Parliament, A4/0053/97.

The other branch of the Directorate General deals with taxes in Europe. Due to the existence of wholly different systems in the Member States, taxation in Europe is not regulated in a standardized manner. This is true in particular in relation to direct taxation, i.e. all types of income tax, inheritance tax, etc. In the area of indirect taxes, i.e. value added tax or taxes on specific products such as alcohol or cigarettes, there has for many years been greater harmonization. The reason for the endeavours where harmonization is concerned is obvious – if products circulating on the Internal Market in the EU as a whole were subject to different taxes in different countries, this would encourage tax evasion and customs fraud.

Directorate D: Indirect taxes and tax management

Directorate D deals with these types of taxes. Harmonization of taxes is most advanced in the area of value added tax and other types of sales tax. In this respect, there is the directive on value added tax, which clearly lays down what the minimum and maximum tax burdens may be within the EU and what product groups come under higher or lower taxation classes (Unit D.1). The second-largest area where a high degree of harmonization already exists is the area of consumption taxes on specific products such as alcohol and tobacco.

Since there is increasing trade on the Internal Market in services such as the routing of traffic and the supply of energy, the European Commission is increasing its endeavours to harmonize related taxes. This is the domain of Unit D.2. As soon as Community laws are approved in this area, Unit D.3 has the task of monitoring application of the laws. It also analyses the compatibility of state aid, which is frequently granted in the form of tax relief, with Community law.

Since it is not always easy to create a joint taxation policy in an Internal Market such as the EU, with tax and administration systems co-ordinated in very different ways, Unit D.4 deals with administrative co-operation between the Member States and thus also with the combating of tax evasion.

Directorate E: Analyses and tax policies

Directorate E deals with further aspects of the tax policy and with analyses and tax policies in the EU and the Member States in general. Although the EU has only very few powers in relation to the way in which its rules of origin affect direct taxation, there are increasing endeavours in relation to tax harmonization where economic activities that can lead to distortion of competition in the EU are concerned. For example, the European Commission has approved notifications that the Member States have to comply with in order to take into sufficient consideration the basic freedoms of the Internal Market in relation to the policy of direct taxation.

There are also directives on the taxation of profits on interest from savings and decisions on the subject of harmful tax competition within the EU. Unit E.2 correspondingly analyses the laws on direct taxes in the Member States. Unit E.3 is responsible for controlling the application of Community law and state aid in relation to direct taxes. Unit E.4 assesses the economic aspects of taxation in relation to market economies in general and where specific branches and economic activities are concerned.

DIRECTORATE GENERAL FOR THE ENVIRONMENT – DG ENV

http://ec.europa.eu/dgs/environment/index_en.htm

The origins of a Community environmental policy go back to the year 1972. Since 1987, articles have also been established in the Community Treaty. The environment thus became one of the Community's main policy areas. The aims of and methods for this policy are explained in Articles 174 to 176 of the Treaty of Nice. In the past, the EU was often the target of bitter criticism, accused of neglecting environmental issues when its economic and trade policy was being worked out. This is why it is now endeavouring to create a sustained development model.

The Directorate General for the Environment (ENV) has a number of main priorities:

- to maintain and improve quality of life by ensuring a high level of protection for natural resources, through effective risk assessment and timely implementation of Community laws;
- to promote efficient use of resources in the production, use and disposal of waste;
- to include environmental issues in different EU policy areas;
- to promote European growth, at the same time taking into consideration the economic, social and ecological requirements of EU citizens and those of future generations;

Table 4.13 Organizational chart, DG Environment

Directorate A Governance, communication and civil protection **A.1** Communication **A.2** Infringements **A.3** Legal matters and governance **A.4** Inter-institutional relations **A.5** Civil protection	**Directorate B** Conservation of natural environment **B.1** Agriculture and conservation of soils **B.2** Nature and biological diversity **B.3** Forest management **B.4** Biotechnology and pesticides	**Directorate C** Air and chemical substances **C.1** Air quality and transport **C.2** Climate, ozone and energy **C.3** Chemical substances **C.4** Industrial emissions

Directorate D Conservation of waters and environmental programmes **D.1** LIFE **D.2** Conservation of waters and seas **D.3** Cohesion policy and environmental sustainability **D.4** Health and urban areas	**Directorate E** International affairs **E.1** International relations, environmental governance and development **E.2** Environmental agreements and trade **E.3** Enlargement and neighbouring states	**Directorate F** Resources **F.1** Personnel **F.2** Finance **F.3** Information technology	**Directorate H** Sustained development and integration **H.1** Sustained development and economic analyses **H.2** Environment and industry **H.3** Research, science and innovations **H.4** Sustained production and consumption

- to accept the global challenges, in particular those posed by climate change and the maintenance of biological diversity;
- to involve all of the actors and target groups in the overall process and to successfully to negotiate strategies and actions.

The Directorate General for the Environment is headed by the Greek Commissioner, Stavros Dimas. The directorate, which has most of its offices in Brussels and employs around 550 staff, initiates and elaborates new laws in the area of the environment. Before it makes policy proposals, it discusses the relevant issues with governmental representatives, industry, non-governmental organizations and experts.

In most cases, the European Parliament has powers of co-decision with the Council; the Council must also hear the opinion of the Economic and Social Committee and the Committee of the Regions before it makes a decision. Another task of the Directorate General for the Environment is to monitor application of approved EU laws. The European Commission can take legal action against Member States or businesses; if these measures have no effect, it can call on the European Court of Justice. In addition, the Directorate General for the Environment represents the European Union on the international stage and attempts to find solutions to trans-national environmental problems. Additional important areas of activity covered by the Directorate General for the Environment are the inclusion of environmental issues in other policy areas (e.g. in the areas of energy, agriculture and transport) and the provision of information on ecological issues.

The central features of the European environmental policy are above all waste disposal, noise pollution, air and water pollution, nature conservation, natural (e.g. environmental catastrophes) and technological risks (e.g. radioactive waste, industrial accidents), the effects of EU enlargement on environmental policy and international co-operation. Running from 2001 to 2010, the Sixth Action Programme for Environmental Protection is focusing on climate change, nature and biological diversity, the environment, health and quality of life, as well as on management of natural resources and waste management. As environmental policy instruments, the Directorate General for the Environment has as its disposal framework provisions – by means of which a series of technical regulations have been approved and the LIFE financial programme was created – action programmes, environmental checks in the Member States, environmental taxes and voluntary international agreements.

Policy areas and division of work

The Directorate General for the Environment is headed by the Danish Director General, Mogens Peter Carl. It is divided into seven directorates. Directorate F is responsible for internal affairs and administration, dealing with personnel issues, finance and information technology. The other six directorates deal with specific thematic aspects of the European environmental policy.

Directorate A: Communication, legal affairs and civil protection

While the first unit within the Directorate, Unit A.1, elaborates and implements the Directorate General's communications policy, Units A.2 and A.3 deal with the legal aspects of the Community's environmental policy. In Unit A.2, infringements of treaty provisions are tracked down and, if necessary, infringement procedures are implemented. Unit A.3 deals with the other legal issues. For example, the laws constituting the *acquis communautaire* must be adapted to facilitate the correct application of international agreements. The fourth unit manages the European Commission's relations with the other institutions of the EU, while the fifth unit deals with issues of civil protection.

Directorate B: Protecting the natural environment

Directorate B of the Directorate General for the Environment is responsible for the protection of the natural environment. Unit B.1 is endeavouring to work out a common strategy for soil conservation. In parallel with this, it also deals with the environmental policy aspects of agriculture. Unit B.2 is responsible for nature conservation and biological diversity. In Europe, almost 1,000 plant species and more than 150 bird species are endangered or have become extinct. The European Commission is attempting to guarantee the survival of flora and fauna, and the conservation of the forests. Unit B.3 deals with the different environmental policy aspects of forestry while Unit B.4 deals with biotechnological developments and the use of pesticides.

Directorate C: Air and chemical substances

Air and chemical substances are the responsibility of Directorate C. Unit C.1 deals with air quality and transport. The Council and the European Parliament lay down limits for carbon monoxide, aerosols and ozone, and the air quality in all the European Member States is tested according to these values. If the limits are exceeded, the Member States are obliged to inform the European Commission of this and to investigate the cause of excessive pollution. Among other things, the proposals for the now infamous European Directive on Particulates originated in this unit. Unit C.1 also deals with the ecological effects of the transport sector.

Unit C.2 deals with issues of climate change, ozone and energy. The aim of the Commission's European Climate Change Programme

(ECCP) is to significantly reduce greenhouse gas emissions and thus to implement the Kyoto Protocol agreed in 1997. (The parties to the protocol agreed to reduce emissions between 2008 and 2012 by 8 per cent compared with the level in 1990.) Unit C.3 is responsible for the use of chemical substances. At present, a directive on the registration, evaluation and authorization of chemical substances (known as REACH), which is controversial within the industry, is being prepared. Unit C.4 deals with emissions from industry. Under the Kyoto Protocol, which came into force in January 2005, the EU opened the largest multinational and multi-sectoral emission trading system in the world in the form of the European Union Greenhouse Gas Emission Trading System (EU ETS).

Directorate D: Conservation of waters and environmental programmes

Directorate D deals with conservation of waters and European environmental programmes. Unit D.1 co-ordinates the Financial Instrument for the Environment Programme, known as LIFE. As one of the most important instruments of the EU environmental policy, LIFE supports projects devoted to environmental protection, nature conservation and sustainable development (both inside and outside the EU). During its third phase (2002–2004), 640 million euros was allocated to LIFE; this figure was increased by 317 million euros for the period 2005–2006.

Unit D.2 deals with conservation of the European rivers, lakes and seas. It works on areas such as sewage management, the quality of bathing water and drinking water, and water pollution caused by the introduction of hazardous substances. The third unit deals with the connections between environmental policy and cohesion policy, i.e. it checks whether European environmental regulations are being taken into consideration when cohesion-related and structural projects are being implemented. Unit D.4 deals with the connections between the environment and health, and looks at the condition of European urban areas affected to a significant extent by air and noise pollution. In June 2004, the European Commission submitted an action plan with the aim of improving understanding of the connections between sources of pollution and health-related effects, examining policy concepts and improving communication.

Directorate E: International affairs

Directorate E of the Directorate General for the Environment is responsible for international affairs. Unit E.1 deals with international environmental governance. The Aarhus Convention signed in 1998 is to safeguard better access to ecological information, increase the involvement of the public in environmental policy decisions and guarantee access to courts in relation to environmental issues. Implementation of the Aarhus Convention is currently one of the most important goals of international EU environmental policy. Unit E.1 is also responsible for developmental policy. A significant amount of EU developmental aid supports ecological projects in the developing countries.

Unit E.2 is in charge of environmental agreements and trade. The European Commission has already signed a series of agreements on behalf of the EU related to a wide variety of issues – e.g. natural diversity (Rio Convention, 1992), climate change (Kyoto Protocol, 1997), industrial accidents (Helsinki Convention, 1992) and the identification and management of chemicals (Stockholm Convention, 2001). Furthermore, Unit E.2 is working on increasing inclusion of environmental aspects in the elaboration and implementation of external trade policy. Unit E.3 deals with issues that arise during the enlargement process. The European Commission aims for the implementation of existing Community environmental laws in the candidate countries of Central and Eastern Europe.

Directorate G: Sustainable development and integration

Directorate G of the Directorate General for the Environment focuses on sustainable development, i.e. it attempts to guarantee that current growth does not become a burden for future generations. Unit G.1 works out the guidelines for this policy. In this area, the European Commission uses a strategy that involves the integration of environmental policy issues into other EU policy areas. This is known as the Cardiff Process.

Unit G.2 is responsible for the integration of industrial policy into this concept. The aim is to overcome the seemingly inevitable conflicts of interest arising between the environment and industry in the context of environmental policy. Companies have made great progress in recent years in the area of environmental protection. Initiatives with regard to research, science and innovation are managed in Unit C.3. The European Commission promotes progress in environmental technologies that prevent the creation of pollutants or save energy or resources. Unit G.4 deals with issues of production, consumption and waste management.

European Environmental Agency (EEA)

http://www.eea.europa.eu/

The European Environmental Agency (EEA) began its work in 1994. This independent agency, located in Copenhagen and run by Jacqueline McGlade from Great Britain, assists other bodies that elaborate and implement European and national environmental policy by preparing environment-specific information. The agency works to support the EU and its Member States in their aim to improve the quality of the environment, to integrate environmental issues into their economic and trade strategies, and to make their policies more sustainable. Second, the EEA appeals to the broad European public with regard to ecological issues. The EEA is a European agency, but it is also open to non-EU states that share its goals. This means that, in addition to the 27 Member States of the EU, Iceland, Liechtenstein, Norway, and Turkey are also members. In 2004, detailed reports were drawn up on the issues of biofuels, the interplay between traffic and the environment in Europe, and energy subsidies and renewable energies.

DIRECTORATE GENERAL FOR ENTERPRISE AND INDUSTRY – DG ENTR

http://ec.europa.eu/enterprise/index_en.htm

The Directorate General for Enterprise and Industry is headed by the German Commissioner and Vice-President of the European Commission, Günter Verheugen. The aim of the Directorate General for Enterprise and Industry (DG ENTR) is to guarantee that Community policies lead to the strengthening of businesses' competitiveness in Europe. The DG ENTR is in particular endeavouring to create an environment in which businesses develop, increase their productivity and create jobs in order to maintain prosperity.

Although the EU fundamentally shapes its policies for enterprise and industry in terms of 'competitiveness', it has in no way lost sight

Table 4.14 Organizational chart, DG Enterprise and Industry

Deputy Director General				
Directorate A Co-ordination of competition	**Directorate B** Industrial policy and economic reforms	**Directorate C** Laws	**Directorate D** Innovation policy	**Directorate E** Furthering competitiveness of small- and medium-sized businesses
A.1 General co-ordination **A.2** International aspects of corporate and industrial policy **A.3** Inter-institutional relations **A.4** Aspects of competition policy	**B.1** Further development of industrial policy **B.2** Competitiveness and economic reforms **B.3** Impact assessment and economic assessment **B.4** Competition aspects of sustained development	**C.1** Legal aspects in relation to the Single Market **C.2** Standardization **C.3** Notification procedures **C.4** General framework for free movement of goods **C.5** Administration of Articles 28-30	**D.1** Further development of innovation policy **D.2** Innovation support **D.3** Financing of small- and medium-sized businesses, entrepreneurs and innovators **D.4** Innovation technology, information and communications technologies (ICT) and eBusiness	**E.1** Improving measures for furthering small- and medium-sized businesses **E.2** Co-operation between businesses and network for supporting businesses **E.3** Crafts, small businesses, co-operatives and mutual societies **E.4** Horizontal aspects of small- and medium-sized business policy

Directorate F	**Directorate G**	**Directorate H**	**Directorate I**	**Directorate R**
Consumer goods	Chemicals and construction industry	Air and space travel, security, defence and armaments industry	Primary and design industries, tourism, Interoperable Delivery of European eGovernment Services (IDABC)	Resources
F.1 Automobile industry **F.2** Pharmaceuticals industry **F.3** Cosmetics and medical products **F.4** Food industry **F.5** Competitiveness of pharmaceuticals industry and biotechnology	**G.1** REACH **G.2** Chemical substances **G.3** Construction industry	**H.1** Air, space, defence and maritime industry **H.2** Space policy and co-ordination **H.3** Space research and possible uses **H.4** Preparatory measures for security research **H.5** Mechanical and electrical equipment **H.6** Pressure equipment	**I.1** Tourism **I.2** Steel, non-iron metals and other materials **I.3** Wood and wood-processing industry **I.4** Textile, leather and toys; corporate social responsibility (CSR) **I.5** European eGovernment Services, Interoperable Delivery of European eGovernment Services (IDABC)	**R.1** Finance **R.2** Personnel **R.3** Data processing **R.4** Communication and information **R.5** Strategic planning and organization

of the social and environmental aspects of a European corporate policy. The realization that Europe is in danger of losing its competitiveness in relation to the USA and other industrial countries, and that the gap between other countries and Europe with regard to innovations and research is widening, has brought the EU and the Member States closer together. The EU as a whole has recognized that the problems engendered by a global economy that is developing ever faster, together with competition that is becoming tougher, can only be tackled by a common EU corporate policy.

The current directives for the EU's corporate and industrial policy can be found in the Lisbon Decision taken by the European Council in 2001. The goal is to make the EU 'the most competitive and dynamic knowledge-based economy in the world, capable of sustainable economic growth with more and better jobs and greater social cohesion'.

The EU's corporate policy is directed towards the whole Community environment, regardless of a company's size, legal form or branch of activity. The goal of its policy is to allow small- and medium-sized businesses and large businesses to grow, further develop and have at their disposal framework conditions that both make them competitive and awaken the corporate spirit within the EU.

This is why the DG ENTR and its directorates have concentrated on the following goals:

- to create framework conditions that further 'competitiveness in businesses;
- to increase the EU's potential, in particular following enlargement;
- to promote the spirit of enterprise and innovations;
- to support close relations between European businesses and the rest of the world.

The legal basis of the EU's corporate policy is contained in Article 157 of the EC Treaty; however, the Directorate General for Enterprise and Industry's areas of activity also include the free movement of goods (Articles 28–30), the Internal Market (Article 95), health (Article 152) and the areas of innovation and research (Title XVIII).

The DG ENTR has to manage a large number of initiatives and programmes that are directed towards the requirements of business. One programme implemented by the DG ENTR was the First Framework Programme for Competitiveness and Innovation (FFPCI), which is running for a period of seven years (2007–2013) and has a budget of more than 4 billion euros. With this programme the EU wants to combine in this area several pre-existing EU activities used in particular to promote innovations. One of the European Commission's aims is to make the EU's means of support more transparent and more comprehensible.

Another programme, the Multi-Annual Programme (MAP), consists of measures aimed at promoting growth and the competitiveness of businesses and corporate initiative, improving and simplifying the administrative and regulatory environment for businesses, improving the financial framework conditions for businesses (in particular small- and medium-sized businesses), and facilitating access by them to the Community's support services, programmes and networks.

Some of these networks include, for example, the Innovation Relay Centres (IRS). The purpose of these networks is to promote the trans-national transfer of technology. They have centres in 71 regions in 33 countries including, obviously, all of the EU Member States, in three candidate countries, and in Istanbul, Norway, Switzerland and Chile. These centres' services are available mainly to small- and medium-sized businesses, but also to large businesses, research bodies and universities.

Another network in the Innovative Regions in Europe (IRE) net-work. Both the Directorate General for Enterprise and Industry and the Directorate General for Regional Policy provide support for this network. The main goal of the network is to facilitate access by regions to new instruments used to promote innovations.

Another important and very well-known network is the Community Research and Development Information Service (CORDIS). This is the European Commission's information service for research and technological development. It provides information, documents and interactive services via its internet site.

Policy areas and division of work

The Directorate General for Enterprise and Industry is headed by the Austrian Director General, Franz Zourek. The ten directorates' areas of activity are divided up into three areas:

- competitiveness and industrial policy (Directorates A, B and C);
- competitiveness and entrepreneurship (Directorates D and E);
- competitiveness of the Internal Market for goods and sectoral policies (F, G, H and I).

Directorate A: Co-ordination of competitiveness

Directorate A has the task of co-ordinating all competition policy measures related to the area of industrial policy. Directorate A specifically supports the work done by the 'competition council'. To achieve the goals contained in the Lisbon Strategy and to make businesses in Europe more competitive, a competition council was established. This council is a body in which representatives of the Member States and a group of Commissioners sit down together and assess and evaluate the competitiveness of the policies and the related Community laws. The competition council is currently focusing on policies in the following areas: research, the Internal Market, competition and businesses. The president of the competition council is the President of the European Commission, José Manuel Barroso, while Mr Verheugen is both Vice-President of the competition council and chairperson of its group of Commissioners. Directorate A of the Directorate General for Enterprise and Industry looks after general co-ordination.

Among other things, Unit A.1 is responsible for the Multi-Annual Programmes (MAPs) for small- and medium-sized businesses, and will also carry responsibility for the new Framework Programme for Competitiveness and Innovation (FFPCI), which will run from 2007 to 2013. Close co-operation is necessary between all participants in and everyone affected by these programmes, and Unit A.1 co-ordinates this co-operation.

Unit A.2 is in charge of the directorate's external relations. This involves fostering relations with countries such as China, the USA and the candidate countries. Unit A.3 on other hand fulfils the important task of managing the Directorate General's inter-institutional relations because Community law as it affects the corporate and industrial policy involves the European Parliament and the Council in the co-decision procedure.

Unit A.4 deals with competitiveness within the context of the competition policy. Here, analyses and assessments are carried out to see if existing Community regulations are really competition friendly and supportive of the competitiveness of European businesses'. Unit A.4 works in particular with the Directorate General for Competition. Furthermore, the Directorate General for Competition consults with the Directorate General for Enterprise and Industry on the introduction of competition procedures via which the Directorate General undertakes analyses of the sector. The directorate receives an average of 800 enquiries each year and these are co-ordinated by this unit.

Directorate B: Industrial policy and economic reforms

In the broadest sense, this directorate is responsible for the question of how the EU's industrial policy can be further developed in order to help European businesses to survive on the global market (Unit B.1). All the reform-related measures and laws that affect the EU economy are analysed in Unit B.2 and checked to see if they promote or hinder the competitiveness of European businesses. Unit B.3 makes economic assessments of the effects that laws have on Member States and different sectors. Sustained development and the protection of the environment as well as social aspects of the labour market are among the EU's main priorities, but these measures should not have a negative effect on the competitiveness of European businesses. Unit B.4 analyses these issues.

Directorate C: Regulatory policy

Although complaints are often made about the EU's regulatory lust, standardization is vitally important when it comes to a product, from toys to cosmetics, being manufactured in one EU country and being sold with a clear conscience in any of the other 26 EU countries.

The European Internal Market, which now consists of 27 countries, today demands better co-ordination than ever if it is to run smoothly. This horizontal form of co-ordination between the directorates and the units in the Directorate General is managed by Directorate C. More precisely, proposed laws and exchanges are managed within the Directorate General. Unit C.1 is responsible for the general legal aspects within the context of the Internal Market. Standardization is an important aspect of the functioning of the Internal Market and in relation to the competitiveness of goods produced in Europe, and Unit C.2 deals with this area. If necessary, the unit gives the European Standardization Office a mandate to develop new standards for products. The unit also monitors harmonization of standards and norms introduced or applied in the EU with EU norms and standards. Units C.3 and C.4 are in charge of the notification procedure and infringement of regulations as well as the general framework for the free movement of goods within the Internal Market. Unit C.3 in particular ensures that norms and standards created in the Member States neither intentionally nor unintentionally erect technical trade barriers, which would prevent the free movement of goods. Member States are notified of treaty infringements if they occur. Directive 98/34 authorizes the EU to request that Member States revise or even abolish related laws.

Unit C.5 is the guardian of Articles 28 to 30 of the treaty. These articles regulate the movement of goods within the European Internal Market and, among other things, prohibit quantitative import restrictions or what are known as 'same effect measures' from being in force in relation to trade between the Member States. Exceptions to this general prohibition can only be made if the importation of a product endangers public safety, order, morals or the health of persons, animals and plants in the affected countries. Examples of related measures taken by the Member States include the ban on importing chicken meat following an outbreak of avian influenza in one of the Member States or the bans following outbreaks of BSE. This unit is responsible for examining the legal and material aspects of such exceptions made by Member States.

Directorate E: Small and medium-sized business competitiveness

Directorate E concentrates specifically on measures that support business. Unit E.1 focuses on concrete steps to promote business and entrepreneurial spirit while improving overall conditions for small and medium-sized businesses – an important component in a knowledge-based economy. Benchmarking and the exchange of best practices among EU-based companies are the most important instruments used by this unit. Unit E.2 works directly with businesses. E.3 helps the skilled trades and small co-operative organizations gain the benefit of EU policies. Unit E.4 provides horizontal oversight, ensuring that various initiatives and policies do not contradict one another.

Directorate F: Industry

Directorate F is responsible for individual industry sectors that are impacted by EU policies. Each industry sector is an important component of the European economy, and many are global market leaders – whether it is the European automobile industry or the pharmaceutical and chemical industries. These sectors are affected not only by EU domestic market law but also by external EU trade relationships. The individual units, each devoted to a particular industry, initiate necessary regulations for each respective area of business. They also monitor industry developments and design industry-specific European policies (F.1 for the automobile industry, F.2 pharmaceutical industry, F.3

cosmetic and medical products, F.4 food industry, F.5 competitiveness in pharmaceuticals and biotechnology). The units are a driving force behind solutions to problems created by trade policy. Moreover, the Commission launches initiatives that support sustainable development and expansion in each industry. As an example, the tourism industry falls under this DG area of expertise.

Directorate G: chemicals and construction

Directorate G is organized in a similar manner. Unit G.2 is responsible for chemical materials and G.3 for the construction industry. G.1 concentrates on the REACH initiative, a new system for registering, evaluating, and authorizing chemical materials inside the EU.

Under the proposed system, all businesses that produce more than one ton of certain chemical substances annually are registered in a centralized database, to improve the risk management of such substances.

Directorate H: Air and space travel, security, defence and armaments industries

Like other industry-specific directorates, Directorate H manages relationships with air and space corporations, and with the defence and maritime industries. Unit H.1 handles air and space, defence, and maritime industries. H.2 focuses on European space policy and co-ordination. H.3 supports space research. Units H.4, H.5 and H.6 deal with security research, mechanical and electronic armaments, and pressure equipment commonly used in these industries.

Directorate I: Basic and design industries, tourism, IDABC

Directorate I is also organized according to economic sectors. I.1 handles tourism, I.2 steel, non-ferrous metals, and other raw materials, I.3 wood and lumber industries, and I.4 textiles, leather, and toys. Unit I.5 is responsible for European eGovernment and interoperable delivery of eGovernment services to public administrations, business, and citizens (IDABC) services. The objective of this programme is to take advantage of technological opportunities to improve efficiencies between business, the general public, and government administrations across Europe.

EMEA – European Medicines Agency

http://www.emea.europa.eu/

The EMEA was founded in 1995. Headquartered in London, the agency is charged with improving public health protection and animal well-being. The EMEA conducts evaluations of medications for humans and animals and co-ordinates control of the medical application of pharmaceuticals within the EU. This is done by co-ordinating a large scientific network of 42 agencies in all 27 Member States and over 3,000 European pharmaceutical experts, who support the scientific work of the agency and its committees. The agency's work is crucial in establishing guidelines for the development of the European pharmaceutical industry.

DIRECTORATE GENERAL FOR ENERGY AND TRANSPORT – DG TREN

http://ec.europa.eu/dgs/energy_transport/index_en.html

This Directorate General is named after the first two letters of the words 'transport' and 'energy' (TREN). Two Commissioners are responsible for these two policy areas. The transport department is managed by Commissioner and Commission Vice-President Jacques Barrot of France. The energy department is under the leadership of Commissioner Andris Piebalgs of Latvia. The Director General Matthias Ruete of Germany has been responsible for development and implementation of the European transport and energy policy since January 2006.

The origins of the European Union reach back to the founding of the European Community for Coal and Steel (ECCS), also known as the Montan Union. The ECCS was founded on 18 April 1951 with the Treaty of Paris with the objective of securing peace in Europe through interdependence. This meant mutual control of the war-making materials of coal and steel as well as the procurement of these resources for reconstruction following the Second World War. The treaty was signed at that time by Belgium, Germany, France, Italy, Luxembourg and the Netherlands. These countries are now referred to as the 'founding states' of the EU. The objectives of the ECCS were quickly achieved and since then the Commission has been striving for a common energy policy. The ECCS treaty expired after 50 years on 23 July 2003. Many of its functions are now conducted within the EU framework.

With the industrial and economic development of the European Union, a common energy policy became increasingly important. The oil crisis of the 1970s made it clear that the industrial countries of Europe were not only extremely dependent on these energy sources but also that these resources are finite.

The infinite demand for finite energy resources such as oil has led again today to responsible industrialized nations rethinking their energy policies. In a global world economy with large, aspiring industrial countries and the increasingly apparent environmental consequences of an industrializing global economy, the EU has also moved to rethink its energy policy.

The Green Paper 'Moving toward a European strategy for energy supply security' was published by the Commission on 29 November 2000. It contains guidelines for European energy policy and provides an impetus for initiatives on the ways in which EU energy policy should develop in the coming decades. The current EU energy policy is designed to promote competition on European energy markets to the benefit of consumers and the entire European economy.

A further objective is to secure the energy supply. Europe currently imports more than half of its energy requirements and is dependent on external energy sources. If the present level of energy consumption continues, the Commission estimates an energy import dependence of up to 70 per cent by the year 2030. This is why European energy policy is consciously focused on promoting renewable energies (air, water, sun, and biofuels). Renewable energies would reduce not only Europe's dependency on finite fossil fuels but also the dependency on energy suppliers located in unstable regions.

An increasingly important aspect of European energy policy is the environmental impact of energy production. The Kyoto Protocol objective of reducing global carbon dioxide emissions is a common goal of the EU.

In contrast to energy policy, the directives of a common transport policy are clearly enumerated in the Treaty of Nice (Articles 70 to 80). A functioning transport policy was and still is seen as the foundation of the European economic area. In order to implement a transport policy in accordance with these directives, and make EU transportation safer and more efficient, the Commission published a White Paper in 2001. The paper contained measures to promote a more efficient and reliable transportation network within the EU. It is an important objective of

Table 4.15 Organizational chart, DG Energy and Transport

Deputy Director General			
Directorate A Resources, inter-institutional relations, communication, and data processing	**Directorate B** Trade policy protection instruments	**Directorate C** Free trade agreements and partnership agreements with ACP countries, Latin America, GCC and Iran; General Preference System	**Directorate D** Trade relationships with neighbouring countries and southeastern Asia
A.1 Personnel, administration, finances, foreign service, programming **A.2** Inter-institutional relations and communication **A.3** Data processing	**B.1** TPPI: General policy, applications **B.2** TPPI: Investigations I; supervision of developing country activities **B.3** TPPI: Investigations II **B.4** TPPI: Investigations III; monitoring and supervision of policy implementation within the EU **B.5** TPPI: Investigations IV	**C.1** Negotiation and administration of trade and free trade agreements with Latin America, GCC and Iran; General Preference System **C.2** Partnership agreements I **C.3** Partnership agreements II	**D.1** Trade issues related to European Neighbourhood Policy; trade relationships with CIS countries and the Balkans **D.2** Negotiation and administration of trade and free trade agreements with Mediterranean countries and southeastern Asia; TREATI

Directorate E	Directorate F	Directorate G	Directorate H
Bilateral trade relationships II; market access, industry trade policy issues, export trade policy **E.1** Standards and certifications; TBT **E.2** Steel, coal, shipbuilding, automobile, chemical, and other industries **E.3** Market access, trade relations with USA, Canada and EFTA **E.4** Export trade policy (exports credits, controls, practices in developing countries)	**F.1** WTO and OECD co-ordination, trade-related assistance **F.2** Dispute support and enactment, trade barrier issues	Services, agricultural trade issues, sustainable development; bilateral trade relations III **G.1** Service transport, GATS, investments **G.2** Agriculture, fisheries, animal and plant health, biotechnology **G.3** Sustainable development (including trade and environment), dialogue with civil society	Textiles, new technologies, intellectual property, public contracts, public procurement, trade analysis; bilateral trade relations IV **H.1** Negotiation and administration of textile agreements, shoes **H.2** New technologies, intellectual property, public procurement **H.3** Trade analysis

the Commission to reach a new balance between the various transport providers in the European transportation system.

Consequently, it is a specific goal of the Union to equip the European transportation network with the latest technologies. The Galileo Project is an EU initiative to construct Europe's own global satellite navigation system, in order to become more strategically and economically independent of the current American global positioning system. Developed in co-operation with the European Space Agency, the satellite system is intended for civilian use, as well as supporting the European transport system.

Policy areas and responsibilities

It is the task of the DG Energy and Transport to implement these directives and to develop appropriate initiatives, programmes and instruments to meet the demands of a common transport policy. Close co-operation and consultation between the DG Energy and Transport and the Directorates General for Competition, Environment, Internal Market and Regional Policy are essential for policy formation.

As in other EU policy areas, Transport and Energy has created agencies to handle specific expert or scientific tasks as well as administrative duties. The agencies that help implement EU transport and energy policies include Euratom and European agencies for Maritime Security, Air Safety, Railways, and the Executive Agency for Intelligent Energy. All units report to the Director General.

Directorate A: General affairs and resources

Units A.1 and A.2 administer general affairs such as personnel and finances. Unit A.3 maintains relationships with the European Parliament and its committees for transport and tourism as well as with industry, research, energy institutions, and the Council. The department also co-ordinates work when new EU legislation is passed. A.4 is responsible for co-ordinating with the appropriate Directorate General all aspects of transport and energy policy that overlap or contradict EU common market or competition law.

Directorate B: Trans-European networks for transport and energy

Directorate B is dedicated exclusively to trans-European energy and transport networks. The Trans-European Network for Transport and Energy (TEN) is considered the nucleus of EU transport and energy policy. Its directives are anchored in European law by Articles 154–156 of the EU Treaty.

Shortly after the founding of the European Common Market in the early 1980s, it became clear that free movement of people, goods, services and capital in the Community could only be achieved within the context of a comprehensive European transport network. The TEN programme works towards the implementation of an integrated European transport network and also aims to improve internal market development as well as economic and social standards for the various regions of the EU. The current TEN programme is divided into two areas: the TEN Transport Programme, which is designed to support the integration of European transport systems (roads, harbours, inland waterways, railways), and the TEN Energy Programme, which supports improvements in energy and telecommunications infrastructure as well as the Galileo satellite navigation system programme. Primary financing of TEN programme projects comes from Member States. The EU has also earmarked supplementary financing.

Co-financing comes from the TEN budget or from the EU structural funds. A website specially designed by the Directorate General contains additional information about Union-financed projects (http://europa.eu.int/comm/transport/extra/web/index.cfm).

Directorate C: Conventional energy sources

A large portion of energy in Europe increasingly comes from conventional energy sources such as gas, coal and petroleum. Directorate C supervises the secure supply of these resources in Member States and the entire EU. In addition, Directorate C monitors energy supply companies to ensure EU legal compliance and that the European energy market is functioning in accordance with EU legislation. A directorate office handles relations with developing countries that are deemed important energy partners for Europe.

Directorate D: New and renewable energy sources, demand management, and sustainable development

The EU has a fundamental objective to reduce dependence on external energy sources and to do this in an environmentally sensitive manner. This can only take place if the entire EU develops new and renewable energy sources and brings them to the market for application. These objectives are pursued by Directorate D with four units. Unit D.1 works on the issue of regulation policy among the individual Member States, so that new energy sources can be incorporated into the electricity grid. Unit D.2 ensures that research and technological development programmes promote sensible development of new energy sources and efficient technological design. D.3 takes this research data and processes it further. D.4 handles general issues of environment-friendly transport and sustainable development.

Directorate E: Overland transport

Directorate E deals with overland based transport, which includes all aspects of rail and road traffic. It is organized in three units. D.1 handles all overland transport policy. D.2 manages railways and interoperability; the latter term refers to the EU objective of improved networking among planners and various forms of transport to promote efficient usage. For example, one goal is that freight trucks loaded at an industrial plant should not undertake a long journey but instead deliver their freight to a special interoperable railway loading station. Then, 2,000 kilometres later, the freight is taken from the railway and delivered to the final destination by lorry. To achieve this, junctions for loading from road to rail must become more intelligent and efficient – after all, time is money. Unit D.3 of the directorate focuses on improving road safety.

Directorate F: Air transport

Directorate F deals with air transport in Europe. The division is responsible for the airline liberalization that has revolutionized medium-distance European air travel over the last decade. Air transport is a growing industry, and increasing interdependence in the air requires a single European policy. Unit F.1 handles air transport policy and the economic regulation of the market as well as the multilateral relationships behind the policy.

Unit F.2 deals with air transport management and airports. F.3 handles the increasingly important issues of environmental impact and safety. This includes noise reduction as well as the widely discussed topic of condensation trails affecting regional climates. Over the last few years, Unit F.4 has been working on the notorious issue of bilateral air travel agreements. The EU objective is to negotiate as a unit rather than as individual states with the United States to conclude an 'open skies' agreement. F.4 also leads this initiative.

Directorate G: Maritime transport and inland navigation

Due to its geographic position and international integration, maritime trade is of great importance to Europe. Over 90 per cent of external trade passes through harbours, and 43 per cent of domestic goods are transported via inland waterways. In addition, the number of people employed in this industry is very significant. With three departments, Directorate G handles all maritime-related issues. These include maritime transport policy, maritime security, short-distance maritime travel, inland navigation, and harbours as well as high-speed sea lanes and intermodality.

Directorate H and I: Nuclear energy and supervision

Not all Member States operate nuclear power plants; indeed, some declared the phasing out of nuclear energy a political objective in the 1990s. Nuclear power remains a controversial European topic, of course, particularly as a subject of the extraordinary Euratom agreement, and Directorates H and I divide the tasks of addressing the questions relating to it. Eight departments deal with all essential aspects of nuclear policy, including plant operation, nuclear waste, radiation safety and reconstitution facility supervision, as well as production and enrichment facilities, reactor inspection, storage of fissile material, and materials inventory. The aim is to ensure that substances do not end up in the wrong hands.

Directorate J: Safety – personal, material, and facility security

The final Directorate J broadens the perspective to include all energy and transport facilities. Acknowledging that energy and transport infrastructure are the nerve centres of the modern European economy and lifestyle, Directorate J responsibilities include air and sea transport safety, power plant protection and infrastructure as well as the transport of hazardous material. Following the events of 11 September 2001 in the USA, and the subsequent attacks on the transport infrastructure in Madrid and London, the importance of these departments and their work has increased significantly.

The Euratom Supply Agency

http://ec.europa.eu/euratom/index_en.html

The Euratom Supply Agency is one of the first agencies of the European Union. In 1958, leaders agreed by treaty to form the European Atomic Energy Community. Its purpose is defined in Article 1: 'It shall be the task of the Community to contribute to the raising of the standard of living in the Member States and to the development of relations with the other countries by creating the conditions necessary for the speedy establishment and growth of nuclear industries.' The Euratom Supply Agency was founded in 1960 to fulfil the anticipated duties of the European Atomic Energy Community. The agency reports to the Energy Commissioner. It is headquartered in Luxembourg and led by Director General Christian Waeterloos.

EMSA – European Maritime Security Agency

http://www.emsa.europa.eu/

Tragic oil tanker accidents in European waters and the devastating consequences for the environment prompted the EU to create the European Maritime Security Agency, or EMSA. EMSA began its work in 2003 under the leadership of Director General Willem de Ruiter and maintains a temporary headquarters in Brussels until a permanent home in Lisbon is completed. The mission assigned to EMSA by the Commission and Member States is to regulate maritime security, ship pollution, and passenger safety by providing the best technical and scientific support possible.

Agency employees are experts in their field, assiduously monitoring approved Union laws and their application. Findings are reported to EU lawmakers with the objective of improving European waterway safety. Consequently, a close working relationship between EMSA and the affected industries, as well as domestic and international authorities, is extremely important. EMSA supervisory board members include representatives from the national industries that are affected.

EASA – European Aviation Safety Agency

http://www.easa.europa.eu/home/index.html

The European Aviation Safety Agency, located is Cologne, is led by Director General Patrick Goudou of France. EASA is responsible for civil aviation security in Europe.

One of the most important objectives of the agency is the harmonization of aviation security and environmental regulation within the EU. The agency, which is an independent EU legal entity, was created in 2002 by a Council and the European Parliament directive.

The Commission and all EU law-making bodies expect EASA to employ highly specialized professionals who are experts in all aspects of aviation safety. Employees develop aviation safety regulations and thereby assist European Union lawmakers in formulating directives and implementation of directives as well as co-ordinating with aircraft safety inspectors and organizations and persons who rely on air transport.

In addition, EASA assists the European Commission with enforcement of EU regulations and the implementation of safety measures. The agency is also charged by the EU to negotiate with third-country aviation authorities and to ensure safety and environmental impact compliance with international aviation organizations. EASA also provides support for the EU and Member States within the framework of co-operation and assistance for third-party countries.

ERA – European Railway Agency

http://era.europa.eu/

Expanding alongside the EU is the European railway network. There are 27 different countries with 27 different national rail companies, and in each individual country there are different tracks and track gauges as well as dissimilar technologies with non-integrated safety standards. Up to now, the development of an integrated railway system in Europe has been impeded by various national regulations.

The European Railway Agency was founded by directive in 2004, with the headquarters being established at this time in Lille/Valenciennes, France. The agency is charged with technical support for the Commission and Member States regarding improvements in railway interoperability within the EU. This includes meeting all safety standards and precautions of the European rail system (e.g., training railway employees), so that all national railways can operate unimpeded throughout the European network.

EACI – Executive Agency for Competitiveness and Innovation

http://ec.europa.eu/energy/intelligent/contact/index_en.htm

The EACI (formerly the Intelligent Energy Executive Agency) is a newly founded agency with the task of implementing the EU Commission initiative to develop an 'intelligent energy programme'. The Intelligent Energy Programme was created to promote efficient energy consumption as well as renewable sources of energy. Further objectives include the removal of market barriers and the sensitization of consumers, energy providers, and other participants to a new European energy policy and associated legal directives. In the first four years (2003–2006) of the programme, nearly 250 million euros were made available to raise the percentage of renewable source energy and to improve energy consumption efficiency.

The 'Intelligent Energy – Europe' programme has pursued these objectives with such initiatives as ALTENER, which promotes renewable energies, including wind and water production, on both local and national levels. The SAVE initiative focuses on promoting more efficient and rational energy consumption in private homes and industrial facilities. The STEER initiative is designed to promote wider distribution of new fuel technologies and their application (e.g. biofuels) in the transport sector. The initiative also develops measures for increasing energy efficiency in the areas of traffic and transport. The COOPENER initiative seeks close international co-operation with third-party countries to promote renewable energies and prudent consumption in Africa, Asia and Latin America.

DIRECTORATE GENERAL FOR COMPETITION – DG COMP

http://ec.europa.eu/competition/index_en.htm

Under the political leadership of Dutch Commissioner Neelie Kroes and in accordance with Article 3(g) of the Treaty of Nice, the Directorate General COMP seeks to 'create a system that protects internal market competition from distortion'. DG COMP can be described as a kind of European antitrust agency. The Directorate General views its work as an important contribution to promoting economic efficiency and creating an advantageous environment for innovation and technical progress. DG COMP's other responsibilities include the protection of the interests of European consumers, as well as ensuring the competitiveness of European business, products, and services on global markets.

The Commission applies competition law in the following situations:

- where companies or national authorities hinder competition through illegal agreements or anti-competitive actions (cartels or pre-arrangements);
- where one or more companies misuse their power against weaker businesses (for example those acquired through mergers);
- where member state governments violate competition laws (state subsidies).

The most common illegal activities requiring Commission intervention include the following:

- Violation of antitrust law in the form of prearranged price-fixing, sales agreements, investments, or production and supply quotas. (One example of such a violation, involving prearranged geographical sales limits between the French company Gaz de France and the Italian gas supplier ENI, was investigated by the Commission in October 2004.)
- Abuse of dominant market position through production or sales limits, to the detriment of the consumer. (In 2004, the Commission levied a fine of 497 million euros against Microsoft, which had refused to make available certain information about its Windows operating system, thereby obstructing the development of alternative, functional products for multimedia player software.)

- The granting of state subsidies, which provide the recipient with an economic advantage, favour a specific industry, distort competition, or limit trade between Member States. (One high-profile dispute involved the aircraft manufacturers Airbus and Boeing. While the American company Boeing was criticizing European state subsidies in the form of low-cost credit to finance construction of the Airbus A380 Superjumbo, Airbus complained that the government in Washington was supporting the development of new Boeing aircraft with tax breaks and contracts from the Defence Department.)

In order to fall under the jurisdiction of EU authorities, agreements or co-ordinated action must concern trade between Member States. In this way EU competition rules and those of individual Member States are clearly defined. In practice, EU and national rules are often applied simultaneously. Likewise, EU competition law can apply to agreements and action initiated in third- countries (e.g. offshore mergers), if these agreements and actions affect competition and trade within the European Union. The Council uses Commission recommendations to take decisions on competition guidelines and directives. A qualified majority is required.

Parliament does not play a central role in setting competition policy: it advises the Council. The Commission is the most important body for European competition policy because it makes recommendations for regulating competition and holds responsibility for implementation of competition rules. The DG COMP investigates alleged cases upon request by a Member State or on its own initiative. If no treaty violations are identified, the investigation is closed. If the Commission discovers actual violations, it recommends appropriate sanctions. The Commission has the power to prohibit agreements and actions that contravene EU competition rules (e.g. it may prohibit mergers or set conditions for approval); alternatively, national authorities and courts can issue penalties of their own. Under certain conditions, the Commission may grant amnesties. However, these are usually temporary and often conditional upon the modification of a questionable agreement.

The Competition Directorate General also handles international competition policy, particularly treaties within international associations such as the World Trade Organization or the OECD. As part of EU competition policy, the Commission has established several bilateral agreements with non-European countries and regions. The Commission

Table 4.16 Organization chart, DG Competition

		Deputy Director General		
Directorate R Strategic planning and resources **R.1** Strategic planning, personnel and finances **R.2** Information technology **R.3** Document administration, information, and communications	**Directorate A** Policy and strategic support **A.1** Antitrust policy and strategic support **A.2** Merger policy and strategic support **A.3** Priorities for the implementation and control of decisions **A.4** European competition network **A.5** International relations	**Directorate B** Energy, raw materials, chemicals and pharmaceutical industry **B.1** Energy, water **B.2** Raw materials, chemicals and pharmaceutical industry **B.3** Merger oversight	**Directorate C** Information, communications, and media **C.1** Telecommunications, postal services, co-ordination of information society **C.2** Media **C.3** Information technology, internet, consumer electronics **C.4** Merger oversight	**Directorate D** Services **D.1** Financial services (banks, insurers) **D.2** Transport **D.3** Trade, distribution, additional services **D.4** Merger oversight
Directorate E Consumer products and manufacturing **E.1** Consumer products and food industry **E.2** Manufacturing, including machinery and automotive **E.3** Merger oversight	**Directorate F** **F.1** Antitrust I **F.2** Antitrust II **F.3** Antitrust III	**Directorate G** State subsidies I: Cohesion and competitiveness **G.1** Regional subsidies **G.2** Restructuring of industry companies **G.3** Research and development, innovation, and venture capital **G.4** Environment and energy	**Directorate H** State subsidies II: Network industries, liberalized sectors and services **H.1** Postal and other services **H.2** Financial services **H.3** Telecommunications and media	**Directorate I** Subsidy policy and strategic co-ordination **I.1** Subsidy policy **I.2** Strategic support and control of decisions **I.3** Subsidy network and transparency **I.4** Implementation and controls

also supports the development of reliable and economically viable competition policies for EU membership candidates.

Policy areas and responsibilities

The Directorate General is led by the British Director General Philip Lowe and consists of 10 Directorates. Directorate R primarily has administrative duties. Its three units deal with strategic planning as well as personnel and financial administration, data processing, and information/communications policy. Directorates A to I each specialize in various aspects of competition policy.

Directorate A: Policy and strategic support

Directorate A deals with the overall co-ordination and strategic planning of European competition policy as well as general issues of competition law and co-ordination with existing EU policies. The directorate is organized into five units. Unit A.1 is responsible for antitrust policy planning. Unit A.2 co-ordinates merger policy. A.3 deals with issues related to implementation and control of decisions. Unit A.4 deals with the European Competition Network (ECN). The ECN includes the EU competition authority as well as the 27 national competition authorities and is designed to facilitate close co-operation between the various agencies. Unit A.5 is responsible for international relations in the area of competition law, a field that is growing in importance as globalization continues. The EU Commission maintains close contact with competition authorities in third-party countries and with international organizations such as the WTO, OECD and EEA.

Over the course of past and future EU expansions, it has been necessary to promote the formation of effective antitrust authorities and to develop competition law in individual candidate countries.

Directorate B: Energy, raw materials, chemicals and pharmaceuticals

Directorates B to E are organized by industry. The first Unit of directorate B is concerned with the energy and water industries. Competition rules for companies providing essential services to business and society (e.g. electricity or water supply) are less strict. Delivery of these services should not be subject to harsh competitive conditions. Unit B.2 deals with raw chemical materials, chemicals and pharmaceuticals. In 2004 the Commission broke up a cartel of three European companies, BASF, Akzo Nobel and UCB, which had attempted to drive up global market prices for choline chloride (Vitamin B), carve up the market among themselves, and thus disable competition. Unit B.3 examines mergers and takeovers in the energy, raw materials, chemical and pharmaceutical industries.

Directorate C: Information, communications and media

Directorate General C is responsible for information, communications and media. It is organized into three units. Unit C.1 is charged with telecommunications, postal services, and all issues related to the information society. C.2 specializes in media, while C.3 handles information industries, the internet and consumer electronics. In a high-profile 2004 case, the Commission opened an investigation into abusive practices by Deutsche Telekom, which had been charging high broadband access fees to competing providers, thereby limiting the competitors' ability to enter the ADSL services market. Profitable operation by competitors was made impossible, and the fees were agreed to represent a market barrier. By obstructing meaningful price competition on the ADSL market, Deutsche Telekom had been abusing its dominant position and had to agree to drastically reduced fees. Unit C.4 examines mergers and takeovers in the information, communications, and media industries.

Directorate D: Services

Unit D.1 is responsible for financial services, primarily banks and insurers. D.2 deals with the transport sector. In 2004, for example, the Commission approved a co-operative agreement between Alitalia and Air France. The Commission had previously determined that the airline alliance would lead to a serious lack of competition on a total of seven routes between France and Italy. However, when it was established that several new competitors had entered the market, initial doubts about fair competition were dispersed. Unit D.3 handles trade, distribution and additional services, while D.4 oversees mergers in the service sector.

Directorate E: Consumer products and manufacturing

The first unit of Directorate E enforces European competition laws for consumer goods and food. In October 2004, after years of antitrust investigations, the Coca Cola Corporation agreed to conditions that significantly opened up the European market for carbonated beverages.

The Commission is constantly working to challenge the commonly held view that European competition rules seemingly do not apply to agricultural food production. One example is the fine of 16.7 million euros levied in April 2003 against a French beef cartel, which had involved six French organizations fixing minimum prices and maintaining in import restrictions on foreign beef imports into France.

Unit E.2 deals with the manufacturing sector, including machinery and automobile production. Unit E.3 oversees merger activities in the consumer products and manufacturing industries.

Directorate F: Antitrust

The three units of Directorate F are devoted exclusively to antitrust activities conducted by the Directorate General for Competition. Units F.1, F.2 and F.3 handle alleged and actual cases of cartel formation by detecting unlawful agreements between companies and, where necessary, issuing sanctions.

Directorate G: State subsidies I – Cohesion and competitiveness

Directorates G to I deal with state subsidies. According to Article 87 of the Community Treaty, 'any aid granted by a Member State or through State resources in any form whatsoever which distorts or threatens to distort competition by favouring certain undertakings or the production of certain goods' is not compatible with the European internal market. Directorates G, H and I oversee the numerous exceptions that are in place.

In this context, Directorate G is responsible for cohesion and competitiveness. Unit G.1 deals with regional subsidies. The office examines the compatibility of regionally granted subsidies and Union-allocated structure and cohesion funds within the framework of European competition law. Subsidies which are designed 'to promote the economic development of areas where the standard of living is abnormally low or where there is serious underemployment' may be granted an exception to general competition regulations.

Units G.2 to G.4 are responsible for horizontal (i.e. industry-overlapping) subsidies. The competitiveness of the entire economy must benefit from the effects of these kinds of state subsidies. Areas of application include the following:

- restructuring of industrial companies (Unit G.2);
- research and development, innovation, and venture capital (Unit G.3);
- environment and energy (Unit G.4).

Directorate H: State subsidies II – Network industries, liberalized sectors and services

Directorate H manages state subsidies for network industries, liberalized sectors and services. Unit H.1 oversees subsidies for postal services and other providers. Unit H.2 handles financial services, while H.3 deals with telecommunications and media. In the case of certain services that are in the public interest, such as postal delivery, telecommunications, energy supply and state broadcasters, exceptions may allow for particular state subsidies. The Commission must often find a sensitive balance between pursuing the public interest by satisfying the basic needs of citizens and allowing unrestricted exercise of free-market mechanisms.

Directorate I: State subsidy policy and strategic co-ordination

The first of the three Directorate I units is the planning office, which handles basic issues related to subsidy policies of the EU and its Member States. It is also responsible for overall political and strategic planning. Unit I.2 provides strategic support. I.3 ensures transparency of subsidy actions implemented by the Commission. The final unit, I.4, oversees the proper implementation and control of EU subsidy policy.

DIRECTORATE GENERAL FOR ECONOMIC AND FINANCIAL AFFAIRS – DG ECFIN

http://ec.europa.eu/dgs/economy_finance/index_en.htm

The EU policy of an economic and monetary union is defined by Articles 98–124 in the Treaty. Article 99 states that the policy is an issue of shared interest. Additional articles describe the establishment of a monetary union, provisions of admission to the euro zone, and regulations for institutional and political implementation of the EU's monetary policy. The European Central Bank and the Commission are given important roles to play with these articles. The Commission's strong role in this area is underscored by Council votes, which in most cases have provided qualified majorities. This voting method provides the Commission with particular influence on the end result.

The Directorate General Economic and Financial Affairs serves the European Commission by fulfilling a broad and complex range of tasks. The challenges are multi-faceted: the economic supervision of the euro zone and the EU overall, for example, and analysis of whether and to what degree EU economies are converging. Economic forecasts, which are generated and published semi-annually, must be developed with precision, and this is an extremely difficult task when 27 Member States are considered within the analyses. In addition to many other responsibilities, as part of the Stability and Growth Pact, the Commission is responsible for monitoring Member States' fiscal policy and delivering an annual report on EU public finances. The Commission also oversees EU financial markets and their integration as well as the financing of economic development programmes. It is also responsible for economic relations with third-party countries.

Policy areas and responsibilities

The centre of these activities is the Directorate General for Economic and Financial Affairs, which is led by Klaus Regling of Germany. Economics and Finances is the most complex DG of the entire Commission. It employs a large number of special advisors as well as a unit for internal auditing. The DG consists of a total of seven directorates.

Directorate R (resources) is responsible for internal administration and strategic planning for this very complex Directorate General. Numerous advisors are engaged, including those responsible for relations with the European Parliament.

Directorate A: Studies and research

Directorate A is focused on economic studies and research. Unit A.1 manages econometric models and medium-term studies. Unit A.2 deals with economic databases and statistical co-ordination, and Unit A.3 handles corporate analysis and surveys. Unit A.4 is responsible for economic forecast models and analysis of the economic situation in the 27 Member States.

Directorate B: Economic assessment

Directorate B conducts in-depth economic assessment of each of the 27 Member States. It is the heart of Commission expertise within the economic and monetary union. Unit B.1 deals with Germany, Estonia, Austria, Portugal and Finland; B.2 with Belgium, France, Luxembourg, Hungary and the Netherlands; and B.3 with Greece, Spain, Italy, Cyprus and Malta. Unit B.4 handles Great Britain, Ireland, Sweden, Denmark and Latvia, while B.5 works with the Czech Republic, Lithuania, Poland, Slovenia and Slovakia. Unit B.6 provides quality control support and is responsible for coherence in the oversight of the individual Member States' economies.

Directorate C: Economic and monetary union

Directorate C is particularly focused on economic and monetary union and handles all issues related to the euro currency.

Unit C.1 oversees monetary policy matters in the euro zone and other Member States. It also manages the European Exchange Rate Mechanism (ERM2), a list of currencies linked to the euro within a 15 per cent margin of fluctuation. This means that non-euro currencies of the various EU states are connected closely to the euro through a system of European central banks. If the markets begin to produce fluctuations and a currency becomes a victim of speculation, the European Central Bank and other central banks will attempt, usually successfully, to maintain stability through co-ordinated intervention.

Table 4.17 Organization chart, DG Economic and Financial Affairs

Deputy Director General			
Directorate A Economic studies and research	**Directorate B** Economies of Member States	**Directorate C** Economy of the euro zone and the EU	**Directorate D** International economic and financial affairs
A.1 Economic models medium-term analysis **A.2** Economic databases and statistical co-ordination **A.3** Business surveys **A.4** Forecasts and economic conditions **A.5** Economic and scientific information and publications	**B.1** EU countries I: Germany, Estonia, Austria, Portugal, Finland **B.2** EU countries II: Belgium, France, Hungary, Luxembourg, Netherlands **B.3** EU countries III: Greece, Spain, Italy, Cyprus, Malta **B.4** EU countries IV: Denmark, Ireland, Latvia, Sweden, Great Britain **B.5** EU countries V: Czech Republic, Lithuania, Poland, Slovakia, Slovenia **B.6** Coherence in the economic monitoring of member states	**C.1** Currency issues in the euro zone and remaining Member States; EMS II **C.2** Public finances, particularly within the euro zone **C.3** Co-ordination of Member State and euro zone economic policies **C.4** Transition issues related to EMU **C.5** Labour markets, including wages, tax and incentive systems, human capital, and productivity	**D.1** Economies of candidate countries and the western Balkans, expansion-related economic policy **D.2** Economies of G7 countries and related multilateral issues, economies of Asian and Latin American countries; trade policy, external EMU issues **D.3** Economies of third countries in the Mediterranean area as well as Russia and CIS countries; Neighbourhood Policy economic issues **D.4** Horizontal issues and co-ordination of financial assistance; development policy, multilateral bank relations

Directorate E	Directorate L	Directorate R
Economic analysis	Financial operations, programme administration and EIB group relations	Resources
E.1 Financial markets and financial intermediaries	**L.1** EIB group relations and new financial instruments	**R.1** Personnel and administration
E.2 Internal markets and domestic product and service markets, competition policy, competitiveness analysis	**L.2** Programme administration (small and medium-sized business)	**R.2** Financial management and controls
E.3 Structural funds and Common Agricultural Policy	**L.3** Bonds, credit, and joint venture programmes	**R.3** Strategy management and controls, inter-institutional relationships
E.4 Environment, transport and energy policy	**L.4** Accounting and risk management	**R.4** Public relations
	L.5 Asset administration and securities	**R.5** Administration of information technology resources
	L.6 Venture capital operations and small/medium-sized business financing for EIB and EIF	
	L.7 Co-ordination, planning and legal issues	

Unit C.2 of this directorate has the task of monitoring the public finances of the so-called 'euro' Member States, with a particular focus on the obligations of euro zone countries. This includes politically sensitive issues such as determining whether a Member State is violating the 3 per cent limit on new debt. In this context, new debt refers to a country spending more than it is taking in as part of its regular budget and financing the remainder with credit. If this is the case and the national deficit exceeds 3 per cent of GDP, the EU may, upon recommendation of the Commission, initiate excessive deficit procedures. This process has several levels of escalation, first an official admonishment from the Commission, a formal Council declaration, deficit reduction measures as well as financial penalties in the billions.

To avoid such a situation, all euro members as well as EU countries not included in the euro zone should co-ordinate their budgetary and economic policies. Unit C.3 fulfils the task of monitoring this co-ordination, whereas Unit C.4 handles transition issues related to individual Member State economies joining the economic and monetary union. Each country that plans to introduce the euro currency must consider a long list of questions. Joining the euro zone means alterations to all the financial instruments that a country has at its disposal. When the option of currency fluctuation as domestic policy is removed, other economic factors relating to wages, taxation, duties, investment incentives, etc must also be readjusted.

Consequently, Unit C.5 attempts to retain oversight of complex labour market issues in all Member States, especially matters related to wages, taxation, social services, human capital and productivity.

Directorate D: International economic and financial affairs

With the monetary union and increasing globalization, the functions of Directorate D are growing in importance. It is known officially as the Directorate for International Economic and Financial Affairs. Unit D.1 is responsible for all issues related to EU candidate countries. The unit also works with countries in the western Balkans and on all economic policy matters related to expansion. Unit D.2 handles economic and associated multilateral issues with G8 countries as well as financial policy relations with Asia and Latin America, trade policy issues and their impact on the euro.

Unit D.3 deals with economic policy relations with the Mediterranean countries, Russia, and Commonwealth of Independent States (CIS) countries. The unit also handles economic aspects of the EU

Neighbourhood Policy, which attempts to create a ring of stable and EU-friendly states around Europe through bilateral economic and political co-operation agreements.

The final unit, D.4, manages all horizontal issues of international economic and financial support that cannot be designated according to the regions. It handles development assistance policy and relations with multilateral institutions such as the World Bank or the European Bank for Reconstruction and Development (EBRD) in London.

Directorate E: Economic assessment service

Directorate E describes itself as an economic assessment service. Unit E.1 is responsible for financial markets and financial service providers. The unit handles analysis of one of the most important aspects of today's free market economies: the organizational form of money that is available for investment. Large financial markets in London or Frankfurt are subject to the same scrutiny as investment funds or banks. Unit E.2 deals with the internal market and national product and service markets as well as competition policy. The unit analyses how markets for products and services are functioning and how efficiently resources are being allocated. Competition policy plays a special role in determining if a company is competing fairly. E.2 also examines competitiveness. Unit E.3 deals with structural funds and agricultural policy from an economic and financial perspective, while Unit E.4 handles environmental, transport and energy policy. Unit E.5 oversees the financial integration of markets and capital flow.

Directorate L: Financial operations, programme management and EIB relations

The six directorate of DG ECFIN deals with financial operations, programme management, and relations with the European Investment Bank and the European Investment Fund. Unit L.1 handles the complex relationships between the Commission and the European Investment Bank and its investment fund. In many cases, the fund is the implementing agency for corporate financial assistance instruments of the EU. This means that most corporate assistance programmes are issued by the Commission but administered by the European Investment Fund. Unit L.2 is responsible for EU programmes designed to help small and medium-sized businesses that use the EU internal market to their advantage. The Commission strives to make complex financial guidelines for receiving assistance as easy to understand as possible SMEs. Unit L.3 deals with new credit processing, and Unit L.4 monitors accounting and risk management in the EU. Unit L.5 handles asset management and securities. Unit L.6 manages venture capital financing for small and medium-sized businesses.

DIRECTORATE GENERAL FOR BUDGET – DG BUDGET

http://ec.europa.eu/dgs/budget/index_en.htm

Led by Commissioner Grybauskaite of Lithuania, Budget is a core Directorate General of the Commission. Virtually every political

Table 4.18 Organization chart, DG Budget

Deputy Director General			
Directorate R Resources	**Directorate A** Expenditures	**Directorate B** Equity capital, evaluation, and financial planning	**Directorate C** Central financial services
R.1 Information and communications **R.2** Overall co-ordination, personnel and financial resources **R.3** Financial information systems **R.4** Data processing infrastructure and user support services	**A.1** Budgetary procedures and oversight, ABB and relations with budget committee **A.2** GAP and structural policy **A.3** Internal policy areas **A.4** External policy areas **A.5** Administrative tools and allocation of data processing resources **A.6** Allocation of personnel resources **A.7** Implementation of budgetary plan (support and reports)	**B.1** Long-term financing models, financial controls and forecasts, budgetary issues related to expansion **B.2** Administration and revenues **B.3** Control of traditional equity capital and support for candidate countries **B.4** Control of VAT and GNP; ACOR secretariat **B.5** Evaluation	**C.1** Financial regulations **C.2** Calls for tender, treaties and financial assistance **C.3** Financial processes and controlling systems **C.4** Help desk, financial information and training **C.5** User-based administration of financial information systems

decision taken by the Commission involves DG Budget. The DG must assess the degree to which decisions affect budgetary law and the impacts political proposal on the budget. Budgetary authorization grants the EU, and thus the Commission, budgetary resources for a specified period and for specific purposes.

DG Budget is responsible for developing an annual EU budget proposal and generating EU financial forecasts every five years. The forecasts lay out broad EU budgetary guidelines, including all its programmes and policy areas.

The 2005 budget for the EU and its 450 million residents was 105 billion euros – less than 1.24 per cent of the EU's Gross Domestic Product. This is less than half of the national budget of the Federal Republic of Germany, which was 254.3 billion euros, for a population of only 82 million. The EU budget includes expenditure on agriculture and regional policy as well as the other EU areas of activity. Expenditure is divided up as follows:

Table 4.19 Draft of the EU's overall budget plan for 2005

Expenditures	**Billion euros**
Common Agricultural Policy	49.11
Structural projects (incl. regional policies)	32.40
Internal policy areas (e.g. research, energy, transport)	7.69
External policy areas (co-operation with third-party countries)	4.99
Administrative expenses	6.31
Reserves	0.45
Assistance to candidate countries	2.98
Compensation payments	1.3
Total	105.23

DIRECTORATE GENERAL FOR COMMUNICATIONS – DG COMM

http://ec.europa.eu/dgs/communication/index_en.htm

The Directorate General for Communications is led by Vice-President Margot Wallström of Sweden. The DG keeps the media and general public informed about the activities of the Commission and explains the content and objectives of its policy measures. Conversely, the Commission Representatives also report on news and viewpoints in Member States.

Table 4.20 Organizational chart, DG Communications

Deputy Director General/Commission spokesperson			
Spokesperson duties			
Representatives in Member States			
Directorate A Strategy	**Directorate B** Representations	**Directorate C** Multimedia Communications	**Directorate D** Resources
A.1 General Affairs and Inter-institutional relations **A.2** Communication Project and Strategies **A.3** Research and Political Analysis	**B.1** Geographical Coordination **B.2** Thematic Support	**C.1** Audiovisual Services **C.2** Web and Contact Centre **C.3** Editorial Content and Support	**D.1** Programming Budget **D.2** Human Resources Management **D.3** Finance and Infrastructure **D.4** Control and Evaluation **D.5**. Informatics

The Directorate General performs the following duties:

- developing a coherent communications strategy for the Commission;
- managing and co-ordinating activities of representations in the Member States;
- facilitating contacts between the Commission and the media.

The DG maintains close contact and co-ordination with Commission agencies that handle public relations activities internally.

In 2005 the DG COMM introduced a comprehensive plan of action containing 50 separate measures as well as the Plan D for democracy, dialogue and debate. The directorate is currently following its 2006 White Paper on the communication of European policies. Achieving closer contact with citizens through improved listening, explaining and local contact is a core component of the strategy. Despite continual adjustments, the primary objective of both the Commission and the Directorate General COMM remains the improvement of the image of the EU by convincing the public of the usefulness, importance and legitimacy of EU policies and activities.

Instruments in pursuit of these objectives include partnerships with Member States, business and civil society, information systems such as EuropeDirect or the Europe by Satellite (EbS) television service, and 35 representative offices in capitals and regions of the Union.

Organization

Claus Sørensen of Denmark leads the Directorate General Communication and also oversees the spokesperson's service and the internal auditing service. The DG is further divided into four directorates and representations in the Member States, mainly supervised by the Deputy Director General.

Service of the Spokesperson

The Service of the Spokesperson represents the official voice of the European Commission to the media and keeps accredited journalists informed of ongoing and future Commission activities. It also manages the daily noon media briefings held in the Commission press room (on the first floor of the main Berlaymont building). The Commission's Spokesperson Johannes Laitenberger is responsible for commenting on all Commission activities and provides information on behalf of President Barroso and the entire Commission. He also conducts the press conferences. Commission members may appear personally at any time before the media. This is typically to explain or comment on specific proposals or to appear with guests of state.

The Brussels press corps has direct contact with a number of media representatives located in the Berlaymont building, each of whom specializes in a particular subject area. The spokespersons participate in parliamentary meetings, ministerial council meetings and European summits, and are available to the press on these matters. In 2004 Spokesperson Services organized 115 press conferences and 100 technical briefings in addition to daily media briefings. Moreover, the office published 1,543 press releases, 306 memos, and 549 speeches during the same period.

An additional responsibility of Spokesperson Services is monitoring, that is, media evaluation for the Commission. Several summaries a day are generated through agency bulletins. The most diverse assortment of periodicals from around the world is reviewed. These reports are then made available to Commission members and their spokespersons as well as to Directors-General.

Directorate A: Strategy

Directorate A of the Directorate General is responsible for information and communications policy. Unit A.1 handles general affairs and co-ordinates the inter-institutional relations. Unit A.2 develops overall strategies and activities designed to bring the European public closer to the EU. The 'Information and communication strategy of the European Union' and the Communication White Paper are two examples of its work. Unit A.3 conducts and evaluates opinion polls. Since 1973 the Commission has published studies on the position and development of public opinion and it uses the information to support the drafting of legislation and to assess its own work. The Unit is also responsible for European surveys, also known as the Eurobarometer, which carry out in-depth work on topics that have included the euro currency, the European constitution, and EU expansion.

Directorate B: Representations

Directorate B is responsible for the representations and the DG's networks in the 27 Member States.

Unit B.1 handles the co-ordination and analysis of work performed by Commission representatives in the 27 Member States. Commission representatives in Member States serve as a link between the Brussels-based Commission and the European general public. They represent the Commission, provide information about political, economic and social developments in EU countries, and act as an intermediary between the Commission, the media, and citizens of Member States.

Unit B.2 manages EU information centres and networks include Europa Direct citizen information offices, which, as the first point of contact, are charged with informing citizens about the EU in general, organizing events, and distributing information materials to the European Documentation Centres (EDC), which make documents and publications freely available to the general public through libraries.

Directorate C: Multimedia Communications

Directorate C likewise works intensively to develop opportunities for interaction between the European Union and its citizens.

Unit C.1 provides audiovisual media support services by offering studios and teams, as well as expanding video, audio and image content on the internet. The Unit also operates the Europe by Satellite

(EbS) television news service and the Mediathek AV library in support of Euronews cable news channel handles media evaluation and operates the EuropeDirect citizen hotline, which responds to online and toll-free telephone enquiries from all Member States. Unit C.2 also manages the European internet service EUROPA, which continually expands content in 23 different languages. In 2004 over a billion page impressions were tallied and nearly 400,000 users visited the site each day. C.2 is also responsible for European Commission publications, which include brochures and leaflets with general information on the *acquis communautaire* and current EU topics of emphasis. They are translated into the official EU languages, and 14 million copies are printed for distribution.

Directorate D: Resources

Directorate D handles primarily internal, financial and administrative functions. Unit D.1 handles the budget and is also responsible for the overall programming. Unit D.2 is responsible for personnel and administration. Unit D.3 oversees calls for tender and grants the service, construction and supplier contracts requested by DG COMM each year for main offices and representations in the EU Member States. DG COMM also provides financial support for organizations that deliver EU information to citizens of Europe with the goal of educating people about European issues. This financial support is likewise administered by D.3. Unit D.4 controls and evaluates the DG's activities, while Unit D.5 manages data processing.

5

External relations

HUMANITARIAN AID DEPARTMENT – ECHO

http://ec.europa.eu/humanitarian_aid/index_en.htm

The RELEX group department of humanitarian aid was launched in 1992 with the objective of making emergency assistance available to people in dire need. A 1996 directive clearly articulated EU policy regarding humanitarian aid. According to the Council, 'people in distress, victims of natural disasters, wars and outbreaks of fighting, or other comparable exceptional circumstances have a right to international humanitarian assistance where their own authorities prove unable to provide effective relief'.[i]

European humanitarian assistance is designed to achieve the following:

- save and preserve human life in acute emergencies and natural disasters;
- provide care for people in need due to protracted crises, such as conflicts and wars;
- assist refugees and displaced persons where they are and help with their repatriation;

[i] Directive 1257/96 on humanitarian aid from 20 July 1996

- finance transport of aid so that assistance reaches the target group;
- provide rehabilitation and reconstruction work so that humanitarian aid is effective and disaster victims can help with recovery (self-help);
- contribute to the development of early warning systems and the financing of preventive measures;
- support civilian efforts to protect victims of conflict, in accordance with applicable international agreements.

Additional designated aid services include feasibility studies of humanitarian efforts, co-ordination of humanitarian projects and the formulation of consequent action, technical training of workers, and increasing the general public's awareness of the issue of humanitarian relief.

Table 5.1 Organizational chart, ECHO

ECHO – Humanitarian aid			
ECHO 1 African, Caribbean and Pacific countries **1.1** Southern Africa **1.2** Caribbean, Indian and Pacific Oceans **1.3** Horn of Africa **1.4** Central Africa **1.5** Western Africa	**ECHO 2** Central and eastern Europe, CIS countries, Mediterranean region, and the Near East **2.1** Europe, central Asia, Mongolia **2.2** Mediterranean region and the Near East	**ECHO 3** Asia, Central and South America, Iraq **3.1** Central and South American countries **3.2** Southeast Asia **3.3** Southern Asia **3.4** Afghanistan, Pakistan, Iran **3.5** Iraq **3.6** DIPECHO	**ECHO 4** Questions of principle, relations with European organizations, donors, and partners; support and co-ordination of programme planning; general support during conflicts
ECHO 5 Personnel, training, administrative support, information technology	**ECHO 6** Finances and auditing	**ECHO 7** Information and communications	**ECHO 8** Legal issues and questions regarding decision-making mechanisms

Humanitarian aid may be allocated by one of three separate resolution processes. In order to react quickly to emergency situations, ECHO director António Cavaco has been delegated authority to make decisions in especially urgent cases. In situations requiring a larger financial allocation, the Commissioner responsible for humanitarian aid, currently Louis Michel of Belgium, can reach decisions through an authorization process. A written procedure (*see* Chapter 2.3) is required for all resolutions not covered by these processes. The Commission is also responsible for controls, administration, monitoring and action assessments.

In 2003 and 2004, the department concentrated its relief efforts on three areas of emphasis. Of special importance were the recognition of and intervention in regions facing the greatest need for humanitarian assistance (e.g. eastern Africa and Afghanistan) and an increased focus on 'forgotten crises' (such as those in the western Sahara and Myanmar). Basic strategy also received more attention: disaster relief, children's welfare, and the integration of immediate assistance, rehabilitation, and economic development.

Policy areas and responsibilities

ECHO is led by Director General António Cavaco of Portugal. It is organized in eight units. ECHO 1, ECHO 2 and ECHO 3 are responsible for humanitarian aid in specific global regions, while ECHO 4 manages relations with partner organizations. Administrative Units ECHO 5 to 8 primarily deal with internal processes. ECHO 5 handles human resources, training, internal administration and information technology. ECHO 6 deals with finances and auditing service. ECHO 7 is in charge of information and communications policy, and ECHO 8 handles legal issues and questions regarding decision-making mechanisms.

ECHO 1: African, Caribbean and Pacific countries

ECHO 1 works with African, Caribbean and Pacific countries, also known as ACP. The unit consists of five sub-units. The first deals with southern Africa, the third with the Horn of Africa, the fourth central Africa, and the fifth western Africa. Sub-unit 2 handles the Caribbean as well as the Indian and Pacific Oceans. The significance of humanitarian aid for the African continent is visible in the unit's organization. The drought in Ethiopia as well as political conflicts in Sudan, Democratic Republic of Congo, and the Ivory Coast are all crises where the EU has provided sustained humanitarian aid in recent years.

ECHO 2: Central and eastern Europe, CIS countries, the Mediterranean and the Near East

Sub-unit 1 of the ECHO 2 Unit is responsible for Europe, central Asia and Mongolia. Important projects include support for the politically unstable northern Caucasus (especially Chechnya), and central Asia (Tajikistan and Uzbekistan). Sub-unit 2 works with Mediterranean countries and the Near East. Since the rekindling of the Near East conflict, ECHO has acted to improve the situation among the civilian population. The often extremely poor living conditions in the Palestinian autonomous areas are alleviated with food, water and construction projects. Refugees and Syria, Jordan and Lebanon also receive aid.

ECHO 3: Asia, Central and South America, and Iraq

Sub-unit 1 of the ECHO 3 Unit handles Central and South American countries. Sub-unit 2 administers humanitarian aid for crisis regions in southeastern Asia (e.g. Indonesia, Thailand, Laos, Vietnam and China), while sub-unit 3 deals with southern Asia (e.g. Sri Lanka, India and Bangladesh). The fourth sub-unit is responsible for Afghanistan, Pakistan and Iran, while the fifth focuses on relief efforts in Iraq. Between March 2003 and December 2004, ECHO made 100 million euros available for humanitarian aid in Iraq. ECHO also supported activities of the few relief organizations remaining in the war zone. Finally, sub-unit 6 administers the disaster prevention and protection programme DIPECHO, which is designed to safeguard the population in particularly disaster-prone areas.

ECHO 4: Basic strategy, relations, co-ordination, and planning

Unit ECHO 4 is devoted to a small number of important inter-institutional functions related to humanitarian aid. It handles general issues of preparation, planning and co-ordination of ECHO relief programmes and strategies. In dire emergencies ECHO 4 assumes responsibility for relief operations. ECHO 4 manages co-ordination with other EU organizations, e.g. the European Parliament, which in the past repeatedly initiated development and improvement of humanitarian aid response.

Although ECHO is one of the most significant donors of humanitarian aid in the international community, most projects are implemented by partner organizations on the ground. ECHO has nearly 200 partners with whom Framework Partnership Agreements (FPA) have been concluded. Unit ECHO 4 also administers relations and negotiations with these organizations.

DIRECTORATE GENERAL FOR EXTERNAL RELATIONS – DG RELEX

http://ec.europa.eu/external_relations/index.htm

Co-operation among European Union states in international relations is still relatively new. This is likely due to the sensitive nature of this political arena – a common foreign policy is often seen by independent states as an encroachment on a core area of national responsibility. Drastic international events in the late 1980s and early 1990s – the end of the Cold War, the reunification of Germany, and conflict in the former Yugoslavia – were occasion for the 12 members at that time to pursue a new path based on shared action.

With the implementation of the Maastricht Treaty of the European Union (EUT) on 1 November 1993, the Common Foreign and Security Policy (CFSP) went into effect alongside previous areas of shared policy. However, European international relations consist of much more than the CFSP and the European Security and Defence Policy (ESDP). In order to define the EU's roles on the global stage, established policy areas such as trade, development co-operation and humanitarian aid as well as the international aspects of other policy areas must be considered.

Article 11 of the European Union Treaty identifies the following as primary objectives of the Common Foreign and Security Policy:

- preserving common values, basic interests, and the independence and integrity of the Union;
- strengthening EU security;
- preserving peace and strengthening international security;
- the promotion of international co-operation;
- developing and strengthening democracy and rule of law as well as monitoring human rights and basic liberties.

As the primary instrument for implementing CFSP, Article 12 of the EU Treaty first provides for a common strategy that establishes areas of vital common interest, precise objectives, a timeframe, and necessary resources. Three common strategies – for Russia, Ukraine and the Mediterranean – have been implemented so far. Second, there are common positions, jointly agreed EU positions that Member States must adopt (e.g. the common position on the struggle against the illegal diamond trade as a contributor to conflict prevention and reconciliation in

Table 5.2 Organization chart, DG External Relations

Deputy Director General			
Directorate A CFSP and ESDP; Commission co-ordination and support **A.1** European correspondent; CFSP co-ordination and analysis; G8 **A.2** Legal and institutional issues; common procedures, sanctions, Kimberley Process **A.3** Security and stability; anti-terror, Treaty on the Non-Proliferation of Nuclear Weapons (NPT), disarmament **A.4** Conflict prevention, crisis management, CFSP and ESDP in relation to ACP countries	**Directorate B** Multilateral relations and human rights **B.1** Human rights and democratization **B.2** United Nations; treaty office **B.3** OECD and European Council	**Directorate C** North America, eastern Asia, Australia, New Zealand, EEA, EFTA, San Marino, Andorra, Monaco **C.1** United States, Canada **C.2** Japan, Korea, Australia, New Zealand **C.3** EEA, EFTA, San Marino, Andorra, Monaco	**Directorate D** European Neighbourhood Policy co-ordination **D.1** Overall co-ordination of European Neighbourhood Policy **D.2** Sector co-ordination of European Neighbourhood Policy

Table 5.2 *(continued)*

Directorate E Eastern Europe, southern Caucasus, central Asian republics **E.1** Russia **E.2** Ukraine, Belarus, Moldova **E.3** Southern Caucasus and central Asia	**Directorate F** Near and Middle East and southern Mediterranean **F.1** EuroMed and regional issues **F.2** Gulf states, Iraq, Iran, Yemen **F.3** Mashriq and Israel **F.4** Maghreb	**Directorate G** Latin America **G.1** Horizontal issues **G.2** Central America, Mexico **G.3** Andes pact **G.4** Mercosur, Chile	**Directorate H** Asia (excluding Japan and Korea) **H.1** Horizontal issues **H.2** China, Hong Kong, Macao, Taiwan **H.3** India, Bhutan, Nepal **H.4** Pakistan, Afghanistan, Sri Lanka, Bangladesh, Maldives **H.5** Southeastern Asia
Directorate I Means administration, information, inter-institutional relations **I.1** Personnel and administration **I.2** Budget and finance issues, comptroller's office **I.3** Computer resources **I.4** Inter-institutional relations **I.5** Information and communications	**Directorate K** External service **K.1** Foreign Service personnel planning **K.2** Rights and responsibilities **K.3** Infrastructure of delegations **K.4** Budget **K.5** Local personnel **K.6** Career development **K.7** Security of delegations	**Directorate L** Strategy, co-ordination and analysis **L.1** Inspection of delegations **L.2** Studies and research **L.3** Co-ordination and analysis	

Africa). Third, opportunities exist for closer co-operation within the framework of joint actions; joint actions in the context of CFSP include, for example, the support of the Palestinian Authority in its efforts to combat terrorist activities originating in territories under their control.

The Directorate General for External Relations (DG RELEX) supports the common EU foreign policy, especially with regard to its legal and economic instruments. The primary responsibilities of the DG RELEX are the following:

- nurturing bilateral relations with third-party countries and managing the Commission delegations (approximately 130 of them) with ambassadors in these countries;
- co-ordinating the Commission's participation in the Common Foreign and Security Policy;
- managing Commission relations with international organizations such as the United Nations, OSCE and the European Council.

Former Austrian foreign minister Benita Ferrero-Waldner is the Commissioner responsible for co-ordinating foreign policy activities and ensuring that the Commission assumes clear and persuasive policy positions. She works with the High Representative for the Common Foreign and Security Policy Javier Solana and the foreign minister of the country holding the Council Presidency. They jointly represent EU in matters of foreign policy and implement the CFSP. (The position of High CFSP Representative was created by the Treaty of Amsterdam, which went into effect on 1 May 1999. The Representative supports the Council in preparing and implementing political decisions and handles negotiations with third-party countries on behalf of the Presidency and the Council to ensure the CFSP's coherence and transparency.)

Because of the sensitivity of this policy area, the power-sharing arrangement between EU institutions that exists in the area of foreign relations is different from that of traditional common policy areas (e.g. trade and internal market) . First, a resolution requires the unanimity of the Member States. Second, the authority of the Commission and Parliament in relation to the Council is limited. The Commission has the (no longer exclusive) right to make recommendations for CFSP legislation. It is responsible for implementing the budget and enjoys a certain weight in the formulation and co-ordination of policy. The Parliament is briefed regularly and can pose questions and offer recommendations to the Council.

Policy areas and responsibilities

The Directorate General for External Relations is led by Eneko Landaburu of Spain. It consists of 11 directorates, and their fields of activity are delineated geographically and by subject. Directorate I primarily handles administrative duties, including personnel issues, administration, inter-institutional relations, electronic data processing, information and communications.

Directorate A: Common Foreign and Security Policy (CFSP) and European Security and Defence Policy (ESDP): co-ordination and support for the Commission

Directorates A to C are led by the first Deputy Director General and deal with CFSP, multilateral relations, North America, East Asia, Australia, New Zealand, EEA and EFTA. Directorate A handles the co-ordination of the Commission's contributions to CFSP and ESDP (European Security and Defence Policy). As a rule, the Director General represents the Commission on the Political and Security Committee (PSC). This committee, which consists of national envoys at the ambassadorial level, prepares European reactions to events affecting external and security policy, and works with the General Affairs and External Relations Council (GAFRC).

Unit A.1 hosts the European Correspondent for the Commission who, along with his counterparts in the Member States, prepares the meeting of the Political and Security Committee (PSC) as well as CFSP-related agenda items for the General Affairs and External Relations Council (GAERC). Since 1977 the unit has also handled ongoing EU participation in G8 summits. Unit A.2 deals with institutional and legal issues in the areas of CFSP and ESDP. It sets up common procedures for interaction with individual countries (e.g. Russia), regions (e.g. the Middle East), or with regard to particular thematic areas (e.g. weapons of mass destruction). It co-ordinates EU sanctions that target third-party countries (e.g. the weapons embargo against China) and works to implement the Kimberley Process, an initiative founded in May 2000 to act against the trade in African blood diamonds.

The primary topic areas for Unit A.3 are stability and security, anti-terror, the Treaty on the Non-Proliferation of Nuclear Weapons, and disarmament. The unit handles basic strategic issues related to the European Security and Defence Policy (ESDP). The common ESDP is designed to work on a national, sub-national and global level in the context of the CFSP. It aims to incorporate adjacent political, economic, and social aspects into European security policy alongside the purely military considerations. A.3 is also responsible for anti-terror policy and deals with nuclear non-proliferation (e.g. in Iran and North Korea) and nuclear disarmament. However, the Secretariat General of the Council of Ministers exercises greater influence in these areas.

Unit A.4 deals with opportunities for conflict prevention (e.g. through developmental aid, trade policy instruments, humanitarian aid, social and environmental action, diplomatic instruments and political dialogue) and the various components of EU crisis management (e.g. the deployment of police forces, strengthening the rule of law, and civil administration). The unit is also responsible for the implementation of CFSP and ESDP for ACP countries.

Directorate B: Multilateral relations and human rights

The first unit of Directorate B is responsible for human rights and democratization, for which the European Union provides financial support. The EuropeAid co-operation office is in charge of identifying eligible projects and implementing aid (*see* Chapter V.5). Units B.2 and B.3 are responsible for multilateral relations. B.2 co-ordinates co-operation with the United Nations, in the form of either financial support of UN programmes or political dialogue. B.2 also operates the Treaty Office that generates all bilateral and multilateral EU treaties. Unit B.3 co-ordinates relations with the Organization for Security and Co-operation in Europe (OSCE) and the Council of Europe. Primary areas of co-operation are the promotion of democracy, human rights and the rule of law, as well as conflict prevention and crisis management.

Directorate C: North America, eastern Asia, Australia, New Zealand, EEA, EFTA, San Marino, Andorra and Monaco

Directorate C is responsible for ensuring close relations between the EU and the most important industrialized countries. Its three units are organized geographically. Unit C.1 handles bilateral relations with the United States and Canada. Numerous meetings take place throughout the year between the EU and these countries (on the ministerial, ambassadorial and expert levels). Current issues discussed at the USA/EU summit in June 2004 included democratization in Iraq, the situation in Darfur, political developments in the Middle East, and the fight against terrorism. Unit C.2 handles bilateral relations with Japan, Korea, Australia and New Zealand, while C.3 manages multilateral relations with the European Economic Area (EEA) and the European Free Trade Association (EFTA) and bilateral relations with Norway, Iceland, Liechtenstein and Switzerland, as well as with the mini-states San Marino, Andorra and Monaco.

Directorate D: Co-ordination of the European Neighbourhood Policy (ENP)

Directorates D to F are led by the second Deputy Director General. Directorate D of the DG RELEX is dedicated to the European Neighbourhood Policy (ENP), which was established in 2003 for countries that will not join the EU in the foreseeable future. These include Ukraine, Belarus, Moldova, Georgia, Armenia, Azerbaijan, Morocco, Algeria, Tunisia, Libya, Egypt, Israel, Jordan, Lebanon, Syria, the Palestinian Authority, and to a certain degree Russia. An emphasis on common values, political co-operation, economic integration, and cultural dialogue is designed to promote security, stability and prosperity inside and outside the EU, and prevent historical rifts from recurring.

Unit D.1 handles general ENP co-ordination. The office generates timeframes and guidelines, while monitoring and evaluating the development and success of strategy. Unit D.2 is charged with the ENP's thematic co-ordination. For example, co-operation takes place in social and economic development, trade and energy.

Directorate E: Eastern Europe, southern Caucasus and central Asian republics

The responsibilities of Directorate E are likewise organized geographically. Unit E.1 handles bilateral relations between the EU and Russia, for which a course was charted in May 2003 during a summit in St Petersburg. Russian-European long-term co-operation is based on four areas:

1. economy;
2. freedom, security and justice;
3. external security; and
4. research, education and culture.

Unit E.2 also co-ordinates bilateral relations with Belarus, Ukraine and Moldova, while E.3 deals with the southern Caucasus (Armenia, Georgia and Azerbaijan) and the central Asian republics (Kazakhstan, Kyrgyzstan, Turkmenistan, Uzbekistan and Tajikistan). Co-operation is designed to promote institutional, legal and administrative reforms and support of the private sector.

Directorate F: Near and Middle East and southern Mediterranean

Directorate F of the Directorate General RELEX works with the Mediterranean region as well as the Near and Middle East. Unit F.1 is responsible for the regional partnership between the European Union and the Mediterranean region, which was defined as a priority by the 1995 Barcelona Processes and continues to develop. The partnership is built on political, social and economic co-operation. European-Mediterranean partners include the 27 Member States and the 10 Mediterranean countries Algeria, Egypt, Israel, Jordan, Lebanon, Morocco, the Palestinian Authority, Syria, Tunisia and Turkey.

Unit F.2 oversees relations with the Gulf Co-operation Council (Saudi Arabia, Kuwait, Bahrain, Qatar, Oman and the United Arab Emirates) as well as Iran, Iraq and Yemen. F.3 handles bilateral relations with the Near Eastern countries. The political, economic, social, humanitarian and security aspects of the Israeli–Palestinian conflict and the role of the EU in its solution are the central areas of responsibility. Unit F.4 is in charge of the Maghreb countries (Tunisia, Algeria and Morocco).

Directorate G: Latin America

Directorates G and H are led by the third Deputy Director General. Directorate G of the DG RELEX is responsible for relations with Latin America. Unit G.1 deals with general issues of Latin American development and ensures coherence of European strategy programmes. A variety of trans-national EU programmes provide support for the continent. AL-INVEST promotes the development of small and medium-sized businesses through European investment. URB AL supports European-Latin American city relationships. ALFA promotes university exchanges. Unit G.2 co-ordinates bilateral and regional relations with Mexico and the central American states (Costa Rica, El

Salvador, Guatemala, Honduras, Nicaragua and Panama). Unit G.3 facilitates political, economic and trade policy dialogue with individual countries of the Andes Pact region (Bolivia, Columbia, Ecuador, Peru and Venezuela). The common struggle against the drug trade is an important emphasis of the relationship. Finally, Unit G.4 works with Mercosur countries (Argentina, Brazil, Paraguay, Uruguay) and Chile. The EU maintains active political dialogue, provides technical assistance, supports trade and promotes investment.

Directorate H: Asia (excluding Japan and Korea)

The EU maintains close relations with Asian countries in terms of trade, investment, anti-terrorism, education and the environment. Co-operation often takes place within the context of existing regional organizations. Noteworthy are ASEAN (the Association of South East Asian Nations) and SAARC (the South Asian Association for Regional Co-operation). Trans-national co-ordination of Europe's strategy on Asia is managed by Unit H.1.

H.2 co-ordinates relations with China, Hong Kong, Macao, Taiwan and Mongolia. In light of the rapid economic development of the country, the strategic Sino-European relationship and China's regional role have become a major aspect of EU Asia policy. Unit H.3 is responsible for India, Bhutan and Nepal. During a November 2004 summit, India and the EU officially launched a strategic partnership. Unit H.4 manages bilateral and regional relations with Pakistan, Afghanistan, Sri Lanka, Bangladesh and the Maldives. H.5 works with the populous and in some cases impoverished nations of southeastern Asia (Brunei, Myanmar, Cambodia, Indonesia, Laos, Malaysia, the Philippines, Singapore, Thailand and Vietnam.).

Directorate K: External Service

Although the European Union is not an internationally recognized legal entity, it does maintain diplomatic relations with other states. Directorate K of the DG RELEX operates external services on behalf of the Commission with 130 delegations worldwide. They are instrumental in the implementation of EU foreign policy. Commission delegations represent the EU and European interests in third-party countries and analyse political, economic and social developments in guest countries for the EU and its institutions. Important political areas for these delegations are common trade policy and developmental co-operation. In addition, agriculture, fisheries, the environment, health and security are key issues. The implementation of CFSP also requires delegations to conduct political analyses and make policy recommendations. Each delegation lends a breadth of expertise to both the planning and the implementation of projects. The units of Directorate K manage the administration of External Service. K.1 is responsible for personnel planning and protocol issues. K.2 establishes guidelines for personnel rights and responsibilities. K.3 is responsible for delegation infrastructure. K.4 handles budgetary issues. K.5 manages local personnel. K.6 deals with career development and education, while K.7 handles security for Commission delegations.

Directorate L: Strategy, co-ordination, and analysis

The three units of Directorate L handle planning, co-ordination and strategy challenges. L.1 oversees management, administration and performance of Commission delegations. L.2 conducts forward planning for Directorate General RELEX by producing studies on possible foreign policy developments. Finally, L.3 is responsible for economic analysis.

European Union Satellite Centre (EUSC)

http://www.eusc.europa.eu/

The European Union Satellite Centre (EUSC) is an autonomous EU agency; its headquarters are in the Spanish city of Torrejón de Ardoz. Under the leadership of Director Frank Asbeck of Germany, the EUSC supports EU decision-making processes within the framework of the Common Foreign and Security Policy, with a focus on the European Security and Defence Policy. The agency provides satellite images and other pictures for the European Union. These are used to facilitate early recognition of possible crisis areas and allow timely preparation of diplomatic, economic and humanitarian measures by political decision-makers. The Centre contributes to conflict prevention, support of peace-keeping efforts in crisis situations, delivery of humanitarian assistance during natural or humanitarian disasters as well as nuclear non-proliferation and disarmament. Third-party countries may also enter associative agreements with the EUSC, particularly European

NATO states that are not EU members and international organizations. They assist in the EUSC's work and have access to agency reports and standards.

European Union Institute for Security Studies (EUISS) *http://www.iss-eu.org/*

The European Union Institute for Security Studies (EUISS) is an independent agency of the EU. Like the Satellite Centre, it was launched in 2002. The institute contributes to a common European security culture and serves as an interface between political decision-makers and external experts in the process. Led by Nicole Gnesotto of France and located in Paris, the facility concentrates on scientific research projects related to security and defence policy, while providing reports and analysis for EU organizations (including the EU Council and the High Representative for CFSP). The analytical capacity of EU bodies is thereby supplemented and intensified by the expertise of scientists and specialists. The agency is also dedicated to the development of a transatlantic dialogue on security issues that affect the EU, Canada and the United States. Semi-annual conferences take place to promote the exchange of information and the improvement of transatlantic relations.

European Defence Agency (EDA) *http://www.eda.europa.eu/*

The third autonomous agency within the CFSP and ESDP is the European Defence Agency (EDA), which was created by the Council of Ministers in July 2004 to foster the development of European security and defence policy. The Brussels-based agency is currently led by Nick Witney of the United Kingdom. The facility is designed to improve defence capabilities, support arms co-operation, adapt the defence industry and technology to new requirements, and make European munitions markets more competitive. National solutions to defence policy challenges must be more closely co-ordinated within a European context so that a more coherent and efficient defence system can be attained. The EDA budget reached nearly 2 million euros in 2004.

DIRECTORATE GENERAL FOR DEVELOPMENT – DG DEV

http://ec.europa.eu/development/index.en.cfm

The Directorate General Development (DEV) is responsible for generating a European development policy. Its objectives are articulated in Article 177 of the European Community Treaty: the policy of development co-operation should support 'sustainable, economic and social development in developing countries; gradual harmonious incorporation of developing countries into the global economy; and the campaign against poverty'. The Community Treaty constitutes only 'a complement to the policies pursued by Member States' and does not

Table 5.3 Organizational chart, DG Development

Deputy Director General			
Directorate A General issues and operational support	**Directorate B** Development policy and sector issues	**Directorate C** Horn of Africa, eastern and southern Africa, Indian and Pacific Oceans	**Directorate D** Western and central Africa, Caribbean and OCT
A.1 Programme planning, strategic planning, financing **A.2** Relations with United Nations, Member States and OECD donors **A.3** Relations with EU and ACP institutions, civil society and NGOs **A.4** Human resources, computing **A.5** Information and communications	**B.1** Development policy, coherence and future development **B.2** Economic co-operation and PRPS processes **B.3** Social and human development **B.4** Environment and rural development **B.5** Transport, infrastructure and urban development	**C.1** Relations with Pacific region countries **C.2** Relations with countries in the Horn of Africa, eastern Africa and the Indian Ocean **C.3** Relations with countries in the region of southern Africa	**D.1** Relations with countries and regions of the Caribbean and OCT **D.2** Relations with countries of the western Africa region **D.3** Relations with central African and Great Lakes region countries

represent a substitute for the development policies of individual EU Member States.

The most important thematic areas of European development work include the following:

- interplay of trade and development;
- promotion of regional integration and co-operation;
- macroeconomic policy for economic development and general access to social services;
- support for transport systems;
- ensuring general nutrition and the development of rural areas;
- assistance in building efficient and trustworthy institutional structures.

Associated with these sectoral areas are a series of horizontal (i.e. overlapping) issues that must be considered with development work. This includes the promotion of human rights, gender equality, children's rights and environmental protection. The DG DEV plans and finances developmental activities in these policy areas. The European office for co-operation (EuropeAID) is responsible for implementing most aid instruments designed to assist third-party countries. It also oversees the practical administration of all phases of implementation at the community level.

One of the most important responsibilities of DG DEV is the development of relations with sub-Saharan African countries, Caribbean countries, and countries in the Pacific and Indian Oceans. (These relations were fully overhauled in 2000, when the existing 1975 Lomé Accord was replaced by the Cotonou Co-operation and Development Agreement as a reaction to significant political, social and economic changes. Cotonou is designed to strengthen political dimensions of the partnership, allow new flexibility, and provide African, Caribbean and Pacific (ACP) states with more individual responsibility.) DG DEV is also responsible for relations with the overseas countries and territories (OCT).

The Commission negotiates with ACP countries and OCT on both national and regional levels. It designs and oversees strategies for development co-operation, and maintains political dialogue regarding co-operation strategies, conflict prevention and crisis management, while pursuing economic co-operation such as economic partnership agreements (EPA).

Internal partners of the Directorate General Development include, in the first instance, the other RELEX members (ECHO, RELEX, AIDCO, TRADE). The Commission discusses development policy with Member States and makes every effort to co-ordinate with international organizations such as the World Bank, OSCE and the United Nations. Local representatives from government, civil society and business are indispensable to EU development work.

The three primary instruments of European development policy are developmental assistance, political co-operation and trade. The STABEX and SYSMIN systems as well as the general preference system (GPS) of the Common Trade Policy form a basis for facilitating import of products from developing countries. The EU budget, the European Development Fund (EDF) and the European Investment Bank (EIB) provide financial subsidies and loans.

According to the Community Treaty, upon recommendation of the Commission and a simple Parliament hearing, the Council can take the necessary steps to provide financial, humanitarian and technical assistance.

Policy areas and responsibilities

Like the office for humanitarian aid ECHO, DG DEV is under the leadership of Commissioner Louis Michel of Belgium. The Directorate General Development is divided into four directorates. Directorates A and B handle horizontal issues, while C and D are responsible for geographic regions.

Directorate A: General affairs and operational support

Directorate A of DG DEV is in charge of general, operational and co-ordinating tasks. Unit A.1 is responsible for programme and strategic planning as well as financial and budgetary management. The unit manages operational, legal and budgetary co-ordination to ensure coherence in European development policy. Unit A.2 administers relations with the United Nations network, individual EU Member States, and other OSCE donor countries. As previously mentioned, co-ordination of the various sources of developmental aid is necessary to maximize success. A.3 maintains close contact with remaining EU institutions and those of the ACP area. Furthermore, the unit is in continuous dialogue with civil society and non-governmental organizations. Units A.4 and A.5 are responsible for personnel and computing as well as information and communications policy.

Directorate B: Development policy and thematic issues

In contrast to Directorates C and D, Directorate B deals with thematic areas of development policy. Unit B.1 oversees cohesion in development policy and designs future perspectives in preparation for continued globalization and EU expansion.

In Unit B.2 thematic emphasis is on economic issues. One instrument of economic support is a system of general tariff preferences and reductions for developing countries that facilitate access to the common market. The STABEX and SYSMIN systems are designed to stabilize volatile export earnings in developing countries. Whenever minimum export profits are not achieved, losses are compensated with payments from the EU budget.

The PRSP (Poverty Reduction Strategy Papers) initiative, which was launched by the International Monetary Fund and World Bank in 1999, contains comprehensive macroeconomic, structural and social programmes aimed at reducing poverty. Unit B.3 handles the social and human elements of poverty reduction efforts. The most important sub-areas are education, health, HIV/AIDS, population growth, social justice, gender equality and cultural support.

Unit B.4 ensures that environmental concerns are considered in developing countries. It generates strategies for sustainable development and guidelines for preserving forests and water resources. The unit also works to create a strategic framework for agricultural development and the sustainable cultivation of natural resources in the fight against rural poverty.

Last, Unit B.5 handles development in the area of transportation, which is necessary to ensure vital trade connections and access to health care, education and work. Unit B.5 is also responsible for infrastructure support and urban development.

Directorate C: Horn of Africa, eastern and southern Africa, Indian and Pacific Oceans

The Directorate General Development handles relations between the European Union and ACP countries. In late 2002, Country Strategy Papers (CSP) were negotiated with most ACO countries, which determine the framework of co-operation between the EU and individual countries for the period 2002–2007. Parallel to this, the Commission is formulating a Regional Strategy Paper (RSP) that is designed to stimulate a higher degree of economic integration and co-operation between countries across regions. The DG DEV is thus involved in planning diplomatic and political relations. Its area of operation reaches well beyond developmental assistance alone.

Unit C.1 is dedicated to relations with Pacific Ocean countries. With the conclusion of the Cotonou Agreement in June 2000, the number of Pacific ACP nations increased to 14. Thematic emphases of co-operation with Pacific states are multifaceted. For Nauru, for example, development of the energy sector is a top priority. For Fiji, it is promoting education in rural areas. Unit C.2 handles relations with the Horn of Africa, eastern Africa, and the Indian Ocean region. As an example, the Commission promotes democratic and responsible government in Burundi and supports non-governmental groups in Tanzania. Unit C.3 works with countries in southern Africa where the fight against HIV/AIDS is a central issue.

Directorate D: Western and central Africa, Caribbean, and OCT

Regional and bilateral relations with Caribbean states are administered in Unit D.1. It is also responsible for overseas countries and territories that have a constitutional relationship with one of four Member States: France, Great Britain, Denmark and the Netherlands. As in the ACP countries, the Commission pursues a policy of poverty elimination, support of sustainable development, and integration into regional and global economic systems for OCT areas.

Units D.2 and D.3 work with countries and regions in Africa. D.2 administers relations with western Africa. This includes the Portuguese-speaking nations of Angola, Guinea-Bissau, Mozambique, and São Tomé and Príncipe, who each concluded development and co-operation agreements with the Commission in the early 1990s. Unit D.3 co-ordinates bilateral and regional relations with states in central Africa.

DIRECTORATE GENERAL FOR ENLARGEMENT – DG ELARG

http://ec.europa.eu/enlargement/index_en.htm

Following an intensive preparation and negotiation process, on 1 May 2004 eight central and eastern European countries as well as Malta and Cyprus joined the European Union. The expansion from 15 to 25 Member States was the largest, though not the first, in EU history. In 1973 the number grew to 15 members. Bulgaria and Romania became members in 2007. Turkey and Croatia have candidate status.

European states wishing to enter the EU must fulfil certain political and economic criteria. The principles of freedom, democracy, observance of human rights, and the rule of law were established in 1992 by the Maastricht Treaty. In June 1993 these directives were elaborated in detail in the Copenhagen Criteria.

There are four basic conditions for EU membership:

- institutional stability as a guarantor of democracy;
- a fully functioning market economy;
- the ability to compete on the free market with other Member States;
- the capability to meet the challenges associated with political membership and economic and monetary union.

Accession to EU membership is a protracted and complex process. Each accession requires a unanimous decision by the Council and the approval of the European Parliament, which must achieve an absolute majority of parliamentary votes. The modalities of accession are determined by an accord between the Member States and the applicant country, which must be ratified by all treaty states. Accession to the European Union obligates the adoption of community *acquis*. This means the application of 80,000 pages of EU law. Furthermore, the accord requires an efficient administration, a strong justice system, and a high level of security on the external borders of acceding countries, as they in turn become the external borders of the expanded Union. Meticulous preparation by both the EU and the acceding country is absolutely essential.

Table 5.4 Organizational chart, DG Enlargement

Directorate A	Directorate B	Directorate C	Directorate D	Directorate E
Acceding countries	Candidate countries	Additional western Balkan countries	Financial instruments	General affairs and resources
A.1 Expansion strategy and co-ordination	**B.1** Turkey	**C.1** Regional co-operation	**D.1** Financial instruments and co-ordination	**E.1** Strategic planning, internal controls, data processing
A.2 Bulgaria	**B.2** Croatia	**C.2** Federal Republic of Yugoslavia	**D.2** Ongoing financial support	**E.2** Personnel
A.3 Romania	**B.3** Information, communications and inter-institutional relations	**C.3** Albania, Bosnia-Herzegovina	**D.3** Horizontal programmes	**E.3** Financial processing
A.4 Task force Turkish-Cypriot community		**C.4** Former Yugoslav Republic of Macedonia	**D.4** Programme for the western Balkans	**E.4** Evaluation
			D.5 Development of administrative capacity, TAIEX, TWINNING	**E.5** Operational auditing

Policy areas and responsibilities

The Commissioner responsible for enlargement policy is Olli Rehn of Finland. The Directorate General in charge of enlargement is led by Director General Michael Leigh of Great Britain. DG ELARG (*élargissement*) handles all aspects of the expansion process. It is separated into five directorates, which contain three to five units. Directorates A to D handle specific policy areas, while directorate E is chiefly responsible for general and internal issues and resources. This includes primarily strategic planning, internal controls and evaluation, personnel and financial matters, and data processing.

Directorate A: Acceding countries

Directorate A works with countries that are scheduled to be admitted to the Union. In January 2007 this was Bulgaria and Romania. The directorate oversaw negotiations with these acceding countries and monitored their success in achieving targeted objectives as they prepare for accession. Unit A.2 was responsible for Bulgaria, A.3 for Romania. Accession negotiations with Sofia and Bucharest were opened in February 2000. Accession partnerships have existed between the EU and the two countries since March 1998. Objectives that must be achieved before accession were established as part of the accession partnership framework. Reform of public administration and the justice system must continue in both Bulgaria and Romania. Further advancement was also required in the area of human rights and minority protection (for example, improvements in the situation of Roma in Bulgaria).

Romania in particular must adhere to structural reform directives. Bulgaria still shows deficiencies in the energy and transport sectors as well as with infrastructure investment. The Commission publishes annual reports on the progress of acceding countries. Unit A.1 handles the underlying tasks of co-ordinating the Commission's enlargement strategies and ensuring smooth accession processes. Unit A.4 makes up the Task Force for the Turkish Cypriot community. The unit generates measures for economic development of the northern part of Cyprus and its rapprochement with the European Union.

Directorate B: Candidate countries

Unit B.1 focuses on the largest and most controversial candidate country: Turkey. It first applied for EU membership on 4 April 1987.

A customs union has been in place since 1995. The 2004 annual report noted observable progress in political reforms, primarily due to a series of constitutional and legal modifications. Upon recommendation by the Commission, the European Council of heads of state and government decided in December 2004 to open accession negotiations with Turkey. Cautions about human rights abuses, the implementation of freedom of speech and religion, as well as the rights of women and minorities were issued. Similar to the units that work with Bulgaria and Romania, B.1 is organized into a series of sections. Each handles a different policy area and harmonization with European community *acquis*. Unit B.2 works on Croatia's accession process. After Slovenia, it is the second accession candidate to emerge from the former Yugoslavia. Accession negotiations with Croatia likewise began in 2004. A stabilization and association agreement, designed to prepare the country gradually for accession has been in effect between the EU and Croatia since 1 February 2005.

Unit B.3 is responsible for information and communications policy relating to EU enlargement. In May 2000 the Commission established a 'communications strategy for enlargement', which is intended to inform citizens of future Member States about the processes and effects of EU expansion. Information compiled by the Commission is submitted to the public for discussion by local European delegations, governments of Member States, candidate states and the media. It is in the Commission's interest to involve large portions of society (e.g. teachers, politicians, business representatives) in the project.

Directorate C: Western Balkans

The Commission pursues a political strategy that encompasses the entire western Balkans. The policy is designed to support the establishment of a stable and prosperous region, and in 1999 the Stabilization and Association Agreement was launched for this purpose. The programme offers financial and political support for the countries of southeastern Europe. This includes trade preferences, support for domestic political reforms, technical advice, and treaty agreements.

Unit C.1 is responsible for regional co-operation in the western Balkans. The three additional units of Directorate C work with one or more countries in the region. Serbia, Montenegro and Kosovo are administered by C.2. In the last few years, these three countries have received significant financial, practical and political support from the EU to promote conflict resolution, reconstruction and reforms.

The same is true for Unit C.3, which manages Bosnia and Herzegovina. Albania, which is also administered by C.3, has been negotiating a Stabilization and Association Agreement with the EU since January 2003. The document is designed to promote democratic reforms within the country and economic integration with the EU. Unit C.4 handles the former Yugoslav Republic of Macedonia, which applied for EU membership in March 2004. The application is currently under review by the Commission.

Directorate D: Financial instruments

DG ELARG has access to a series of financial support instruments designed to facilitate harmonization with the EU's political and economic system for acceding countries and the governments of the western Balkans. The most important objectives of the PHARE programme are the strengthening of public administration and structures, the harmonization of national laws with the community *acquis*, and the creation of greater economic and social cohesion. (Rural and agricultural development is administered by the Directorate General for Agriculture with its SAPARD programme. Environmental and transport issues are handled by the Directorate General for Regional Policy through the ISPA programme. Unit D.1 is responsible for co-ordinating pre-accession financial support instruments.

Unit D.2 handles continued financial support following the accession of EU candidates. The unit consists of several geographically organized sub-units, which provide financial assistance to ensure the harmonious transition from candidate status to membership. Unit D.3 develops programmes, which support overlapping objectives (e.g. the promotion of small and medium-sized businesses, trade, educational improvement, job opportunities and environmental initiatives). With the accession of the eight central and eastern European states on 1 May 2004, the focus of European accession assistance has moved south. Unit D.4 administers financial assistance programmes for countries in the western Balkans.

Finally, the instruments TAIEX (Technical Assistance Information Exchange Office) and TWINNING provide short-term technical support and valuable information and skills for new Member States, acceding countries, and governments in the western Balkans to enable them to introduce, apply and implement the community *acquis* and to build modern and efficient administrations and structures. In close co-operation with expert teams from Member States, candidate countries carry out projects to introduce and implement specific aspects of community *acquis*. These assistance projects and programmes are administered by Unit D.5.

Table 5.5 Organizational chart, Office for Co-operation

EuropeAid – Office for Co-operation Deputy Director General			
Directorate A	**Directorate B**	**Directorate C**	**Directorate D**
Europe, southern Mediterranean region, Near East, and Neighbourhood Policy	Latin America		Asia and central Asia
A.1 Geographic co-ordination and oversight Europe **A.2** Geographic co-ordination and oversight Mediterranean and Near East **A.3** Central administrative functions Europe, Mediterranean region and Near East **A.4** Nuclear security **A.5** Finances, contracts and auditing Europe, Mediterranean region and Near East **A.6** Partnership activities	**B.1** Geographic co-ordination and oversight Latin America **B.2** Central administrative functions Latin America **B.3** Finances, contracts and auditing Latin America	**C.1** Geographic co-ordination and oversight ACP countries I **C.2** Geographic co-ordination and oversight ACP countries II **C.3** Coordination ACP internal, OCT-related and pan-African issues and horizontal aspects **C.4** Central administrative functions ACP countries **C.5** Finances, contracts and auditing ACP countries **C.6** Peace facility **C.7** Water facility	**D.1** Geographic co-ordination and oversight Asia and central Asia **D.2** Central administrative functions Asia and central Asia **D.3** Finances, contracts, and auditing Asia and central Asia

Table 5.5 *(continued)*

Directorate E	**Directorate F**	**Directorate G**
Quality improvement support	General support of activities	Resources
E.1 Macroeconomic support	**F.1** Quality improvement working group	**G.1** Programming and budgetary issues
E.2 Business, trade and regional integration	**F.2** Administrative committees	**G.2** Co-ordination of information and communications strategy
E.3 Social and human development	**F.3** Financial, contractual, and legal issues	**G.3** Personnel
E.4 Governance, human rights, democracy, gender equality	**F.4** Relations with EU institutions, international organizations and donors	**G.4** Training and knowledge management
E.5 Security and migration	**F.5** Relations with civil society and non-governmental organizations	**G.5** Information systems and office technology
E.6 Natural resources	**F.6** Information, communications and central contact point	**G.6** Document administration and office infrastructure
E.7 Infrastructure		**G.7** Resource expertise

EuropeAid – OFFICE FOR CO-OPERATION – AIDCO

http://ec.europa.eu/europeaid/index_en.htm

The European Union Office for Co-operation (EuropeAid) was created by a European Commission resolution in January 2001 and is managed by the Commissioner for External Relations and European Neighbourhood Policy. It is the central administrative body of EU foreign aid, which is distributed worldwide. Over 150 countries, regions and facilities in eastern and southern Europe, Africa, Latin America and Asia receive support from EuropeAid. In addition to support for countries and regions, EuropeAid initiates projects for environmental protection, human rights and food safety. In 2002 foreign financial aid totalled 6 billion euros. Contributing 10 per cent of worldwide foreign assistance, the EU is one of the most important international donors for development policy.

The EuropeAid Co-operation Office – known internally as AIDCO – administers development aid instruments that have been made available by the Commission. In addition to administering the budget from the Commission, the office also manages funds from the European Development Fund (EDF). AIDCO allocates funds according to objectives set by the Directorates for External Relations and Development. EuropeAid is involved in all phases of the project cycle. It selects projects and programmes to support, examines them, generates resolutions for their financing, and implements, supervises and evaluates them.

The office co-operates with other Commission agencies that share responsibility for foreign relations. As part of an extensive decentralization strategy, tasks that are most effectively handled on the ground are entrusted to local Commission delegations in third-party countries. EuropeAid manages contacts with likely donors and maintains an active dialogue with businesses and non-governmental organizations that work with the Commission to implement development projects.

EuropeAid is the result of the sweeping administrative reform of European foreign assistance that began with the new millennium. Previously, the Directorates General responsible for foreign relations administered financial assistance independently. Administration is now centralized at the Office for Co-operation. The objectives of the reform are improved quality and flexibility in project administration, faster response times, and a strengthening of the visibility and transparency of EU development work. On the other hand, the pre-accession instruments PHARE, ISPA and SAPARD, the EU's humanitarian activities and the Common Foreign and Security Policy (CFSP) are not part of EuropeAid's responsibilities. They are administered by the Directorates General for Enlargement (ELARG), Humanitarian Aid (ECHO), and External Relations (RELEX).

Policy areas and responsibilities

EuropeAid is under the leadership of Director General Koos Richelle of the Netherlands. It is divided into seven directorates. Directorate A to D are arranged regionally. Directorate E administers overlapping, horizontal assistance programmes. Directorates F and G handle support activities (G primarily supports internal processes and F provides support for EuropeAid activities).

Directorate A: Europe, southern Mediterranean, Near East, and Neighbourhood Policy

Directorate A is responsible for EU developmental support for eastern and southeastern Europe, the southern Mediterranean region, the Near East, and Neighbourhood Policy countries, which include Algeria, Armenia, Azerbaijan, Belarus, Egypt, Georgia, Israel, Jordan, Lebanon, Libya, the Republic of Moldova, Morocco, Syria, Tunisia, Ukraine and the Palestinian Authority. Current decentralization reforms have had an impact on the AIDCO organizational chart.

Units A.1 and A.2 of Directorate A handle the geographic co-ordination and oversight of projects that are prepared and implemented locally by Commission delegations. Within this framework, Unit A.1 is responsible for projects in Europe, and A.2 handles projects in the Mediterranean region and the Near East. Examples include agricultural development programmes in Egypt and support for the banking sector in Bosnia-Herzegovina. (Support for the Federal Republic of Yugoslavia and the former Yugoslav Republic of Macedonia is primarily provided by the European Agency for Reconstruction [EAR] – *see* below.)

Unit A.3 is responsible for centrally administered EuropeAid activities. Although third-party country delegations now handle a large portion of projects and programmes, projects of an overlapping nature that affect several countries in a geographic region continue to be managed from the Commission headquarters. Examples include support for democratic stabilization in the western Balkans and the promotion of cross-cultural, inter-faith dialogue in the Mediterranean region. This approach is also used in the remaining AIDCO directorates, which are organized geographically.

Unit A.4 is dedicated to supporting nuclear security in the countries of eastern and southeastern Europe and the CIS states. Unit A.5 handles financial, contractual and auditing issues that affect the geographical area of responsibility of Directorate A. Unit A.6 administers 'twinning operations', implemented by the EU to support the establishment of modern, efficient administrations in potential accession candidate countries.

Directorate B: Latin America

The organizational structure of Directorate B, which is responsible for Latin America, is the same as that of Directorate A. Unit B.1 co-ordinates and oversees projects and programmes for Latin America that are implemented locally. Successful projects include the improvement of the water infrastructure in Nicaragua and conflict resolution in Columbia through the strengthening of local and regional institutions. Unit B.2 administers numerous centralized activities for Latin America, including projects for social cohesion and regional co-operation in the energy sector. Last, Unit B.3 is responsible for Latin American project finances, contracts and auditing.

Directorate C: Southern Africa, Caribbean region, and Pacific Ocean

Two units of Directorate C co-ordinate assistance projects for ACP countries. Unit C.1 works with ACP countries and overseas countries and territories (OCT) in eastern and southern Africa, the Indian and Pacific Oceans, while Unit C.2 works with those in western and central Africa and the Caribbean. Examples include projects such as an economic rehabilitation programme for the Republic of Haiti, a career-training project in Niger, and a development programme for the Zambian private sector. Unit C.4 is dedicated to overlapping and centrally administered activities. One example is the establishment of a regional Caribbean network to fight HIV/AIDS. C.3 is a support working group that examines ACP, OCT and pan-African issues. Unit C.5 handles financial, contractual and auditing matters.

In addition, Directorate C includes two independent units. C.6 deals intensively with the problems of war, which make development assistance in many countries impossible. In this area, European programmes concentrate on a few important issues. In the aftermath of open conflict, these include support for refugees, the disarming of soldiers, and the clearing of landmines. In the long term, work focuses on reintegrating communities, strengthening justice systems, and supporting final conflict resolution.

Unit C.7 administers the EU water facility for African, Caribbean and Pacific countries. With a budget of 500 million euros, this is the largest European water and sanitation project so far.

Directorate D: Asia and Central Asia

Directorate D works with Asia and Central Asia. Unit D.1 co-ordinates and oversees projects and programmes implemented by local delegations. Examples include a co-operation programme between the EU and the Chinese government for primary education in western China. Unit D.2 handles centrally administered activities for Asia and central Asia, which are often designed to facilitate regional co-operation among affected countries (i.e. within the framework of SAARC [South Asian Association for Regional Co-operation] or ASEAN [Association of Southeast Asian Nations]) and pursue of diverse objectives, such as environmental protection, inter-regional trade, and improved communications. Unit D.3 is responsible for finances, contracts and auditing.

Directorate E: Quality control

The primary task of Directorate E is to optimize the quality of EU development co-operation. The planning and implementation of AIDCO-administered aid must be coherent and effective. Quality control of development assistance is organized by topic.

E.1 is responsible for macroeconomic support measures. Instead of individual EU projects, direct subsidies are often forwarded directly to the national budgets of partner countries. This is contingent upon a stable and sustainable macroeconomic policy – i.e. fiscal and monetary responsibility combined with structural improvements. Unit E.2 is responsible for business, trade and regional integration. Concepts for greater support of the business sector in developing countries (e.g. through private sector investment and assistance) and the reform of state enterprises are of central importance.

Human and social development is addressed by Unit E.3. It concentrates on health, education, employment and social justice. Unit E.4 handles the critical areas of good governance, human and civil rights, the rights of children, the disabled and indigenous peoples, democratization, the strengthening of civil society, and gender equality. Unit E.5 deals with issues of crisis management, migration, police reform, anti-terrorism, and the fight against organized crime. E.6 handles natural resource management in developing countries, while E.7 provides support for infrastructure such as transport, water, energy, telecommunications, and urban development, as well as information and communications technology.

Directorate F: General support

Directorate F handles general tasks and provides support for EuropeAid activities. Unit F.1 is a working group for general quality-control issues. Unit F.2 maintains relations with numerous administrative bodies made up of national representatives who ensure the co-operation of Member States in European development assistance. It has long been agreed, however, that Member States should concentrate on overall strategic issues and allow individual Commission projects to handle detailed management. Unit F.3 deals with financial, contractual and legal issues. F.4 and F.5 maintain relations with other EU institutions, international organizations, and other donors, i.e., civil society and non-governmental organizations. Last, Unit F.6 handles information and communications policy and is the central point of contact for the general public.

European Agency for Reconstruction (EAR)

http://www.ear.europa.eu/

The autonomous European Agency for Reconstruction was formed in December 1999 by the European Council and launched in February 2000 in the Greek city of Thessaloniki. Led by Richard Zink of Germany, the agency administers the most important EU aid programmes in the Federal Republic of Yugoslavia (i.e. in the Republic of Serbia, in Kosovo, and in the Republic of Montenegro), as well as in the former Yugoslav Republic of Macedonia. (EU aid programmes for Albania, Bosnia-Herzegovina and Croatia are prepared and implemented by delegations at the local level; EuropeAid operates all regional programmes.)

EAR maintains operational centres in Pristina, Belgrade, Podgorica and Skopje and works with a budget of 1.6 billion euros. Programme objectives include the support of good governance, the establishment of institutions and the rule of law, the development of free markets, the investment in critical physical infrastructure, environmental protection, social development and a stronger civil society.

DIRECTORATE GENERAL FOR TRADE – DG TRADE

http://ec.europa.eu/trade/index_en.htm

The Directorate General for Trade is the sixth service with responsibility for external relations. Led by Commissioner Peter Mandelson of the United Kingdom, the Directorate General is responsible for the European Union international trade policy (i.e. EU trade relations with third-party countries). According to Article 131 of the Community Treaty, the Common Trade Policy (CTP) of the Union should 'contribute, in the common interest, to the harmonious development of world trade'. Alongside development and monetary policy, trade policy completes the economic foreign relations agenda of the EU.

DG Trade has a number of concrete objectives:

- liberalization of markets through the removal of trade barriers;
- creating and updating general international trade regulations, which ensure fair trade and mitigate the effects of globalization;
- integration of social issues such as the environment, food safety, agriculture and culture into the crafting of European trade policy.

As a first priority, the Commission naturally pursues the political and economic interests of Member States when developing and representing EU trade policy. Through unified action and representation, the already considerable trade influence of the 27 EU countries continues to grow. Since 1994, the Union has been working closely with the World Trade Organization (WTO), which consists of nearly 200 members and integrates developing countries alongside industrialized states.

Concrete regional projects include the improvement of relations with neighbouring countries and the establishment of a Mediterranean free trade zone within the framework of the Barcelona Process.

The responsibilities of DG Trade are as follows. Taking EU trade interests and Council directives as a basis, the directorate negotiates bilateral, regional and multilateral agreements in addition to managing their implementation and control. It also co-ordinates with Directorates General that have an effect on trade relations (e.g. Internal Market, Consumer Protection, Competition, Environment and Transport).

Co-ordination with the other Directorates General of the RELEX group (Foreign Relations, Development, Enlargement, and so on) is designed to ensure broad coherence between the European trade policy and the overall foreign policy objectives of the EU. DG Trade also integrates the general public and industry associations into EU trade policy.

According to Article 133 of Community law, the Commission is responsible for recommending, negotiating and implementing EU trade policy. The European Council reaches decisions on agreements and legislation with a qualified majority. The European Parliament is consulted and fully informed before all resolutions, but it only votes on highly important agreements.

Policy areas and responsibilities

Led by David O'Sullivan of Ireland, the DG Trade is divided into eight directorates. The units of Directorate A handle administration and

Table 5.6 Organizational chart, DG Trade

Deputy Director General			
Directorate A Resources, inter-institutional relations, communications, and data processing **A.1** Personnel, administration, finances, foreign service, programming **A.2** Inter-institutional relations and communications **A.3** Data processing	**Directorate B** Trade defence instruments **B.1** TDI: General policy, claims **B.2** TDI: Investigations I; oversight of third-party country measures **B.3** TDI: Investigations II **B.4** TDI: Investigations III; support and oversight of implementation in the Community **B.5** TDI: Investigations IV	**Directorate C** Free trade and partnership agreements with ACP countries, Latin America, GCC, and Iran; GPS **C.1** Negotiation and administration of trade and free trade agreements with Latin America, GCC, and Iran; General Preference System **C.2** Partnership agreements I **C.3** Partnership agreements II	**Directorate D** Trade relations with neighbourhood countries and southeastern Asia **D.1** Trade aspects of the European Neighbourhood Policy; trade relations with CIS countries and the Balkans **D.2** Negotiation and administration of trade and free trade agreements with Mediterranean countries and southeastern Asia; TREATI

Table 5.6 *(continued)*

Directorate E	Directorate F	Directorate G	Directorate H
Bilateral trade relations II; market access, industry policy trade issues, export trade policy	Co-ordination WTO and OECD, dispute support and provisions dealing with trade barriers	Services, agricultural trade issues, sustainable development; bilateral trade relations III	Textiles, new technologies, intellectual property, public procurement, trade analysis; bilateral trade relations IV
E.1 Standards and certifications; TBT **E.2** Steel, coal, shipbuilding, automobile, chemical, and other industries **E.3** Market access, trade relations with the United States, Canada, and EFTA **E.4** Export trade policy (export credits, controls, practices of third-party countries)	**F.1** Co-ordination WTO and OECD, trade-related assistance, GATT; 133 Committee **F.2** Dispute support and provisions dealing with trade barriers	**G.1** Service sector, GATS, investment **G.2** Agriculture, fisheries, plant and animal health, biotechnology **G.3** Sustainable development (including trade and the environment), dialogue with civil society	**H.1** Negotiation and administration of textile agreements, shoes **H.2** New technologies, intellectual property, public procurement **H.3** Trade analysis

personnel, and inter-institutional relations, as well as communications and information policy. Directorates B to H concentrate on specific thematic areas of European trade or on geographic regions in which the EU engages in trade. Directorates C to H are under the leadership of the Deputy Director General.

Directorate B: Trade defence instruments (TDI)

The five units of Directorate B, which are also under the direct responsibility of the Director General, work primarily with trade defence instruments or trade policy protection measures to ensure the implementation of fair global trade.

The EU has three basic trade protection instruments:

- anti-dumping measures to protect EU industries from the unfair competitive practice of dumping;
- anti-subsidy measures to penalize government-subsidized imports from third-party countries that endanger EU industries;
- protective measures that, in accordance with WTO agreements, may be levied against the import of goods that is seen as constituting unfair competition.

Unit B.1 is the general grievance office. In Units B.2 to B.5, complex investigative processes are used to determine possible illegalities, to which the Commission may introduce a temporary response – usually higher tariffs. Final reprimands are issued by the Council. In 2004 the Council issued protective tariffs in nine cases of export dumping. Affected industries included cotton bedding from Pakistan and salmon and trout from Norway and the Faroe Islands.

Unit B.2 monitors trade protection investigations in third-party countries. The Commission publishes an annual report on the most important third-party country processes that target the EU or its Member States. B.2 also ensures that third-party countries are fulfilling their commitments and adhering to international trade rules. Unit B.4 oversees the correct implementation of trade protection measures within the Community.

Directorate C: ACP, Latin America, GCC, and Iran

Directorate C is primarily responsible for the further development of EU trade relations with ACP countries, Latin America, Iran, and the countries of the Gulf Co-operation Council (Bahrain, Kuwait, Oman, Qatar, Saudi Arabia, United Arab Emirates). Three units in Directorate C work with these countries and regions, for which the European Union in most cases represents the most important trading partner. C.1 focuses on regional and national trade agreements. Units C.2 and C.3 manage Economic Partnership Agreements (EPA). For Latin American and ACP countries, economic and trade policy co-operation is closely linked to development policy.

Co-ordination of the General Preference System (GPS), which is designed to promote economic development and stronger trade in developing countries through tariff advantages, also falls under the responsibility of Unit C.1. Depending on the results of negotiations, products from developing countries can benefit from either a total tariff elimination or a significant reduction of tariff duties. GPS policy guidelines are reviewed by the Commission every 10 years.

Directorate D: Neighbouring countries and southeastern Asia

Directorate D handles trade relations with EU neighbouring countries and the states of southeastern Asia. Unit D.1 deals with trade policy issues related to the European Neighbourhood Policy (ENP) and trade relations with CIS countries and the Balkans. The Commission works towards creating a larger free trade zone with acceding and candidate countries. Economic relations with countries of the former Soviet Union and the Balkans continue to be strengthened through partnership and co-operation agreements.

Within the framework of the Barcelona Processes, launched in 1995, the Commission is pursuing the aim of creating a free trade zone among the EU and Mediterranean countries by 2010. Bilateral trade relations with Asian countries and trade policy co-operation between the EU and the regional organization ASEAN are administered by Unit D.2 as part of the 'Trans-National Trade Initiative EU-ASEAN' (TREATI). D.2 is also responsible for Mediterranean trade policy.

Directorate E: North America, Oceania, and EFTA

Directorate E manages trade relations with the North American states (USA and Canada), Australia and New Zealand as well as the EFTA countries (Iceland, Liechtenstein, Norway, Switzerland). Because of the European Economic Area (EEA) agreement, which integrates Iceland, Liechtenstein and Norway into the common European market, these countries are of great importance to EU trade.

The United States is the most important trading partner of the European Union. The mutual interdependence of these economic powerhouses and occasional trade disputes (e.g. ongoing subsidy disputes between aircraft-making giants Boeing and Airbus) require the continuous examination and revision of trade relations. Unit E.3 is charged with this task. The unit is also responsible for the Market Access Strategy, implemented in 1996 and designed to reduce trade barriers to EU exports through practical information policy and operational measures.

Units E.1 and E.2 of the directorate handle EU trade policy dealing with manufactured goods. In general, the Commission works for considerable tariff reductions on manufactured goods and the broad elimination of technical trade barriers (TBT) through the introduction of universal technical standards and guidelines. Planning is carried out by Unit E.1.

E.2 is responsible for specific industry sectors (e.g. the steel, coal, shipbuilding, automobile and chemical industries). Unit E.4 administers European export trade. Its duties include the examination of agreements and rules on export credits and their integration into European law.

Directorate F: Co-ordination with the WTO, dispute support and TBR

The EU speaks with one voice on matters relating to trade and the WTO. Unit F of DG Trade co-ordinates relations between the European Union and the World Trade Organization (WTO) and represents European trade interests on behalf of the 27 Member States at multilateral negotiations. The Director General for Trade and the Director of Unit F.1 exert considerable influence. In the context of the '133-committee', they meet regularly with Council representatives to define the Commission's trade policy position. Unit F.1 manages strategies for trade-related assistance (TRA) as part of the Doha Development Agenda (DDA) plan and is designed to help developing countries achieve economic progress through international trade.

Unit F.2 deals with issues relating to the Dispute Settlement Mechanism (DSM) set up in 1995 by the WTO. Parties to disputes can use the DSM to assert their rights under the multilateral trade agreement. F.2 also administers Trade Barrier Regulation (TBR) rules, which offer a mechanism for EU businesses and industries to proceed against trade barriers that hinder access to third-country markets.[ii] The TBR is the only offensive trade instrument available to the Community.

Directorate G: Services, agricultural trade, and sustainable development

In addition to bilateral trade relations with the Far East (i.e. China, Mongolia, Hong Kong, Macao, Taiwan), Directorate G is divided into

[ii] The regulation of trade barriers allows EU businesses to lodge a trade complaint with the Commission. If the application is successful, the conflict may be resolved through discussion, the WTO dispute resolution process or punitive measures.

several thematic areas of activity. Unit G.1 is responsible for trade in services. In accordance with the WTO's General Agreement on Trade with Services (GATS), set up in 1995, the Commission pursues a policy of continued liberalization of the services market, the EU's largest economic sector. In addition, G1 develops conditions for transparent, coherent and multilateral rules regarding foreign direct investment (FDI).

Trade in agricultural products is monitored by Unit G.2. As the leader in import and runner-up in export of agricultural products, the EU is interested in clear trade regulations for agricultural and fishery products. In the wake of the failed WTO conference in Cancun in September 2003, the Commission has expressed an increased interest in a compromise regarding the controversial topics of import tariffs and export subsidies.

Since environmental protection has increased in importance on the world stage, Unit G.3 of DG Trade has been systematically researching the potential impact of trade policy measures on the environment and sustainable development. The unit is also exploring opportunities for trade to assist in achieving environmental policy objectives. G.3 uses Sustainability Impact Assessment (SIA) to identify the economic, social and ecological consequences of trade agreements and recommends measures for mitigating negative effects. Unit G.3 also maintains the dialogue with civil society.

Directorate H: Intellectual property, GPA and trade analysis

Geographically, Directorate H is responsible for trade relations with Japan, the EU's fourth-largest export market. Unit H.1 concentrates mainly on trade in textiles and footwear. Unit H.2 handles issues related to new technologies, intellectual property, and public procurement. The Commission is working for an effective and worldwide implementation of the World Trade Organization programme for Trade-Related Aspects of Intellectual Property Rights (TRIPS). It is also working towards a liberalization of public procurement that would go far beyond the current Government Procurement Agreement (GPA). Finally, Unit H.3 conducts analyses of trade interests and strategies.

6

General services

SECRETARIAT GENERAL – SG

http://ec.europa.eu/dgs/secretariat_general/index_en.htm

The primary responsibility of the Secretariat General is to ensure the efficient implementation of the Commission's political priorities. It co-ordinates internal Commission activities, provides strategic planning and programming, and ensures smooth decision-making processes in the College of Commissioners. The Secretariat General also co-ordinates public Commission activities and maintains relations between the Commission and other EU bodies. This central administrative instrument for implementing Commission policy is under the sole leadership of President José Manuel Barroso.

In addition, the Secretariat-General is responsible for simplifying the Commission's administrative processes and dealing with current topics and events. When fundamental issues that affect the entire EU (e.g. the future of the European Union or implementation of the economic and socio-political Lisbon Strategy) arise, the Commission can assign special projects to the Secretariat. The SG handles topics of structural underlying importance (e.g. institutional issues, policy of openness and transparency, relations with civil society, data protection) and provides official information on EU decision-making processes.

Organization

The Secretariat General is currently led by Catherine Day of Ireland who also directly oversees an auditing service. The Secretariat works closely with the Commission President and is divided into eight directorates.

Directorate E handles overlapping administrative tasks such as resources, correspondence, document management and computing.

Directorate A: Registry and Commission decision-making processes

Directorate A is the registry or administrative headquarters of the European Union. In Unit A.1, oral procedures (plenary and working group meetings of Commission members, cabinet head meetings, and special cabinet meetings) are prepared and recorded. Typically, this includes compiling agendas and meeting materials. Written procedures are the usual medium for decision-making and are the responsibility of Unit A.2. The unit also handles delegation procedures, i.e. the procedural authorization of one Commission member to act on behalf of the whole college. Unit A.3 is entrusted with electronic data transfer for internal Commission decision-making processes.

Directorate B: Relations with civil society

Directorate B of the Secretariat General manages relations with civil society. The first unit of the directorate ensures the correct application of Community law. Together with sectoral directorates, this unit plays the role of 'guardian of contracts'. Unit B.2 maintains close contacts with civil society and promotes transparency in the Commissions work. The Commission holds regular consultations designed to strengthen public dialogue and give citizens opportunities to express opinions on general and institutional topics.

Recent topics of particular interest include the simplification of the *acquis communautaire* and the future of the European Union. The Commission has also established a framework for coherent and productive interaction with members of civil society (e.g. non-governmental organizations and interest groups). Unit B.3 is responsible for archiving systems, especially the historical archive, which co-ordinates the storage of documents and records. At the beginning

Table 6.1 Organizational chart, Secretariat General

Secretary General Deputy Director General			
Directorate A Registry and organization of Commission decision-making processes **A.1** Verbal processes and document distribution **A.2** Written processes, authorizations, and transfer of authority **A.3** Electronic document delivery	**Directorate B** Relations with civil society **B.1** Application of Community law **B.2** Transparency and civil society **B.3** Archiving policy and document administration policy **B.4** Rules of conduct	**Directorate C** Planning and administrative co-ordination **C.1** Strategic and administrative co-ordination **C.2** Co-ordination of administrative and budgetary policy **C.3** Publications and General Report **C.4** Secretariat of the auditing sub-unit	**Directorate D** Policy co-ordination **D.1** Task force Lisbon Strategy **D.2** Policy co-ordination I **D.3** Policy co-ordination II
Directorate E Resources and general affairs **E.1** Planning and resources **E.2** Correspondence and document administration **E.3** Computing **E.4** Information and databases	**Directorate F** Relations with the Council **F.1** Committee of permanent representatives I **F.2** Committee of permanent representatives II **F.3** Shared decision-making processes	Directorate G Relations with the EP, European citizen representatives, economic and social committee, committee of regions and national parliaments **G.1** European Parliament I **G.2** European Parliament II **G.3** Economic and social committee, committee of regions, European citizen representative, and national parliaments	**Directorate H** Institutional affairs **H.1** European constitution **H.2** Institutional affairs and improved lawmaking **H.3** Governance

of the Barroso Commission administration, Directorate B received a fourth unit, which handles professional rules of conduct that apply to Commission administration employees. The 'Codex of good administrative behaviour' commits employees to impartiality, coherence and high-quality performance in their work.

Directorate C: Planning and administrative co-ordination

Directorate C is concerned with co-ordination tasks. Unit C.1 is responsible for overall strategic planning and co-ordination within the Secretariat-General, whereas Unit C.2 manages administrative and budgetary policy. Unit C.3 handles Commission publications, including the annually published *General Report on the Activities of the European Union*, which is compiled on the basis of contributions by individual Directorates General. The document is an account of the preceding year's activities and is available online. Unit C.4 serves as the office for the Audit Progress Committee, which provides support for the individual audit services of the various Directorates General.

Directorate D: Policy co-ordination

Directorate D handles one of the core responsibilities of the Secretariat-General: content co-ordination of Commission policies. It ensures that the activities of the various Directorates General correspond with one another. The directorate thereby contributes to greater efficiency in the Commission's work.

In this context, Directorate D is intensively involved in assembling the Commission's annual programme. It compiles the suggestions of the Directorates General and prepares the programme so that the President can present it to the European Parliament upon approval by the College of Commissioners.

In 2005 the Commission identified the following political priorities:

- boosting economic growth through improved competitiveness and stronger cohesion;
- stability and security for a greater number of increasingly mobile citizens through enhanced security and the full implementation of the concept of EU citizenship;

- assumption of new foreign policy responsibilities by managing neighbour and partnership relations with countries bordering the south and east of the EU.

The task of co-ordinating the myriad Commission policies belongs to Units D.2 and D.3. In Unit D.1, a task force was assembled to ensure the successful implementation of the Lisbon Strategy. The plan is intended to initiate new perspectives on employment, growth, the environment, and social welfare but has achieved only modest success so far.

Directorate F: Relations with the Council

Directorate F of the Secretariat General is responsible for relations with the Council of Ministers. Its primary task is to co-ordinate the activities of the various Commission offices in Council committees to ensure coherent and persuasive Commission positioning. The directorate also generates reports to the Commission on the debates in the Council of Ministers and Committee of Permanent Representatives.

Although the Council is a single unit, it functions in several different configurations. The Committee of Permanent Representatives does preparatory work for the Council of Ministers and carries out tasks delegated to it. It consists of two levels. One committee is made up of the ambassadors themselves (COREPER II). The second is a meeting of their representatives (COREPER I). Both groups are responsible for a variety of topic areas. COREPER II Trades prepares issues regarding general affairs and external relations, economics and finances as well as justice and the interior. COREPER I is responsible for employment, health and social welfare, competitiveness, transport and energy, agriculture and fisheries, as well as education and culture.

The units of Directorate F of the Secretariat-General are oriented around this structure. Unit F.1 co-ordinates relations with COREPER I, while Unit F.2 works with COREPER II. The third unit is responsible for the co-decision legislative procedure that is anchored in the Treaty of Nice (Article 251). The agreement regulates the interplay of Parliament, the Council and the Commission for a large portion of law-making procedures.

Directorate G: Relations with the European Parliament, the European Ombudsman, the European Economic and Social Committee, the Committee of Regions, and the national parliaments

Directorate G handles relations between the Commission and Parliament. The continuous broadening of Parliament's responsibilities (e.g. through the expanded application of the co-decision legislative procedure and greater influence on budget processes) and its growing significance make careful co-operation essential.

Directorate G continuously monitors the activities of the various parliamentary committees as well as the discussions taking place in the framework of plenary sessions in Strasbourg and Brussels. The directorate has two primary objectives. The first is to be in a position to inform Directorates General and Commission offices of the content of parliamentary consultations. The second is to ensure appropriate representation of Commission interests in the European Parliament. Commission positions represented in Parliament are determined internally at the cabinet level by the Group for Interinstitutional Relations. This group supports the Commission President and the Commission member responsible for parliamentary affairs – currently Margot Wallström of Sweden – during important meetings (e.g. conferences with the President of Parliament).

In addition, Directorate G is responsible for collecting and forwarding the many written enquiries, which members of Parliament address to the Commission. Through the relevant Directorates General and offices process the enquiries, Directorate G verifies the correctness of formulations and conformity with Commission positions. Units G.1 and G.2 are charged with these duties.

Unit G.3 is responsible for relations with the Economic and Social Committee (ESC) and the Committee of Regions (CoR), which often need to be consulted by the Council or Commission during the legislative process. The unit also handles complaints directed towards the European Ombudsman and ensures that they are answered. Finally, G.3 maintains relations between the Commission and the national parliaments of Member States.

Directorate H: Institutional affairs

Directorate H of the Secretariat General deals with institutional affairs. It handles general questions and generates ideas for thematic issues that will affect the future development of the European Union. Unit H.1 deals with the European constitution, which was accepted on 18 June 2004 but whose ratification process has since stalled. Unit H.2 monitors the status of pending reforms to European institutions and supports improved law-making. Unit H.3 deals with European governance: it searches for opportunities to strengthen democracy in Europe, increase participation in decision-making among the European public, and thereby promote the political legitimacy of EU organizations.

LEGAL SERVICE – SJ

http://ec.europa.eu/dgs/legal_service/index_en.htm

A further core office of the Commission is the Legal Service, abbreviated from the French Service Juridique (SJ). The Legal Service is headed by Director General Michel Petite of France. The service reports directly to the Commission President and it participates in every decision made by the Commission. The Legal Service examines each resolution for its lawfulness, to ensure that it does not conflict with the treaties of the European Union. It also checks whether a Commission action is warranted or even required on the basis of a directive or guideline.

For this purpose, the Legal Service is divided into working groups of lawyers who specialize in specific areas. Examples of group

Table 6.2 Organizational chart, Legal Service

Deputy Director General			
Group organizations and institutions	Group external relations	Group internal market	Legal examiners
Group corporate law	Group budget, administration and personnel	Group employment and social affairs	Codification
Group justice, freedom and security, civil law, criminal law	Group agriculture and fisheries	Group competition and mergers	Documentation and information
Group state subsidies and dumping			Information systems

topics include political organs and institutions, corporate law, the internal market, competition and mergers. Certain departments are also entrusted with the final examination of rulings as well as with codification.

Without the support of the Legal Service, virtually no decision could be taken by the Commission and this is why the office is so highly valued by the other Commission agencies. The Legal Service also represents the Commission in external legal disputes, particularly those before the European Court of Justice.

OFFICE FOR OFFICIAL PUBLICATIONS – OPOCE

http://publications.europa.eu/index_en.html

With its headquarters in Luxembourg, the Office for Official Publications for the European Union – internal abbreviation OPOCE (Office des Publications Officielles des Communautés Européennes) – is the publishing house for all EU organizations. As such, it is an inter-institutional facility. Its beginnings are rooted in the Publishing Service of the European Coal and Steel Community (ECSC), and its archive contains the product of 50 years of publishing activity. Under the current leadership of Martine Reicherts, the institution is responsible for all European Union publications (print, e-books, CD-ROM, websites, and internet databases) and their distribution (via information offices, delegations, representatives, and European information networks). By publishing and distributing high-quality information and legal texts, the office hopes to bring the European general public and expert communities closer to the EU and make a contribution to European law-making processes and policy. The Office of Official Publications also plays a leading role in the area of new technology. The importance of the internet for distributing information has increased dramatically in recent years.

Among the most important Office publications are the *Official Journal of the European Union* and the *General Report on the Activities of the European Union*. The former has been published daily in all 20 official languages, and, upon request, in other languages, since the entry of 10 new Member States on 1 May 2004. (The first issue appeared on 30 December 1952 in German, French, Italian and Dutch.) The annual *General Report* describes the most important political decisions and other activities of the European Union. In 2004 the Office of Official Publications employed over 500 people and published 7,080 titles.

Table 6.3 Organizational chart, Office for Official Publications of the European Communities

Office for Official Publications		
Directorate R **Resources**	**Directorate A** Official Journal and Access to Law	**Directorate B** Publication and distribution
R.1 Personnel **R.2** Public calls for tender **R.3** Budget and accounting **R.4** Infrastructure	**A.1** EUR-Lex **A.2** Official Journal **A.3** Quality control	**B.1** Publications **B.2** Multimedia **B.3** Distribution **B.4** CORDIS

Organization

The Office for Official Publications is divided into three directorates. Directorate R handles personnel issues, public calls for tender, and announcements regarding jobs, deliveries and services, budgetary and accounting issues as well as internal office infrastructure. Directorate A is responsible for the *Official Journal*. It also manages EUR-Lex, the internet portal for public access to EU law, and ensures quality control. Finally, Directorate B is responsible for publishing and distributing the office's titles. Emphases include the multimedia distribution of publications as well as the design of CORDIS (Community Research and Development Information Service), the European Commission information service for research and innovation activities.

EUROPEAN ANTI-FRAUD OFFICE – OLAF

http://ec.europa.eu/dgs/olaf/index_en.html

The European Anti-Fraud Office (OLAF, from the French Office Européen de Lutte Anti-Fraude) was launched by the Commission on 28 April 1999. Primary responsibilities of the facility are to protect the financial and economic interests of the European Union and to expose fraud, corruption or any other misconduct in EU organizations and facilities. European citizens should be confident that EU offices are responsible, transparent, and cost-effective. The office benefits from full independence in its activities. It is however part of the Commission authority and reports to the Vice-President Siim Kallas of Estonia, who, as a Commission member, is responsible for administration, auditing and anti-fraud activities.

OLAF conducts independent investigations, especially in cases where customs fraud, tax evasion, misuse of subsidies, or corruption is suspected.

The office's primary areas of responsibility are shown in Table 6.4.

In cases of reasonable suspicion in any EU organization, institution, agency, or office, OLAF may conduct internal administrative reviews to uncover corruption or abuse of power among officials.

Primary office activities include the following:

- In cases of reasonable suspicion, the office may conduct internal administrative investigation of any EU organization, institution, agency, or office to root out corruption or official misconduct.

Table 6.4 Organizational chart, European Anti-Fraud Office

Directorate A Policy, legislation, legal affairs	**Directorate B** Investigations and operational activities	**Directorate C** Intelligence, operational strategy, and information service
A.1 Legislation, legal affairs, relations with other EU organizations, facilities, offices, and agencies **A.2** Strategic programming, reports, advising committee, external relations **A.3** Customs, co-ordination of capital resources, co-ordination of penalties **A.4** Agriculture and structural policy issues; penalties **A.5** Direct disbursements; penalties, confiscation **A.6** Euro currency protection	**B.1** Internal investigations; Eurostat **B.2** Internal investigations **B.3** External assistance for PHARE and TACIS **B.4** Direct disbursement, including PHARE and TACIS **B.5** Shared investigations with other organizations **B.6** Agriculture **B.7** Customs **B.8** Structural issues	**C.1** Intelligence; strategic analysis and evaluation **C.2** Information service **C.3** Operational intelligence; information and technical support

- It works in conjunction with its counterparts in the Member States (e.g. investigation bureaus, police and justice authorities) to investigate international illegal activities. OLAF deploys a special task force in cases involving products that present a disproportionate harm to the EU (e.g. tobacco and alcohol); it co-ordinates European and national exposure and prosecution of large smuggling rings. The office also provides national authorities with essential support and expertise. An exchange of ideas between OLAF and Member States takes place in a specially conceived consulting committee for anti-fraud co-ordination, known as CoCoLaF (Comité consultatif pour la Co-ordination de la Lutte contre la Fraude).
- OLAF participates in the development and implementation of a general strategy for anti-fraud enforcement in the European Union. The office contributes to improved preventive measures by making recommendations for tightening existing laws and introducing new legislation.

Investigations are conducted under the leadership of the Director General of OLAF in co-ordination with the Parliament and Council. The Director serves a term of five years and is appointed by the Commission. Since 2000 OLAF has been led by Franz-Hermann Brüner of Germany. To ensure the independence of the Anti-Fraud Office, the Director is strictly prohibited from requesting or accepting instructions from national governments or other EU institutions. If the Director believes that the Commission is inappropriately influencing OLAF, he has the option of summoning the European Court of Justice. Furthermore, a supervisory board ensures the independence and impartiality of the office. The board consists of five members who do not belong to any EU institution but are experienced in the activities of the Anti-Fraud Office. It oversees and monitors all activities and may express an opinion at any time, upon the request of the Director General or on its own initiative. However, the board does not participate in the daily operations of the office.

The activities of the Anti-Fraud Office span a wide range of economic and political areas. Between 2003 and 2004 cigarette smuggling remained a central challenge. OLAF also deals with fraudulent origin information for a series of imported products as well as funds misappropriation both inside and outside the EU. Internal investigations have been conducted in virtually every institution of the Union. The number increased by 9 per cent between July 2003 and June 2004, from 585 cases to 637. Of those, 275 led to the opening of an investigation.

The Anti-Fraud Office attributes this increase to growing trust in its operations.

Organization

The European Anti-Fraud Office is divided into three directorates, in addition to several consultancies and four units that report directly to the Director General on administrative issues (OLAF/1), communications policy and public relations (OLAF/2), external relations (OLAF/3), and legal advice and punitive measures (OLAF/4).

The units of Directorate A handle relations with the remaining EU bodies and the advisory committee; anti-fraud enforcement and penalties for customs and trade; agricultural and structural measures; and protection from misuse and counterfeit of the common euro currency. Directorate B is responsible for investigations and operational activities. Internal investigations (especially within the Eurostat office of statistics), reviews of external and direct EU assistance as well as shared investigations with other organizations also take place here.

The European Technical and Scientific Centre (ETCS) has been an integral part of the Anti-Fraud Office administrative structure since its launch on 1 October 2001. The centre works intensively to combat the misuse of the European common currency, especially coin counterfeiting. It lends technical and scientific expertise primarily in support of facilities that combat the production and distribution of counterfeit money in Europe (e.g. Europol).

EUROPEAN PERSONNEL SELECTION OFFICE – EPSO

http://europa.eu/epso/index_en.htm

The European Personnel Selection Office (EPSO) began its work on 1 January 2003 and since then has been conducting open personnel selection processes for the European Union – including the Council, Commission, Parliament, Court of Justice, Court of Auditors, Economic and Social Committee, Committee of Regions, and the European Ombudsman. The current Director is Erik Halskov of Denmark.

Like the Office of Official Publications, the Personnel Selection Office is an inter-institutional facility. Recruiting was previously handled by each organization individually. Now, centralized hiring ensures coherent and efficient planning and organization in the selection process. (EPSO employs the latest information technology in its application procedures for maximum efficiency.) The European Public Affairs office provides updated information about hiring and career opportunities and serves as a central contact point for the general public. The Office simplifies the application process for job-seekers and ensures uniform hiring practices. (*See* Chapter 3 for further information on Commission application and hiring processes.)

Table 6.5 Organizational chart, European Personnel Selection Office

European Personnel Selection Office		
Directorate A Selection procedures and recruiting mechanisms I	**Directorate B** Selection procedures and recruiting mechanisms II	**Directorate C** Budgetary and personnel issues and operational support
Directorate D Personnel selection policy, legal issues, information, communications, and customer service	**Directorate E** EPSO, information technology and infrastructure, databases	**Directorate F** Administration and control of reserve lists, selection process for contract employees

The annual budget of the Office for Personnel Selection is nearly 10 per cent smaller than the previous recruitment costs of individual institutions combined. Recently, the primary objective of the office has been to offset the increased workload presented by EU enlargement. Since 2003 EPSO has managed rapidly growing selection and hiring processes.

Organization

The Office for Personnel Selection is divided into six directorates. Directorates A and B handle regular selection competitions and other recruitment mechanisms. Directorate C is responsible for budgetary and personnel issues as well as operational support. Directorate D deals primarily with legal issues, communications and information. Directorate E manages electronic activities (i.e. websites, online application procedures and databases) for the office, while Directorate F administers the use of reserve personnel lists and oversees selection procedures for temporary and contract employees.

EUROSTAT – ESTAT

http://epp.eurostat.ec.europa.eu/

Headquartered in Luxembourg, the Eurostat Office provides high-quality statistical information services. The Statistical Office of the European Community, abbreviated to ESTAT, supplies the Union with statistics that allow comparisons between European countries and regions. The legal basis for the compilation of Community statistics was established in 1997 by Article 285 of the EC Community Treaty: 'The Council shall adopt measures for the production of statistics where necessary for the performance of the activities of the Community.'

The principles of impartiality, objectivity, scientific independence, cost-effectiveness, and confidentiality in Community statistical work are contractually binding. The Commissioner responsible for economic and monetary issues, Joaquín Almunia of Spain, oversees the service.

The EU believes that the generation of reliable and significant statistics is an important responsibility in support of an efficiently functioning democratic society. Political decision-makers at European, national and regional levels rely on statistical findings to formulate sound policies. The European public and the media use statistical data to make a realistic assessment of economic conditions and corresponding political action. Overlapping EU and international statistics provide an opportunity to learn more about other EU Member States and third-party countries.

Eurostat does not work alone. It is also a part of the phased introduction of the European Statistical System (ESS), which is designed to produce comparable statistics at the European level. In addition to Eurostat, the ESS includes the statistical offices, ministries, agencies and central banks that are responsible for statistical analysis in the 27 Member States as well as Norway, Liechtenstein and Iceland. Eurostat collects data from all of these statistical sources. It then examines, compiles and, where necessary, harmonizes various national statistical information.

Table 6.6 Organizational chart, Eurostat

Directorate A Resources **A.1** Personnel and administration **A.2** Employment programme and relations with Member States **A.3** Budget **A.4** Legal issues and inter-institutional relations	**Directorate B** Main indicators and statistical instruments **B.1** Main indicators **B.2** Computer-assisted administration and information systems **B.3** Statistical information technology **B.4** Reference databases **B.5** Research	**Directorate C** Economic and financial statistics **C.1** Economic resource accounting – methodology **C.2** Economic resource accounting – production **C.3** Public finances and taxation **C.4** Balance of payments **C.5** Taxation **C.6** Certification of resource accounting and state finances
Directorate D Internal market, employment, and social statistics **D.1** Labour market **D.2** Living conditions and social safety net **D.3** Business **D.4** Energy and transport **D.5** Education and culture **D.6** Health and food safety **D.7** Information society and services	**Directorate E** Agriculture, fisheries, structural fund and environment statistics **E.1** Structural agriculture statistics **E.2** Agricultural production statistics **E.3** Sustainable development, fisheries, rural development and forestries **E.4** Structural funds **E.5** Environment	**Directorate F** Foreign relations statistics **F.1** Demographics and migration **F.2** International trade **F.3** Technical co-operation with European third-party countries **F.4** Technical co-operation with international institutions **F.5** Co-operation with international institutions

Eurostat co-operates with international organizations such as the United Nations and OECD to improve statistical systems of acceding states and developing countries. The office works closely with national statistics authorities in central and eastern Europe, the former Soviet Union, Mediterranean countries, and several African states.

Each year Eurostat publishes a multitude of printed and electronic materials. Of particular note is the Eurostat yearbook, which contains socioeconomic data for all EU Member States and an overview of political and economic developments.

Organization

Eurostat is led by Director General Günter Hanreich of Germany. Directorate A is chiefly concerned with personnel, budgetary and legal issues as well as relations with members and other institutions. Directorate B is responsible for statistical instruments such as information systems, reference databases and statistical research.

Directorates C to F deal with various thematic areas of statistics. Directorate C works with economic and financial statistics (e.g. economic statistics, public finances, taxation, and prices). Directorate D produces statistical information on the internal market, employment and social affairs (e.g. labour market, living conditions, health, and services). Directorate E is responsible for agriculture, fisheries, structural funds and environment statistics, while Directorate F compiles statistics on external relations (e.g. demographics, foreign trade and co-operation with international institutions).

7

Internal services

PAYMASTER'S OFFICE – PMO

The Office for Administration and Payment of Individual Elements is responsible for the administrative processing of wages and the financial obligations to EU employees and experts. PMO is headquartered in

Table 7.1 Organizational chart, Paymaster's Office

Paymaster's Office		
PMO 1 Salaries and administration of individual financial rights	PMO 2 Missions and experts	PMO 3 Sickness and accident insurance
PMO 4 Pensions	PMO 5 Luxembourg	PMO 6 Ispra
PMO 7 Resources	PMO 8 Budget, internal auditing, and information technologies	PMO 9 Simplification, communication, and co-ordination between sites

Luxembourg and, to a large degree, operates as an integrated part of EU institutions. It is divided into different sections, such as shared with Sickness and Accident Insurance Cover (PMO3), Salaries and Administration of Individual Financial Rights (PMO1), and Missions and Experts (PMO2).

OFFICE FOR INFRASTRUCTURE AND LOGISTICS, BRUSSELS – OIB

http://ec.europa.eu/oib/index_en.htm

At its headquarters in Brussels, the European Commission occupies over 60 buildings, which house the Directorates General and other Commission offices, including the library. The majority of Directorates General are located within the 'European Quarter' in the Etterbeek district of Brussels. The European Council and Parliament are also in the vicinity.

The two most important Commission buildings are the Berlaymont Building, where the Commissioners and their cabinets meet, and the Charlemagne Building, which is adjacent to the Berlaymont. The Charlemagne Building is home to the Directorates General that are responsible for EU foreign relations, i.e. Trade, External Relations and Enlargement.

Table 7.2 Organizational chart, Office for Infrastructure and Logistics, Brussels

Office for Infrastructure and Logistics, Brussels		
OIB 1 Implementation of buildings policy	OIB 2 Space management and maintenance	OIB 3 Purchasing policy and inventory
OIB 4 Reproduction services, mail, and historical archives	OIB 5 Resources	OIB 6 Social welfare infrastructure – Brussels
OIB 7 Building administration and safety	OIB 8 Property projects	OIB 9 Transport and mobility

The Office for Infrastructure and Logistics reports to the DG Personnel and Administration. It is responsible for acquiring or leasing buildings whenever additional space is required and for maintaining existing properties. The office also manages document flow and mail services as well as social facilities for EU employees in Brussels, e.g. day care for children.

One important duty of the office is the administration of historical archives, where Commission files and documents are stored.

OFFICE FOR INFRASTRUCTURE AND LOGISTICS, LUXEMBOURG – OIL

http://ec.europa.eu/oil/index_en.htm

Table 7.3 Organizational chart, Office for Infrastructure and Logistics, Luxembourg

Office for Infrastructure and Logistics, Luxembourg				
OIL1 Building policy – Luxembourg	OIL2 Internal services and building maintenance – Luxembourg	OIL3 Conferences and social support facilities – Luxembourg	OIL4 Finances and support in contractual matters	OIL5 Resources, horizontal co-ordination, safety, and hygiene

Although Brussels is home to the Commission headquarters, several units and Directorates General are located in Luxembourg. The Office for Infrastructure and Logistics in Luxembourg fulfils administrative functions similar to its counterpart in Brussels.

DIRECTORATE GENERAL FOR INFORMATICS – DG DIGIT

http://ec.europa.eu/dgs/informatics/index_en.htm

The Europa website is one of most frequently visited sites in the world. Millions of EU citizens and users from around the world visit it to

Table 7.4 Organizational chart, DG Informatics

	DG Informatics **Director General**	
Directorate A Infrastructure	**Directorate B** Information systems	**Directorate C** Resources and logistics
A.1 User support **A.2** Telecommunications and networks **A.3** Computer Centre **A.4** Technical and office communications solutions	**B.1** Consultation contact with offices, institutions and other EU units **B.2** Interoperability, architecture and methods **B.3** Information systems for personnel administration **B.4** Information systems for planning, financial and document administration	**C.1** Planning and resources **C.2** Finances and contracts **C.3** Logistics

access information about EU developments and future plans. At a time when political and economic events happen at an increasingly fast pace, it is even more important for visitors to have access to current and reliable facts.

The Commission, which is represented in all 27 Member States and in 130 delegations around the world, must have a good information network and cutting-edge technology. In June 2001 the Commission introduced the 'e-Europe' action plan and the 'electronic Commission' in pursuit of three objectives:

1. Internal administrative structures should be modernized, in order to simplify work for the directorates, making their activities and interactions more efficient and less time-consuming. In addition, information exchange with external partners and national authorities and ministries should be made more effective.
2. Second, an efficient system is required for trade issues, e.g. for customs authorities. Goods and products imported into the EU internal market from third party countries are checked according to Community law at the point of entry by EU customs officials. If they do not conform to EU standards – for example, they are not in compliance with EU consumer protection laws – customs can alert

the Commission, in this case the Directorate General for Customs and Taxation. The directorate then quickly informs all EU customs officials and provides information or warnings regarding the goods, so that their impact can be stopped. The same applies to the system of import quotas on certain goods and products from third-party countries, e.g. textiles. An efficient network is necessary so that the Commission – in this case DG Trade – is able to monitor when certain import quotas have been reached. A reliable and efficient information network between customs officials and ministries in Member States is thus an absolute necessity.

3. The third and most important objective of the Commission is to share the political and economic progress of the EU with all citizens and organizations – businesses, consumer organizations and non-governmental organizations – and to incorporate it into its policymaking. At the 'Your Voice' website, citizens can take part in EU policy discussions and find detailed information (www.europa.eu.int/yourvoice/consultations/index_en.htm).

Businesses both inside and outside the EU are affected by European policy. They need to stay informed about the latest developments in their industry. The website 'Your Europe: Information for your business' was designed for this purpose. Here businesses learn about potential partners in other countries and about EU certification for their products (http://europa.eu.int/youreurope/nav/en/business/home.html).

Ultimately, a well-administered website is essential since the Commission also grants public contracts. The information system for public contracts, SIMAP (http://www.simap.eu.int), provides contracting offices and contractors with information on the bidding processes. The Commission website 'Europe for You' (http://europa.eu.int/youreurope/index_en.html) is a portal of EU online offices and national authorities, where citizens can access detailed information and advice on rights and opportunities in the EU and its internal market.

The Directorate General Information Technology is responsible for telecommunications and information technology infrastructure and logistics for the Commission. The system must be efficient and secure as well as extremely powerful. The directorate reports to Commissioner Siim Kallas of Estonia.

Led by Director General Francisco Garcia Moran, the Directorate General DIGIT is divided into two directorates. Directorate A is charged with the co-ordination of all infrastructure and logistics for the Commission network. One crucial assignment is providing technical support for Commission offices and directorates. Directorate B co-ordinates the information services of other EU institutions. It also selects the systems and technologies which ensure that the Commission's technology is at the cutting edge.

DIRECTORATE GENERAL FOR INTERPRETATION – DG INTERPRETATION

http://scic.cec.eu.int/europa/jcms/j_8/home

Like other Commission translation services, the Directorate General for Interpretation reports to Commissioner Ján Figel' of Slovakia. Unlike the translation services, the interpreting service is a central contact point for several institutions. The Council of Ministers, the Committee of Regions, the European Investment Bank and numerous

Table 7.5 Organizational chart, DG Interpretation

DG Interpretation			
Directorate A Interpreting	**Directorate B** Administration and resources	**Directorate C** Interpreting assignments	**Directorate D** Conferences
A.1 Interpreting I **A.2** Interpreting II **A.3** Interpreting III **A.4** Interpreting IV **A.5** Interpreting V	**B.1** Work programme and evaluation, inter-institutional relations, and information technology **B.2** Budget and finances **B.3** Personnel and general administration **B.4** Collaborative administration of freelance conference interpreters	**C.1** Multilingualism and support of interpreter education **C.2** Interpreter assignment planning **C.3** Professional support for interpreters	**D.1** Conference organization **D.2** Meeting facilities management **D.3** Conference technologies

additional EU facilities all use the services of this directorate. It is the DG's responsibility to translate the spoken word into other languages.

Institutions such as the Council meet daily with various committees, ministers from Member States and the Commission. The Committee of Regions also holds regular conferences. Interpreting services are essential when Member States propose legislation.

The conference interpreting service becomes active in dozens of daily Commission meetings. Its interpreters attend over 50 meetings and conferences from various institutions every day. The interpreting service assigns meeting rooms and provides conference interpreters. Depending of the size and type of meeting, only three or four interpreters may be required; alternatively, interpretation into as many as 21 languages may be necessary for important political negotiations.

Interpretation depends on a large number of full-time in-house interpreters (up to 400 civil servants and officials) but also employs freelance and independent interpreters in special cases. Due to the influx of new languages following the most recent round of enlargement, it has become a highly complex task to provide interpreters for all meetings with the required language combinations. Covering several thousand conferences and meetings a year demands exceptional organization. The interpreting service is organized according to the same principles as the translation service. Enlargement has generated a great demand for interpretation from and into the new official languages. Consequently, the Commission is putting great effort into acquiring new qualified interpreters. Interpretation has begun to co-operate with colleges and universities in Member States to meet the growing demand for professionally trained interpreters.

INTERNAL AUDITING SERVICE – IAS

http://ec.europa.eu/dgs/internal_audit/index_en.htm

The Internal Auditing Service is responsible for the Commission's accounting. It examines in detail whether Commission offices conduct accurate accounting. The service hence ensures that the Commission uses the European taxpayer's money as granted to it by Council and Parliament, in accordance with the law.

A key responsibility of the auditing service is providing recommendations to the Commission and its Directorates General in the following areas:

Table 7.6 Organizational chart, Internal Auditing Service

Internal Auditing Service	
Directorate A Horizontal issues	**Directorate B** Auditing processes
A.1 Administration **A.2** Co-ordination and communications	**B.AS.01** Audit supervisor 1 **B.AS.02** Audit supervisor 2 **B.AS.03** Audit supervisor 3 **B.AS.04** Audit supervisor 4 **B.AS.05** Audit supervisor 5 **B.AS.06** Audit supervisor 6 **B.ASP** Auditing staff

- risk management in the assignment and planning of Commission-supported programmes and initiatives;
- the protection of the Commission's assets;
- improved compliance with internal Commission rules;
- generation of correct and reliable auditing figures to prevent the waste of resources;
- improved management and review of internal auditing systems;
- increased efficiency and effectiveness in the Commission's activities to maximize the available resources.

DIRECTORATE GENERAL FOR PERSONNEL AND ADMINISTRATION – DG ADMIN

http://ec.europa.eu/dgs/personnel_administration/index_en.htm

The Directorate General for personnel and administration is responsible for overall personnel administration for EU civil administrators and employees.

Each EU employee is permitted to apply for other positions within the Commission, with other EU institutions, such as the Council or Parliament, or in other EU agencies. The mobility of employees is encouraged to supply all EU institutions with the necessary expertise.

Career mobility, professional development and career training support are administered by the Directorate General ADMIN. The directorate also manages the rights and responsibilities of EU employees and works to inform them of their rights and of staff regulations. As

Table 7.7 Organizational chart, DG Personnel and Administration

DG Personnel and Administration		
Directorate A Personnel and career development **A.1** General issues, policy, and external hiring **A.2** SCOP: Career counselling and development **A.3** Training **A.4** Temporary employment: hiring and administration **A.5** Organization and leadership **A.6** Career development structure and advancement	**Directorate B** Directorate statute: policy, administration, and consulting **B.1** Legal and statutory issues, wages and pensions solutions **B.2** Judicial remediation **B.3** Employment conditions, non-financial rights and responsibilities **B.4** Equal opportunity and anti-discrimination **B.5** Social dialogue, relations with national public officials, and horizontal issues related to enlargement	**Directorate C** Directorate social policy, personnel in Luxembourg, job safety and hygiene **C.1** Social policy and programmes; alumni relations **C.2** Personnel, statutory and personnel policy: Luxembourg **C.3** Medical service Luxembourg **C.4** Medical service Brussels **C.5** Job safety and hygiene
Directorate D Resources **D.1** Budget and support in contractual matters **D.2** Strategic planning, relations with institutions and offices **D.3** Personnel – ADMIN, internal reforms **D.4** European schools **D.5** Communications and information administration	**Directorate DS** Security **DS.1** Protective measures and crisis management **DS.2** Information and prevention **DS.3** Inspection and consulting **DS.4** Technical facility, computer, and telecommunications security **DS.5** Co-ordination	

in comparable circumstances, national authorities, EU staff regulations are adapted to most recently when officials from the new Member States were integrated into institutions.

DG ADMIN administers the wages, pensions and other financial entitlements of nearly 22,000 Commission employees, in addition to any other business relating to EU staff regulations (e.g. questions about promotion). DG ADMIN also manages the EU health insurance plan and premiums paid by the employees, as well as employees' contributions to the Community pension fund. All social support services for employees currently or formerly in service are administered by the Directorate General Personnel and Administration.

The Commission as an institution is committed to gender equality in the recruitment, career development and professional training of its employees.

BUREAU OF EUROPEAN POLICY ADVISERS – BEPA

http://europa.eu.int/comm/dgs/policy_advisers/index_en.htm

Table 7.8 Organizational chart, Bureau of European Policy Advisers

Bureau of European Policy Advisers		
Economic policy analysis group	Political advisor group	Social policy advisor group

Founded during the tenure of Commission President Jacques Delors, and defined at that time as a unit for forward planning, today's Bureau of European Policy Advisers reports directly to the Commission President. The group consists of political analysts from a variety of policy areas. Their responsibility is to provide professional and thoroughly researched EU policy recommendations to the President and to the entire Commission. In contrast to the Directorates General, which are usually organized by operations, the bureau concentrates on large-scale strategic and structural issues in EU development and on the early phases of policy development. BEPA provides support for the President on special matters that involve multiple policy areas. A classic example is life sciences (biology, pharmacy, chemistry) and, more broadly speaking, biotechnology, which lie in the policy areas of different Commissioners.

The bureau is the co-ordinating office for three advisory groups: a group of political advisers, a group for economic policy analysis, and a group for social policy. BEPA responds to enquiries made by the

President and individual Commissioners; analyses early economic, social and political developments in and outside the EU; and presents its conclusions to the College of Commissioners. The President may assign the Bureau to examine the effects of certain programmes or political decisions and make subsequent recommendations. Vitor Gaspar recently assumed the post of Director General.

DIRECTORATE GENERAL FOR TRANSLATION – DG DGT

http://www.europa.eu.int/comm/dgs/translation/index_en.htm

As an internal department of the European Commission, the translation service reports to Commissioner Leonard Orban of Romania, who is responsible for multilingualism in the EU.

All EU institutions, Parliament and the European Council have their own translation services. Because each institution has unique tasks and procedures, this is necessary for maintaining smooth internal processes.

The Commission translation service is responsible for the translation of written documents. A huge number of speeches and presentations for Commissioners and high-ranking officials, as well as information material, press releases, international treaties, political announcements and verbal or written requests from the European Parliament, are translated every day. In 2004 the Service translated 1,270,586 pages for the departments and offices of the Commission alone. This amount of work requires an efficient organization and the latest technical equipment in order to deliver high-quality translations in a short amount of time. The Commission Translation Service is among the largest, most important and technologically best-equipped translation services in the world.

As the guardian of Community law and initiator of Community law legislation, the European Commission has a special responsibility and an obligation to disseminate all laws among the public, the relevant authorities and the governments and ministries of all 27 Member States, from the earliest phases until eventual ratification. This is essential not only for the sake of transparency, but also because each guideline, directive or decision from courts of law, authorities and ministries must be fully understood and incorporated into national

Table 7.9 Organizational chart, DG Translation

Translation			
Directorate A Languages I – Luxembourg	**Directorate B** Languages II – Brussels	**Directorate C** Resources and language technology support	**Directorate D** Strategies
A.DE German language department	**B.DA** Danish language department	**C.1** Personnel administration	**D.1** Demand management
A.NL Dutch language department	**B.EL** Greek language department	**C.2** Financial administration	**D.2** External translation
A.CS Czech language department	**B.EN** English language department	**C.3** Information technology	**D.3** Multilingualism and terminology co-ordination
A.ET Estonian language department	**B.ES** Spanish language department	**C.4** Training	**D.4** Evaluation and analysis
A.HU Hungarian language department	**B.FI** Finnish language department	**C.5** Internal administrative affairs	
A.LT Lithuanian language department	**B.FR** French language department		
A.LV Latvian language department	**B.IT** Italian language department		
A.MT Maltese language department	**B.PT** Portuguese language department		
A.PL Polish language department	**B.SV** Swedish language department		
A.SK Slovakian language department			
A.SL Slovenian language department			

law. Citizens must also be able to read all Community laws in their native language in order to implement them at national and European levels. However, daily work at the Commission has been limited to three official languages (English, French and German) ensure efficient work processes.

With the accession of 10 new Member States, an additional nine languages were introduced into the EU. The Union now has 21 official languages: Czech, German, Danish, Estonian, English, Finnish, French, Greek, Italian, Latvian, Lithuanian, Maltese, Dutch, Polish, Portuguese, Slovakian, Slovenian, Spanish, Swedish, Romanian and, most recently, Gaelic.

The Commission Translation Service, led by Director General Lönnhorts Johanni, has official offices in both Brussels and Luxembourg. Directorate A, which is located in Brussels, is responsible for 11 of the 21 official languages. Directorate B in Luxembourg is responsible for the remaining languages. Language units are organized according to EU policy areas. Consequently, each unit includes translators with a particular expertise in a wide range of fields. Directorate C is responsible for general personnel issues, technical resources and training for 1,650 full-time translators. To ensure a high-quality translation, it is essential that translators stay knowledgeable in their area of expertise.

Directorate D has a central role in handling all requests for translation and is required to set priorities based on the importance of texts and their deadlines. When the internal translation service cannot meet demand, external translation companies are contracted to provide support. Unit D.2 is responsible for all external translation services. Unit D.3 ensures that all translated texts use consistent terminology and establishes new nomenclature in co-ordination with the translation services of other institutions. Unit D.4 evaluates and monitors translation quality and institutes measure to ensure uniform quality in 21 official languages.

8

Important addresses and phone numbers

EuropeDirect Information Network
http://www.europa.eu.int/europedirect
Tel: +800 6 7 8 9 10 11 (toll free from all 27 Member States)
Tel: +32 2 299 96 96 (toll call from other countries and certain mobile networks)

THE EUROPEAN COMMISSION

European Commission
Rue de la Loi 200
B-1040 Brussels
Tel: +32 2 299 11 11

Luxembourg office:
Bâtiment Jean Monnet
Rue Alcide de Gasperi
L-2920 Luxembourg
Tel: +352 43 01 1e

Letters addressed to specific European Commission officials require only the name and the Directorate General of the addressee. The address should appear as follows:

Peter Kaltenegger
Directorate General Agriculture and Rural Development
European Commission
B-1049 Brussels
Belgium

Even if the office is located outside Brussels, letters will be forwarded to the recipient by the Commission postal service.

Directorates General of the European Commission located in Brussels

DG Agriculture and Rural Development
Rue de la Loi 102/130

DG BUDGET
Rue Breydel 4

DG Business and Industry
Rue de la Science 15

DG Communications
Rue de la Loi 200

DG Competition
Rue Joseph II 70

DG Data Processing
Av. de Cortenbergh 6

DG Development
Rue de Genève 12

DG Economic and Financial Affairs
Av. de Beaulieu 1

DG Education and Culture
Rue van Maerlant 18

DG Employment, Social Affairs and Equal Opportunities
Rue Joseph II 27/37

DG Enlargement
Rue de la Loi 170

DG Environment
Av. de Beaulieu 9

DG External Relations
Rue de la Loi 170

DG Health and Consumer Protection
Rue Froissart 101

DG Information Society
Av. de Beaulieu 24/29/31/33

DG Internal Market and Services
Av. de Cortenbergh 100/107

DG Internal Market and Services
Rue Joseph II 79/99

DG Interpreting
Rue Froissart 36

DG Justice, Freedom and Security
Rue de Luxembourg 46

DG Personnel and Administration
Rue de la Science 11

DG Regional Policy
Rue Père de Deken 23

DG Research
Rue de Champs de Mars 21

DG Taxation and Customs Union
Rue Montoyer 51/59

DG Trade
Rue de la Loi 170

DG Translation
Av. de Cortenbergh 1

DG Transport and Energy
Rue Demot 24/28

Other services of the European Commission located in Brussels

Bureau of European Policy Advisers
Rue de la Loi 200

ECHO – Humanitarian Aid Office
Rue de Genève 1

EuropeAid – Co-operation Office
Rue de la Loi 41

European Anti-Fraud Office
Rue Joseph II 30

European Recruitment Office
Av. de Cortenbergh 80

Infrastructure and Logistics Office, Brussels
Av. de Cortenbergh 1

Internal Auditing Service
Rue de la Loi 200

Legal Services
Rue de la Loi 200

Paymaster's Office
Rue Belliard 28

Secretariat-General
Rue de la Loi 200

Shared Research Facility
Square de Meeûs 8

European Union Services and Directorates General in Luxembourg

Eurostat
Bâtiment Jean Monnet
Rue Alcide de Gasperi

Infrastructures and Logistics Office, Luxembourg
Bâtiment Jean Monnet
Rue Alcide de Gasperi

Office for Official Publications
Rue Mercier 2

OTHER EU INSTITUTIONS AND FACILITIES

Allée du Printemps
BP1024
F-67070 Strasbourg Cedex
Tel: +33 3 88 17 40 01

Centre de Conférences
Kirchberg
L-2929 Luxembourg
Tel: +352 43 02 1

Committee of Regions
Rue Belliard 101
B-1040 Brussels
Tel: +32 2 282 22 11

Council of the European Union
Rue de la Loi 175
B-1048 Brussels
Tel: +32 2 285 61 11

Economic and Social Committee
Rue Belliard 99
B-1040 Brussels
Tel: +32 2 546 90 11

European Central Bank
Kaiserstraße 29
D-60066 Frankfurt am Main
Tel: +49 69 13 44 0

European Court of Auditors
Rue Alcide de Gasperi 12
L-1615 Luxembourg
Tel: +352 4398 45410

European Court of Justice
Boulevard Konrad Adenauer
L-2925 Luxembourg
Tel: +352 43 03 1

European Data Protection Supervisor
Rue Wiertz 60

B-1047 Brussels
Tel: +32 2 28 31 900

European Investment Bank
100 Boulevard Konrad Adenauer
L-2950 Luxembourg
Tel: +352 43 79 1

European Ombudsman
Av. du Président Robert Schuman 1
BP403
F-67001 Strasbourg Cedex
Tel: +33 3 88 17 23 13

European Parliament
Rue Wiertz
BP1047
B-1047 Brussels
Tel: +32 2 284 21 11

Luxembourg: Plateau de Kirchberg
BP1601
L-2929 Luxembourg
Tel: +352 43 00 1

BUSINESS AND OTHER ASSOCIATIONS

Eurochambers – Association of European Chambers of Commerce and Industry
Av. des Arts 19 B-1 000 Brüssel
Tel: +32 2 282 08 50
E-mail: eurochambres@eurochambres.be

European Centre of Enterprises with Public Participation
Rue de la Charité 15 B-1210 Brüssel
Tel: +32 2 219 27 98
E-mail: ceep@ceep.org

European Union of the Crafts Industry and of Small and Medium-Sized Businesses
Rue J. de Lalaing 4
B-1 040 Brüssel
Tel: +32 2 230 75 99
E-mail: info@ueapme.com

European Trade Union Confederation
Boulevard Roi Albert II 5
B-1210 Brüssel
Tel: +32 2 224 04 11
E-mail: etuc@etuc.org

European Automobile Manufacturing Association
Rue du Noyer 211
B-1 000 Brüssel
Tel: +32 2 732 55 50
E-mail: info@acea.be

Association of the European Self-Medication Industry
Av. de Tervuren 7
B-1 040 Brüssel
Tel: +32 2 735 51 30
E-mail: info@aesgp.be

European Chemical Industry Council
Av. E. van Nieuwenhuyse 4
B-1160 Brüssel
Tel: +32 2 676 72 11
E-mail: mail@cefic.be

Federation of the European Construction Industry
Av. Louise 66
B-1 050 Brüssel
Tel: +32 2 514 55 35
E-mail: info@fiec.org

Committee of Professional Agricultural Organizations in the EU and General Committee for Agricultural Co-operation in the EU
Rue de Trèves 61

B-1 040 Brüssel
Tel: +32 2 287 27 11
E-mail: ute.papenfuss@copa-cogeca.be

EuroCommerce – European Representative for Retail, Wholesale and Foreign Trade in Europe
Av. des Nerviens 9–31
B-1 040 Brüssel
Tel: +32 2 737 05 98
E-mail: mueller@eurocommerce.be

Union of Co-operative Purchasing Organizations in Europe
Av. des Gaulois 3
B-1 040 Brüssel
Tel: +32 2 732 46 60
E-mail: info@ugal.org

European Savings Bank Federation
Rue Marie-Thérèse 11
B-1 000 Brüssel
Tel: +32 2 211 11 11
E-mail: michaela.koller@savings-bank.com

EU Banking Federation Rue Montoyer 10
B-1 040 Brüssel
Tel: +32 2 508 37 11

European Association of Co-operative Banks
Rue de l'Industrie 26
B-1 040 Brüssel
Tel: +32 2 230 11 24
E-mail: v.heegemann@eurocoopbanks.coop

European Association of National Insurance Companies
Square de Meeûs 29 B-1 000 Brüssel
Tel: +32 2 547 58 11

Community of European Railway and Infrastructure Companies
Av. des Arts 53
B-1 000 Brüssel
Tel: +32 2 213 08 70
E-mail: contact@cer.be

PostEurop – Association of European Public Postal Operators
Av. du Bourget 44
B-1130 Brüssel
Tel: +32 2 724 72 80
E-mail: posteurop@posteurop.org

Eurelectric – European Association of Electricity Supply Companies
Boulevard de l'Impératrice 66
B-1 000 Brüssel
Tel: +32 2 515 10 00
E-mail: eurelectric@eurelectric.org

European Federation of Local Public Energy Distribution Companies
Rue Royale 55
B-1 000 Brüssel
Tel: +32 2 217 81 17
E-mail: jacques.glorieux@cedec.com

European Council of the Liberal Professions
Rue J. de Lalaing 4
B-1 040 Brüssel
Tel: +32 2 511 44 39
E-mail: ceplis@pi.be

European Bureau of the Consumers' Unions
Av. de Tervuren 36
B-1 040 Brüssel
Tel: +32 2 743 15 90
E-mail: consumers@beuc.org

European Environmental Bureau
Boulevard de Waterloo 34
B-1 000 Brüssel
Tel: +32 2 289 10 90
E-mail: eeb@eeb.org

WWF
Av. de Tervuren 36
B-1 040 Brüssel
Tel: +32 2 743 88

List of sources

Europa Server: http://www.europa.eu.int

- European Commission: http://europa.eu.int/comm
- European Treaties: http://europa.eu.int/abc/treaties_de.htm
- Summaries of European Union legislation: http://europa.eu.int/scadplus
- General Report on the Activities of the European Union: http://europa.eu.int/abc/doc/off/rg/de/welcome.htm
- Summary of the European Institutions: http://europa.eu.int/institutions/index_de.htm
- Electronic Directory of the European Institutions: http://europa.eu.int/idea/de

European Parliament: http://www.europarl.eu.int
Council of the European Union: http://www.ue.eu.int
Court of Justice of the European Union: http://www.curia.eu.int
European Court of Auditors: http://www.eca.eu.int
European Central Bank: http://www.ecb.int
European Investment Bank: http://www.eib.eu.int
Economic and Social Committee: http://www.esc.eu.int
Committee of the Regions: http://www.cor.eu.int
European Ombudsman: http://www.euro-ombudsman.eu.int
European Data Protection Supervisor: http://www.edps.eu.int
European Agencies: http://www.europa.eu.int/agencies
Office for Official Publications: http://www.publications.eu.int

Abbreviations

ACP	African, Caribbean, Pacific
ALDE	Alliance of Liberals and Democrats for Europe
ASEAN	Association of South East Asian Nations
ASEM	Asia-Europe Meeting
AU	African Union
CAP	Common Agricultural Policy
CARDS	Community Assistance for Reconstruction, Development and Stabilization
CCP	Common Commercial Policy
CEDEFOP	European Centre for the Development of Vocational Training (Centre Européen pour le Développement de la Formation Professionelle)
CEEAC	Economic Community of Central African States (Communauté Economique des Etats d'Afrique Centrale)
CEMAC	Central African Economic and Monetary Community (Communauté Economique et Monétaire de l'Afrique Centrale)
CEPOL	European Police College
CFCA	Community Fisheries Control Agency
CFP	Common Fisheries Policy
CFSP	Common Foreign and Security Policy
CoCoLaF	Advisory Committee for Co-ordination of Fraud Prevention (Comité consultatif pour la Coordination de la Lutte contre la Fraude)

COM	Common Organizations of Agricultural Markets
CoR	Committee of Regions
CORDIS	Community Research and Development Information Service
Coreper	Committee of Permanent Representatives (Comité des Représentants Permanents)
CPVO	Community Plant Variety Office
CSP	Country Strategy Paper
DDA	Doha Development Agenda
DIPECHO	Disaster Preparedness ECHO
DSM	Dispute Settlement Mechanism
EAGFL	European Agricultural Guidance and Guarantee Fund
EAR	European Agency for Reconstruction
EBRD	European Bank for Reconstruction und Development
EbS	Europe by Satellite
ECB	European Central Bank
ECCP	European Climate Change Programme
ECDC	The European Centre for Disease Prevention and Control
ECHO	European Office for Emergency Humanitarian Aid (L'office Humanitaire de la Communauté Européenne)
ECN	European Competition Network
ECOFIN	European Economic and Finance Ministers Council
ECSC	European Coal and Steel Community
ECTS	European Credit Transfer System
EDA	European Defence Agency
EDC	European Documentation Centre
EDF	European Development Fund
EEA	European Economic Area
EEA	European Environment Agency
EESC	European Economic and Social Committee
EFA	European Free Alliance
EFRE	European Regional Development Fund
EFSA	European Food Safety Authority
EFTA	European Free Trade Association
EG	European Community
EIB	European Investment Bank
EIC	Euro Info Centres
EIF	European Investment Fund
ELSA	European Laboratory for Structural Assessment
EMCDDA	European Monitoring Centre for Drugs and Drugs Addiction

EMEA	European Medicines Agency
EMSA	European Maritime Safety Agency
EMU	Economic and Monetary Union
ENISA	European Network and Internet Security Agency
ENP	European Neighbourhood Policy
ENPI	European Neighbourhood and Partnership Instrument
EP	European Parliament
EPA	Economic Partnership Agreement
EPSO	European Personnel Selection Office
ERA	European Research Area
ERM	Exchange Rate Mechanism
ESDP	European Security and Defence Policy
ESF	European Social Fund
ESS	European Statistical System
ETF	European Training Foundation
ETSC	European Technical and Scientific Centre
EU ETS	European Union Greenhouse Gas Emission Trading Scheme
EuGH	Europäischer Gerichtshof / Court of Justice of the European Communities
EUISS	European Union Institute for Security Studies
EUL/NGL	European United Left/Nordic Green Left
EUMC	European Monitoring Centre for Racism and Xenophobia
EURES	European Employment Services
EUSC	European Union Satellite Centre
EVP/ED	Europäische Volkspartei und Europäische Demokraten / European People's Party and European Democrats
FAO	United Nations Food and Agriculture Organization
FDI	Foreign Direct Investment
FPA	Framework Partnership Agreement
GAERC	General Affairs and External Relations Council
GATS	General Agreement on Trade in Services
GATT	General Agreement on Tariffs and Trade
GCC	Golf Co-operation Council
GMO	Genetically Modified Organisms
GPA	Government Procurement Agreement
GSP	Generalized System of Preferences
ICT	Information and Communication Technologies
IDABC	Interoperable Delivery of eGovernment Services to Public Administrations, Business and Citizens
IE	Institute for Energy

IES	Institute for Environment and Sustainability
IHCP	Institute for Health and Consumer Protection
ILO	International Labour Organization
IMF	International Monetary Fund
IND/DEM	Independence/Democracy Group
IPSC	Institute for the Protection and Security of the Citizen
IPTS	Institute for Prospective Technological Studies
IRMM	Institute for Reference Material and Measurements
ISPA	Instrument for Structural Policies for Pre-Accession
ITU	Institute for Transuranium Elements
JRC	Joint Research Centre
LIFE	Financial Instrument for the Environment
MAP	Multi-annual Guidance Programmes
MEDA	Financial Instrument for the Euro-Mediterranean Partnership
MOEL	Mittel- und Osteuropäische Länder / Central and Eastern European Countries
NAFO	Northwest Atlantic Fisheries Organization
NGO	Non-Governmental Organization
OAMI	Office of the European Union Trademarks and Designs
OCT	Overseas Countries and Territories
OECD	Organisation for Economic Co-operation and Development
OLAF	European Anti-Fraud Office (Office Européen de Lutte Anti-Fraude)
OPOCE	Office of Official Publications for the European Union (Office des Publications Officielles des Communautés Européennes)
OSCE	Organization for Security and Co-operation in Europe
PALOP	African countries with Portuguese as their official language (Países Africanos de Língua Oficial Portuguesa)
PES	Party of European Socialists
PHARE	Instrument for Pre-Accession Assistance
PRSP	Poverty Reduction Strategy Papers
PSC	Political and Security Committee
REACH	Registration, Evaluation and Authorisation of Chemicals
RELEX	External Relations (Relations Extérieures)
RSP	Regional Strategy Paper
RTD	Research and Technological Development
SAA	Stabilization and Association Agreement

SAARC	South Asian Association for Regional Cooperation
SAP	Stabilization and Association Pact
SAPARD	Special Accession Programme for Agriculture and Rural Development
SEA	Single European Act
SIA	Sustainability Impact Assessment
SME	Small and Medium-Sized Enterprises
SPD	Single Programming Document
STABEX	Funds for Stabilizing Developing Countries' Export Losses in the Area of Agricultural Primary Products
SYSMIN	Funds for Stabilizing Developing Countries' Export Losses in the Area of Minerals Products and for Mining Companies
TAC	Total Allowable Catch
TACIS	Financial Instrument for Co-operation between the EU and Eastern European and Central Asian Countries
TAIEX	Technical Assistance Information Exchange Office
TBR	Trade Barriers
TBT	Technical Barriers to Trade
TDI	Trade Defence Instruments
TEN	Trans-European Network
TEU	Treaty on the European Union
TRA	Trade Related Assistance
TREATI	Trans-Regional EU-ASEAN Trade Initiative
TRIPS	Trade-Related Aspects of Intellectual Property Rights
TWINNING	Financial Instrument for Institution Building and Infrastructure Strengthening in Accession Countries
UEN	Union for Europe of the Nations
WCO	World Customs Organization
WEU	Western European Union
WHO	World Health Organization
WTO	World Trade Organization

Author biographies

HÜRREM CANSEVDI

Born and attended school in Munich, degree in German Studies from University of Istanbul. English-language studies at University College of London, followed by Master of Science in European Studies at the London School of Economics and a Masters degree in international policy at the Centre Européen de Recherches International & Stratégiques (CERIS), University of Paris. Various activities in Brussels, including for the European Commission, European Parliament, and the Eurocities conference, as well as publisher of EU legal analyses.

MONIKA STEINEL

Born in Brussels, Monika Steinel attended European schools in Brussels and Munich until 1999, and then pursued studies in history and archaeology in York (Bachelor 1999–2002) as well as contemporary history and international relations at the London School of Economics (Masters 2003–2004). She was involved in election monitoring during the 1999 European elections and has also undertaken various activities in culture-related areas (federal archives, Jewish centre, Pergamon Museum). She is a doctoral candidate at University College London.

DR GERHARD SABATHIL

Dr Gerhard Sabathil has been Head of the Representation of the European Commission in Germany since the beginning of 2004. Born in 1954 in Pforzheim, he has been working for the European Commission for 23 years. Since 2000 he has been Ambassador of the European Commission for Norway and Iceland, based in Oslo, and was previously Head of the Division for the Western Balkans, based in Brussels. From 1992 until 1996, Gerhard Sabathil was Counsellor in the Delegation of the EU Commission in Prague. After completing his doctorate at Munich University, he began work for the German Association of the Chamber of Commerce and Industry in Bonn, before moving onto the General Directorate for Competition of the European Commission in 1984. In 1987, Gerhard Sabathil became a member of the Cabinet of the Commission's Vice President Karl-Heinz Narjes and in 1989 he then became Office Manager of General Directorate for the EU Budget. Since 1996, he has been a guest Professor at the University of Prague.

DR KLEMENS JOOS

Dr Klemens Joos was born in 1969. From 1988 to 1992, he studied business at the Ludwig Maximilians University in Munich. From 1988 to 1990, he acted as personal assistant to a Member of the European Parliament. During this period, the idea came about to establish the company EUTOP International GmbH. EUTOP has specialized in the structural representation of the interests of private businesses and organizations vis-à-vis political and administrative decision-makers.

With his dissertation, published in 1998 and entitled 'Representation of the Interests of German Companies with the Institutions of the European Union', he became the first person to complete an academic study on the framework business conditions involved in representing interests. Dr Joos is also the author of numerous publications on EU-related topics.

EUTOP International GmbH has subsidiaries in Brussels and Berlin and is also represented in Paris, Vienna, Tokyo, Beijing and New York. Since 1990, Dr Joos has been Managing Director (CEO) of EUTOP International GmbH.

BERND KEẞLER

Bernd Keßler was born in 1960. After passing the first state law exam in 1987, he worked as an assistant to Professor Dr Salzwedel at the Friedrich Wilhelm University in Bonn, in the Chair of Public Law.

He interrupted his in-service training to carry out post-graduate studies at the University of Administrative Sciences in Speyer, with a focus on 'Europe and Business'. At the end of 1992, he passed the second state law exam and, in 1993, set up a law practice in Bonn. From the beginning of 1992, during a period of in-service training, he worked as a legal advisor for a Member of the European Parliament. From the beginning of 1993 onwards, he was an advisor to several Members of the European Parliament and to EUTOP. Since 1995, he has been working exclusively for EUTOP and, since 1998, he has been Chairman of the Board of Directors of EUTOP Bruxelles S.A. and, since 2006, Managing Director of EUTOP International GmbH.

Index

NB: 1. page numbers in italic indicate tables
2. other than Commission, Parliament and Union, entries are prefixed with the significant title, eg Data Protection Supervisor, European
3. policies for Directorate Generals and services: entries are found under the significant title, eg Education and Culture

(*as seen in* contents pages)